Migration and Xenophobia

Migration and Xenophobia

A Three Country Exploration

Kyle Farmbry

LEXINGTON BOOKS
Lanham • Boulder • New York • London

Published by Lexington Books
An imprint of The Rowman & Littlefield Publishing Group, Inc.
4501 Forbes Boulevard, Suite 200, Lanham, Maryland 20706
www.rowman.com

6 Tinworth Street, London SE11 5AL

Copyright © 2019 by The Rowman & Littlefield Publishing Group, Inc.

All rights reserved. No part of this book may be reproduced in any form or by any electronic or mechanical means, including information storage and retrieval systems, without written permission from the publisher, except by a reviewer who may quote passages in a review.

British Library Cataloguing in Publication Information Available

Library of Congress Cataloging-in-Publication Data

Names: Farmbry, Kyle, 1970- author.
Title: Migration and xenophobia : a three country exploration / Kyle Farmbry.
Description: Lanham, Maryland : Lexington Books, 2019. | Includes bibliographical references and index.
Identifiers: LCCN 2019009847 (print) | LCCN 2019014176 (ebook) | ISBN 9781498553360 (Electronic) | ISBN 9781498553353 (cloth : alk. paper)
Subjects: LCSH: Emigration and immigration--Social aspects--Case studies. | Refugees--Social conditions--Case studies. | Xenophobia--Case studies. | South Africa--Emigration and immigration--Social aspects. | Malta--Emigration and immigration--Social aspects. | United States--Emigration and immigration--Social aspects. | Refugees--Social conditions--South Africa. | Refugees--Social conditions--Malta. | Refugees--Social conditions--United States. | Xenophobia--South Africa. | Xenophobia--Malta. | Xenophobia--United States.
Classification: LCC JV6225 (ebook) | LCC JV6225 .F37 2019 (print) | DDC 304.8--dc23
LC record available at https://lccn.loc.gov/2019009847

∞™ The paper used in this publication meets the minimum requirements of American National Standard for Information Sciences Permanence of Paper for Printed Library Materials, ANSI/NISO Z39.48-1992.

Printed in the United States of America

This book is dedicated to the hundreds of thousands who namelessly cross borders at risk to selves and loved ones for the purpose of simply seeking a better life.

Kyle

9/29/20

"Rutgers" Newsletter

$50 students
current Exchange member
Other similar programs?

"Pitfalls"

Doreen
NXJ

Lofty
Ambitions

July 2020

Sunday	Monday	Tuesday	Wednesday	Thursday	Friday	Saturday
28	29	30	1	2	3	4
5	6	7	8	9	10	11
12	13	14	15	16	17	18
19	20	21	22	23	24	25
26	27	28	29	30	31	

Contents

Preface		ix
1	Introduction	1
2	Theoretical Context for Racism(s) and Xenophobia	15
3	Migration and Conceptualizations	29
4	South Africa: Aspiration Meets Human Condition	43
5	Malta: Toward an Integrative Strategy	65
6	The United States: History Repeats	81
7	Conclusion	103
Appendix I: Convention Relating to the Status of Refugees		109
Appendix II: Protocol Relating to the Status of Refugee		127
Appendix III: Resolution Adopted by the General Assembly on 19 September 2016		133
Appendix IV: Global Compact for Safe, Orderly and Regular Migration		163
Bibliography		211
Index		217
About the Author		221

Preface

On a late afternoon in mid-September 1988, I sat across a table from Roger Winter, interviewing for an internship I wanted to start as a freshman in college that fall. At the time, Roger served as the Executive Director of the U.S. Committee for Refugees (USCR—now the U.S. Committee for Refugees and Immigrants), an organization at the forefront of advocating on behalf of displaced persons around the world. Founded in 1911, when the United States was in the middle of one of its great waves of immigration, the organization sought to make migration a humane process for those coming to U.S. shores. Over the years, particularly in the latter half of the twentieth century, the organization would advocate for the needs of refugees and asylum seekers fleeing some of the worst humanitarian crises of the day.

Roger hired me to serve as an intern that semester—and in time over subsequent semesters. Over the years, as a result of our interactions and conversations with the policy analysts and staff I would work under during that time (Court Robinson, Bill Frelick, Hiram Ruiz, Carolyn Moore, Ginny Hamilton, Joe Cerconi, to name a few), I would learn about the numerous global situations that contributed to, or were part of, the worldwide flow of refugees, asylum seekers, and other displaced people—conflict in Central America, famine in the Horn of Africa, refugee warehousing in camps and settlements in the Philippines and Thailand, and people fleeing South Africa's then oppressive Apartheid-era regime. I would also learn about the various periods of refugee concentration that framed many of the narratives of refugees and asylum seekers for much of the latter half of the twentieth century.

The interview that afternoon quickly turned into a tutorial that I would find myself reflecting on at different times in the thirty years since it occurred. It would also be my first significant interaction with someone who I would quickly learn was a tireless advocate for refugees, whose intense interest in the well-being of others would model a commitment to a broader humanitarian vision that I hoped to use as an example as I crafted my own career pathway.

About thirty minutes into that first meeting, Roger took off his glasses, paused for a few seconds, and posed a question that I have asked myself continuously over the years.

"Tell me," he asked, "why do people leave?"

The decision to leave is one that many are forced to make as conditions of war, famine, or economic instability often shape their choices (or lack thereof), related to their own survival.

This book is rooted in this question that Roger posed to me in the fall of 1988. Over the past few years, driven in part by the mentorship and influence Roger and others at USCR provided in the late 1980s and early 1990s, I have wondered about choices to depart one's home, one's family, and one's traditions. Given the reality that for many making choices to migrate—as refugees or asylum seekers, the risks are numerous, and the reality that many of the communities where people land may not be welcoming—the question of "why do people leave?" becomes much more complex.

Over the past decade, I have found myself in situations where I have been reflecting on some of the questions I asked in the late 1980s and early 1990s about the decisions people make to leave "home" in anticipation of something new, and hopefully better. Linked to some of these questions of choices to migrate have been questions of what awaits them in the new places where they might find themselves situated.

In 2008, while in South Africa, I visited camps that had been established in the aftermath of a series of attacks against foreigners in communities throughout the nation. As I sloshed through muddy terrain between tents near Cape Town for those seeking shelter from both the seasonal rains and the violence of the communities where they had been living, I found myself wondering about these people. What were their lives like before? What had they left behind in their home countries—whether Zimbabwe, Malawi, Nigeria, Somalia, or elsewhere? What caused them to leave? How did they manage the disappointment of learning that their new realities—in a country many risked great consequences to reach—were far from hospitable?

Like many others, I considered post-Apartheid South Africa as the locale where the embodiment of the "rainbow nation" concept presented by Nobel Laureate Archbishop Desmond Tutu, would reflect the possibilities of a broader humanitarianism. Given such imagery promoted at the time, the xenophobic outbreaks were disheartening. South Africa had, I naively believed, become the bastion of acceptance and a place where goals of human rights, social equity, reconciliation, and social justice were becoming the norm. The violence proved my naiveté and that of others who believed the proclamations of a welcoming "rainbow nation." Our hope had, in some ways, been premature.

My second point of reflection on the choices people make to leave "home" was triggered in July of 2014, when I had the opportunity to visit relatives who at the time were serving as faculty at the University of Malta. During my visit to this small island in the Central Mediterranean, there were several discussions on matters of migration. Malta, being the southernmost nation in the European Union and only a few hundred miles from the Libyan coast, was geographically positioned to receive one of the largest flows of migrants from nations in Central and North Africa who were desperate to find a way into Europe. Just several months prior, a boat carrying 500 such migrants had capsized in the ocean, killing over 350 people. That incident was a small sample of the many deaths that occurred that year. In total, 2014 saw nearly 3,500 deaths in the Mediterranean. People were leaving their home countries for what they thought would provide a better life. For many of them, risking a journey in an overcrowded, unseaworthy boat would be the vehicle through which they could seek this better life.

During my trip, I learned that Malta had been the locale for much refugee activity, as the first two decades of the twenty-first century witnessed surges in the global refugee movement. Malta has a population of slightly under 450,000 people. Between 2002 and 2013 it became a landing site for nearly 17,000 migrants arriving by sea, causing Maltese voices to be raised with concerns about the increase in refugees and asylum seekers. As one official I interviewed explained, "we project, due to political instabilities, the impact of climate change, and other factors, that this number will only increase. What happens when our small nation begins to see ten thousand or twenty thousand people per annum migrating here?"

I also began to question some of the complexities related to the societal changes that much of Europe was beginning to experience. On the one hand, many nations in Europe were beginning to see declining populations. Slowing birth rates were shifting demographics among those traditionally deemed European. Countering these population declines were increases among the numbers of migrants—including those coming through regular and irregular means. As many of the migrants were of different races and religions, coming at a time when anxieties were already high around civilization clashes, the challenges surfaced around what dynamics meant in the realities of these population transitions.

Shortly after my trip, I applied for and received a Fulbright Fellowship to Malta. My hope was to further understand how Malta was addressing the dilemma of large waves of migration. By that time, the number of people migrating, or attempting to migrate to Europe was increasing dramatically. So too were the number of people who weren't successful in their attempts. In conversations with people encountered, I grew to understand some of the complexities related to Malta's place in this debate, as well as some of the broader issues driving the European discourse relevant to migrants and refugees. Time spent with people seeking asylum in Malta and elsewhere, conversations with advocates, government officials, and Maltese people in the middle of this transitional period of population change, helped me to better understand the reasons for leaving. They also helped me understand strategies for adapting when the places where one finds oneself have wavering degrees of hospitality.

The third point of reflection occurred as I tried to make sense of an unraveling civic discourse in my own country of the United States around issues of migration. Like many others, I witnessed the toxic discourse of the 2016 election cycle; as conversations around building walls to keep migrants out, and around implementing travel bans against populations (linked to factors of religion, race, and place of origin), became increasingly normalized. I found my heart sinking in the early months of a new U.S. presidential administration in January and February 2017, when I realized that the rhetoric of marginalization, which had been so prevalent during the election cycle, was a language of intent; as the administration sought to actualize policies that the new president had publicly expounded on a few months earlier as a candidate.

My anxiety around the implementation of new policies, which I came to view as promoting increased marginalization and further dislocation of people seeking a better life for themselves and their families, increasingly seemed to reflect the global growing hostility toward migrants, refugees, and asylum seekers. I questioned the long-term impact on my own nation, as the deepening sense of xenophobia, and a distain for particular groups of "Others" was reinforced at the highest levels of government and in far too many communities across the nation.

SHIFTING THE DIALOGUE

People will continue to move, and the levels of receptivity to the new arrivals will vary. My challenge, and that of scores of others who recognized and committed ourselves to a different reality than what was sadly being actualized, was to put into motion means for better managing conflicts between people as further movement and resettlement occurred. But first, there was a need to better understand the issue of human movement. What hopes might people have for their new places? Why are some people hostile to newcomers, particularly when many of these newcomers are fleeing barely imaginable realities of war, persecution, or extreme realities of a human existence?

As a global wave seemed to be emerging of anti-migrant, and anti-refugee sentiments in communities, I've struggled with questions of how we might shift the dialogue. How can a conversation be developed which relates to people's mobility and the challenges encountered when they arrive in their new environments? How might we better comprehend the forces that lead to such movement, and how might we understand the factors that impact how people are received when they arrive?

Hopefully, this book will play a role in reframing our understanding about the choices people make to leave previous lives and some of the barriers they face as they integrate into their new realities. My goal is to also encourage those initially opposed to the arrival of the newcomers to shift to a perspective of greater acceptance.

A NOTE OF GRATITUDE

I have now learned, as a result of having authored or edited several publications before this one that books are not sole endeavors, they really are the product of the energy, and effort, of many people. My support network at Rutgers University-Newark, Chancellor Nancy Cantor, Provost Jerome Williams, Vice-Chancellor Marcia Brown, Executive Vice-Chancellor Sherri-Ann Butterfield, and Chief of Staff Peter Englot provided the encouragement that enabled me to balance my administrative duties with the research agenda that this book entailed.

The team at the Graduate School-Newark, Sandy Reyes, Viki Hadjikonstantinou, Deseray Graham, Diane Filippone, Karen Sanderson, and Charles Basden provided the stability in the day-to-day roles that enabled me to find time to work on this book. I want to extend a special thanks to Kinna Perry, Adriana Afonso, and Jack Lynch for keeping things in our office running smoothly during times of absence for the Fulbright-related research.

Graduate and undergraduate students Jane Roche, Hourie Tafech, Michael Conteh, Murad Meshanni, Lauren Kaplan, Kathryn Duffey-Jaeger, Jennifer Bucalo, Rebecca Pena, Kelly James, Matthew Holly, Marie-Jeanne Ndimbira, M'Ballou Sanogho, Bronwyn Douman, Alice Benishyaka, and Marie-Elle Sudarkasa helped with background research.

Friends from all over the globe provided vital encouragement in this effort. In the United States, Sara Busdiecker, Amanileo Busdiecker, Steve Levy, Daryl Nann, Mike and Heather Libonati, Priscilla and Danny Marin, Abigail Moore, and Termeh Rassi would sometimes knowingly, and often unknowingly, provide the push needed to move this project along.

In South Africa, Lorenzo Davids, Titania Fernandez, Merlinda Abrahams, Stan Henkman, Noel Daniels, Albert Fritz, Edwin Smith, Desiree Tesner-Smith, Kagiso Phatshwane and Shuaib Domingo helped me understand many of the components of the South African narrative. Many of these friendships span the length of the seventeen years that I have been traveling between the

United States and South Africa—and it is the support of these people that made me excited to call their nation my second home.

In Malta, Romina Baldwin, George Vital Zammit, Sari Albaaga, Ahmed Bugri, Mohammed Hassan, Paul Galea, Maria Pisani, Danielle Van Rooyen, and Umayma Ma welcomed me into conversations about the complexities of the choices to move, and strategies for adapting to a new set of realities that are largely those of circumstance. I particularly owe a debt to everyone with Spark 15, Moh, Sari, Dursaa, Ahlan, Abdo, and Moad. Their leadership will shape the futures of many refugee youth in the years to come.

As has been the case for the past forty-eight years, Larry and Deidre Farmbry have provided the support and guidance that one might wish to receive from one's parents—even when one has long ago reached adulthood. For them, my gratitude is unending.

Finally, it is the asylum seekers and migrants that I have met, and those who I have not encountered, who will have an impact on various efforts to whom I owe the greatest thanks. I have come to realize that the human story is one of migration. At times, the tales of people who make choices to move are linked to a narrative of heroism and at times to a narrative of survival. The true story is one of humans simply doing what needs to be done for themselves and their families in hopeful anticipation of another day.

Chapter One

Introduction

On a morning in early October 2013, roughly 500 people boarded a twenty-meter long boat on the northern coast of Libya. Many of them had travelled for hundreds of miles, from as far away as Eritrea, Ghana, and Somalia, to get to this point of departure. Knowing that the seas in the Central Mediterranean during this time of year are much calmer than during other parts of the year, the people boarding and launching the boat were aware that the chances of reaching land on the other side were greater than when the rougher waters of the fall and winter would arrive.

Several days later, the boat, which had a standard capacity of only thirty-five, approached the island of Lampedusa in the Mediterranean Sea. As it drew closer, a small fire started, driving many of those squeezed onto the vessel to panic. As water began to slip into the vessel, the panic grew, ultimately leading to the sinking of the boat and much of its human cargo. With over 100 people reported dead, and another 200 missing, the sinking of the craft became one of the more widely recognized tragedies in the Mediterranean that fall. Due to the nature of the migratory routes, and the numbers of people willing to take risks like those who were on the tragically lost vessel, there are estimates that there may have been dozens of other crafts that met a similar fate that year.

Located less than 300 miles from the Libyan coast, Lampedusa had become one of the landing points for thousands of migrants over a several year period. At the time of the October tragedy, over 8,000 migrants that year alone had landed on the island's shores. It was the locale where international attention was beginning to focus as people around the world were beginning to understand the scope of the tragedies that were unfolding in relation to migration in the Central Mediterranean. In July of 2013, just a few months prior to the sinking of the ship in October, Pope Francis visited Lampedusa to make a statement about the broader challenges of migration around refugee flows. During the visit, the Pope claimed, "we have lost a sense of brotherly responsibility," and "have forgotten how to cry for those migrants who were lost at sea."[1]

While the Central Mediterranean was experiencing the arrival of people coming from North African points of departure, the eastern Mediterranean was also in the midst of experiencing major flows of arrivals. Images of Syrian refugees landing on beaches in Greece impacted much of the global discourse around the desperation to find stability and peace in conflict-based regions. For many, the image of the lifeless body of three-year-old Alan Kurdi lying on a Turkish beach triggered what would be a series of questions of what might be done.

The tragedies of the Mediterranean helped to bring attention to flight, and its associated risks, occurring all over the world. Somewhere in the desert between Mexico and the United States, someone was attempting to cross a border, risking death from dehydration or at the hands of smugglers. In Somalia, someone would try to flee the realities of the Al Shabaab to Kenya's Dadaab refugee camp, or many of the other camps that exist in East Africa. In Eritrea, someone would attempt to flee the forced conscription of their nation and head into one of the neighboring countries and ultimately into Europe or the United States. Groups of people have always fled situations in hope of finding new realities for themselves and their families. They have also confronted conditions, sometimes harsh, sometimes not, upon reaching their new homes. Migration has been a constant of human existence for as long as human beings have roamed the earth.

Despite the link between migration and human evolution, the first two decades of the twenty-first century have witnessed one of the largest waves of movement since World War II. It is estimated, as we near the end of the century's second decade, that over 65 million people, or one in 135 people living on this planet, are migrants. Their movement is due to several reasons. In some cases, people move due to conflict and resulting concern for safety to self and family. In other cases, increasing strains on human existence caused by shifting environmental or climate change realities are pressing people to move to less impacted regions. In still other instances, growing economic challenges that are surfacing in nations are adding to the reasons why people migrate. Projections of increasing threats in areas of humanitarian crises, environmental change, widening economic disparities, and cultural or religious clashes have led to assumptions that the patterns of migration will only grow. It is believed that millions more will decide to gamble with the safety of self and family to cross inhospitable terrain, to place non-sea worthy boats into water, and to pay smugglers to try and make it from where they are to places where they hope life will be better.

Introduction 3

Sadly, if many of today's migrants are successful, those risking the journey for what they hope will be a better life may not encounter one. Rising incidents of xenophobic reactions have surfaced in nations where many of these migrants aim to re-settle. Over the past several years, as these migrants have increased in numbers, arms initially opened in welcoming gestures have crossed as resistance and opposition to these migrants have arisen. Throughout Europe, politicians have called for closing borders. In the United States, politicians have called for the building of walls, while in parts of Africa and Asia people sit in camps awaiting news of being permitted to enter the broader society in which they might become a part. Much of the world is sadly making it clear that many of those fleeing difficult circumstances are not welcome where they land.

Many government officials are unfortunately caught in positions of recognizing the public opposition to these new arrivals, including societal frustrations of widening economic gaps, fewer jobs, and a rising presence of migrant "Others" who segments of populations are quick to scapegoat as the sources of their economic and social challenges. As public pressure grows, demonstrations at the ballot box have begun to replace governments more hospitable to migrant "Others" with those willing to limit opportunities for entry and the building of new lives.

Migration and Xenophobia: A Three Country Exploration examines the challenges related to migration. It recognizes, as a foundation, several dynamics of this present wave. First, there is the reality that this present-day pattern of movement is not one that will be short-lived. Much of the current migration is driven by regional conflicts framed by the weakening and failures of several state systems. As Libya became the model of a failed state, as the Syrian civil war drives hundreds of thousands of refugees into desperate situations, and as groups such as al-Shabaab, Boko Haram, and Isil grow, we come to understand challenges related to the lives that people are leaving behind. In Central America, as gang activity and violence of the northern triangle helps drive hundreds of people, particularly youth, northward in hope of escaping inhabitable communities in Honduras, Guatemala, and El Salvador, this population grows. While the violence of war and local conflict have certainly served as major push factors, dynamics of environmental change and weakened economic systems, have also encouraged movement. As a result, the crisis of migration is increasingly recognized for its complexity.

REACTIONS TO SUCH MOVEMENT

Reaction to the migration of the early twenty-first century has been wide-ranging. On one extreme are those driven by the deepest humanitarian notions to encourage the development of welcoming environments. Their focus has been on finding ways of facilitating smooth integration strategies for ensuring that migrants are able to adjust, and ultimately contribute to the societies into which they arrive. On the other hand, there are those who have assumed positions counter to those providing an inclusive environment. For them, the migrants are perceived as being a threat or danger to the host society. The narrative presented by such opponents is one that points to the risk that will result from allowing too many people to come from these settings into their nations.

In his 2016 campaign kick-off speech, then U.S.-Presidential candidate Donald Trump noted that Mexicans coming into the country were, "bringing drugs, they're bringing crime. They're rapists and some, I assume are good people, but I speak to border guards and they're telling us what we're getting."[2] In France, National Party leader Marine Le Pen's arguments against immigration provided an example of some of the European perspectives against concepts of integration. In Britain, the success of Brexit was largely a product of concern about the immigrant "Other" and what many view as a rapidly changing British society.

Sadly, economic conditions and socioeconomic tensions from a number of varying causes play a role in shaping the perspectives of migration opponents. Rising unemployment rates provide a foundation for anti-migrant forces to suggest that the migrants are taking the jobs of nationals. A terrorist attack with a name of an immigrant attached as a perpetrator is often used as an argument for closing borders to keep "those people" out. Meanwhile, the silence of politicians and political pundits is often deafening when conversations turn to violence committed by members of native-born populations.

Method

Migration and Xenophobia: A Three Country Exploration examines issues of migration and xenophobia using the experiences of three nations: the United States, South Africa, and Malta. Through the cases, I hope to build a larger dialogue examining issues related to patterns of movement and the xenophobic realities encountered with such migrations. If projections from the United Nations, the World Bank, and the International Organization for Migration that say the world will experience a continued wave of movement between people and place for the foreseeable future are true, then the lessons from the nations examined here have implications for a broader set of realities related to migration. The experiences of these nations represent a microcosm of what is happening globally in relation to nation-based questions on the migration realities of the early twenty-first century.

With each of the cases, I focus on several critical questions that ultimately provide a framework for the specific situations and help to build a larger understanding of the dynamics related to the national experiences connected to the rise of migration and xenophobia. For groups examined, a central question is focused on why choices were made to leave the situations people were fleeing. I try to get an understanding of who some of the people leaving are, and the realities in which they find themselves in attempts to integrate into new settings.

In each of the cases, there is a recognition of the role of institutional frameworks for exploring the management of the challenges. In some instances, the institutions that are engaged in migration discourse have been around for decades, in other instances, they are new. Within considerations of institutional frameworks are both those institutions in the nations and those institutions that stretch across national boundaries. Thus, organizations working in a local and global framework, such as the United Nations High Commission for Refugees (UNHCR), the International Organization for Migration, and other agencies are crucial for understanding the evolving global structures related to migration and the evolution of managing such systems.

Each case explores factors of xenophobia that have arisen in each setting. Through closer examination of questions around why factors of xenophobia emerge, I found myself exploring subtleties related to the discourse around migration and the emergence of hostility toward the migrant "Other." In each case, there is a conversation that needs to be integrated into broader cultural, historic, economic, and sociopolitical contexts. Malta, for example, is a nation that has seen invasion throughout its history. As a result, some of the tensions related to the arrival of migrant "Others" stem from the roots of a nation that has experienced foreign influences from its early stages. South Africa's history as a nation that dealt with challenges of transition from an Apartheid to a post-Apartheid state is one of the critical elements of its story. How South Africa responded to the challenges of people from other nations is a critical element of the nation's transition, as it provides for deep inquiry into concepts of inclusion that framed so much of the post-Apartheid era narrative. Finally, the story of the United States, which has tangled with matters of diversity since its founding as a nation, has a narrative around migration, immigration, and xenophobia, which is critical for exploration in the current discourse. As the nation finds itself re-entering a cycle of waning tolerance of migrant and refugee "Others," the story of how the United States is managing such cycles is vital. In each of the cases, history matters.

Finally, a theme throughout the cases examined is a notion of imagined communities, which help shape the discourse within each nation. As political scientist Benedict Anderson observed, an imagined political communities is ". . . both inherently limited and sovereign."[3] As he noted:

> It is imagined because the members of even the smallest nation will never know most of their fellow-members, meet them, or even hear of them, yet in the minds of each lives the image of their communion. . . . The nation is

imagined as *limited* because even the largest of them, encompassing perhaps a billion living human beings, has finite, if elastic boundaries, beyond which lie other nations. . . . It is imagined as sovereign because the concept was born in an age in which Enlightenment and Revolution were destroying the legitimacy of the divinely-ordained, hierarchical dynastic realm. Coming to maturity at a stage of human history when even the most devout adherents of any universal religion were inescapably confronted with the living pluralism of such religions, and the allomorphism between each faith's ontological claims and territorial stretch, nations dream of being free, and, if under God, directly so. The gage and emblem of this freedom is the sovereign state. . . . Finally, it is imagined as a community, because, regardless of the actual inequality and exploitation that may prevail in each, the nation is always conceived as a deep, horizontal comradeship. Ultimately it is this fraternity that makes it possible, over the past two centuries, for so many millions of people, not so much to kill, as willingly to die for such limited imaginings.[4]

This concept of *imagined communities* creates a framework for considering a proactive process to reflect on the type of nations that stakeholders might want. In the context of considering this are questions of who might be involved with shaping or imagining a broader national community and how they aim to achieve it.

Case One: South Africa

The first case is of South Africa, a nation that I first became fascinated with during the 1980s as a high school student. I learned about many of the anti-Apartheid efforts advocated by global activists at the time. As was the case with many on the political left, I was in support of the anti-Apartheid efforts, including those related to sanctions against South Africa. In February of 1990, I remember watching on TV in my college dormitory room as Nelson Mandela was released from prison. In 1994, I remember the long lines of people waiting to cast ballots for the first time in South Africa's first democratic elections.

In 2002, I began what would ultimately be the first of many visits to South Africa. During these journeys, I witnessed various transitions that would shape the realities experienced by different groups of people there. Like many others visiting South Africa, part of the appeal has been the narrative of a nation that survived Apartheid and was re-building itself with a foundation very different from its predecessor. In 2008, that imagery changed. I watched with sadness as South Africa, a nation I defined through the ideals shared by Nelson Mandela, experienced outbreaks of attacks against foreigners who had migrated there. I became even more concerned when I heard pronouncements by some political figures that seemed to support the anti-migrant violence. "How," I found myself wondering, "did this violence surface—particularly with such tones of xenophobia in the broader society?" I began to consider potential disconnections between what was occurring and the portrayal of the inclusive nation it was presenting itself as.

The chapter on South Africa wrestles with factors of migration framed by the history of the nation's evolution of immigration policies. It discusses the shifting dynamics on who is permitted and who faces challenges related to settling in the nation as a migrant. It also explores the conversations related to migration and xenophobia in the context of an imagined community framework. Central to the imagining context is the role of the re-creation or re-imagining that South Africa has undergone on several occasions since the late 1800s. With each of these re-imaginings, factors of inclusion and exclusion (or purposeful marginalization), have been a central component of the process. While several of these periods of re-imagining will be touched upon, recent periods, post-1994 transitions, the impact of constitutional provisions and the evolution of migration policies will be particularly important parts of the cases examined.

Case Two: Malta

The second case of Malta helped to shape many of the central issues related to xenophobia and migration that I've reflected on in writing this book. Malta's story, as I learned, is shaped by several complexities. First, the nation's geographic position in the central Mediterranean has over centuries situated it for invasion and occupation by people from other lands. There is, as a result, a cultural concern around what newcomers might bring to the nation. Second is Malta's role as a relatively new member of the European Union (EU). As a result, EU policies have an impact on what happens in Malta. In addition, a general tone in policy initiatives related to migration in a European-wide context impacts Malta. Third is a sense of Maltese identity, which is framed in areas of religion, custom, and language that play a role in galvanizing a definition of what Malta is and what it is not.

While conceptualizing and compiling the chapter on Malta, I had several opportunities to visit the nation. In 2014, a visit with family members who were serving as faculty at the University of Malta peaked an initial interest in both the island, and Malta's relationship with increasing migration. Two years later, while on a Fulbright Fellowship, I examined in further detail some of the issues pertaining to migration and xenophobia related to the nation's refugee communities. My extended time in Malta enabled me to engage at a deeper level with many of the people who were at the front lines of developing policies related to migration. Further visits and interactions with many of the individuals and organizations I met during my Fulbright enabled me to explore factors of migration and resistance to migration.

My time in Malta coincided with a shift in policies related to migration, which is still very much under way as I complete this book. Several months before my arrival to Malta in 2016, Britain's Brexit vote occurred, triggered partially by a discussion around how Britain would respond to challenges related to migration. The Brexit vote in the United Kingdom, and the subsequent negotiations toward a withdrawal from the EU, took place during a time when conservative forces were raising concerns about migration in Europe, as well as other parts of the world. As I was completing my Fulbright, and in the subsequent months, I watched as two dynamics transpired that would influence how the nation would be viewed in international discourse. First, Malta assumed the presidency of the EU—making it the first time that this small island nation had done so. Such an opportunity enabled Malta to serve a critical role in shaping the broader European agenda and drawing attention to itself as a nation. Malta's assumption of this role would enable it to leverage a platform focused on advancing its agenda of demonstrating that despite its size in both population and geography, Malta could play a vital role in shaping the future of Europe and the Mediterranean region.

Second, the government of Malta began to reconsider its own policies related to the scores of people from other nations on the island. In November of 2016, the Maltese government requested that thirty-five asylum seekers who had been living there for several years report to the immigration office. The people reported, many under the impression that they were doing so to replace needed immigration documents. Instead, upon arrival, the migrants were arrested and placed in detention. Shortly thereafter, Malta began processes for their deportation.

In response, civic organizations mobilized and pressured the government to rethink its strategy. While the result led to numerous inquiries related to specific approaches in Malta, it also led to broader questions related to the implementation of efforts related to migration policy in Europe. Conversations with policy makers in Malta at various levels indicated that there was division in policy discourse. Some officials were strongly opposed to the actions of the ministries ordering the roundup. Others saw the process as one that served as a partial deterrent and part of a broader strategy for management of migration trends in what is Europe's smallest and most densely populated nation.

By the fall of 2017, government had reversed many of its policies and was engaged in an active discourse on strategies for integration of refugee and migrant populations. In October of that year, the Ministry of European Affairs and Equality approved hiring an officer to work on issues around how to best manage the integration and coexistence of populations from different parts of the world. By mid-December of 2017, the Ministry had formally adopted an integration strategy which mapped out how government practices of encouraging integration would be implemented.

Case Three: The United States

The third case stems from a growing concern I have about the status of my country as a person born and raised in the United States. I have often reflected on a series of ideals expressed in many of our founding documents—and our success through years of struggle and national transformation in achieving such ideals. As a person who came of age in an era when many of the notions of inclusivity and intergroup dialogue were paramount in many of the social teachings that I experienced as a child growing up in the 1970s, I worry about a broad conversation in which concepts of such inclusivity are being tested in the public discourse. As this book was coming together, I was attempting to find a way to react to much of the negative stereotyping that I was hearing in the national presidential discourse in 2015 and 2016, which countered the perspectives that I came to appreciate while growing up. In early 2017 as I was completing an early draft of this book, the reality of the presidentially enacted travel bans and the building of walls between Mexico and the United States were reflections of the xenophobia from the highest levels of power in the United States. My concerns were supported by an emerging reality full of fear and hostility aimed toward the migrant or refugee "Other." How had a discourse supportive of xenophobic notions entered the political and civic narrative of my nation?

One set of migrants whose stories are part of the early twenty-first-century narrative in the the United States, are the youth who entered the country in one of the largest waves of unaccompanied minors in the nation's recent history. The specific challenges these youth face drive their desire to leave their homelands. They are taking incredible risks in how they arrive and attempt to integrate into the United States. On the one hand, their stories elicit questions for a different dialogue than we have had around migration in the United States. On the other hand, they raise questions on the country's shifting moral foundation as policy makers weigh their receptivity to assisting populations of youth in crisis.

This exploration of U.S. xenophobia in this era was vital in driving my interrogation. Part of the challenge I found, as I cast a critical eye on the direction and tone of public discourse in the United States, was that xenophobic notions could be found throughout the nation. Therefore, I had to choose a contemporary issue to engage in a manageable, yet deeper examination of how these various elements of intolerance were surfacing. A close look at elements pertaining to youth migration, particularly for unaccompanied youth from Guatemala, Costa Rica, Honduras, and Mexico, provided my foundation.

The case presented of the United States begins with a historical context through which I provide a basis for examining the current dialogue in the United States, through a lens that considers earlier waves of hostility related to migrant "Others." As I demonstrate, many of the arguments against groups of foreigners in the first two decades of the twentieth century were not too dissimilar from many of the anti-migrant and xenophobic messages of the early twenty-first century. History, and some of the messages presented by those opposed to the arrivals of newcomers, repeats itself.

Organization of the Book

Migration and Xenophobia is divided into seven chapters. This introductory chapter aims to set an overview for the rest of the book. I have attempted to frame some of the guiding notions and provide a brief overview of the cases and contexts that will be examined.

The second chapter explores the notion of xenophobia in several contexts. Specifically, it will examine how factors of xenophobia have surfaced over the years and our understanding of why communities tend to develop a fear, and at times, a hatred of the foreigner. Much of chapter two will examine perspectives of the immigrant "Other" which tends to surface in discourse in various settings. The chapter will be influenced by questions and thoughts related to *otherness*. I draw upon philosophical notions of prejudice, to put such notions in a context for building comprehension of how communities react to the arrival of newcomers.

The third chapter provides a context for the migration and refugee crisis of the first quarter of the twenty-first century, drawing largely upon challenges of the twentieth century. Here, I provide an overview of some of the broader challenges leading to widescale human movement. Drawing upon some of the present migration flows, I present an outline of the scale, as well as the challenges, related to the projection of how immense the crisis is expected to become in the future. The chapter builds a framework for contextualizing migration issues since the middle of the twentieth century—when our current system around refugees was set in place by the 1951 Refugee Convention. It also introduces discussions related to international migration and refugee policy as it has evolved in the early twenty-first century with the recognition of the Millennial Development Goals, the Sustainable Development Goals, and a movement on new approaches for considering migration shaped by the 2016 New York Declaration for Refugees and Migrants, the 2018 Global Compact for Safe, Orderly and Regular Migration, and the 2018 Global Compact on Refugees. Two of my central questions that I introduce in this chapter are: how much does the institutional framework around refugees that was established in the mid-twentieth century actually achieve today, given modern realities of human movement and opposition to such movement? How much do the frameworks re-imagined in the early twenty-first century with the New York Declaration and the Global Compacts on Refugees and for Migrants impact the evolutions of the institutional instruments to shape the sociopolitical and economic environments facing migrants and refugees. Ultimately, I suggest that we might be getting to a point of needing an additional structure for considering migration and our conceptualizations of refugees and migrants as we recognize an increased diversity in what drives people to uproot themselves.

The next three chapters present in-depth cases on migration, xenophobia, and a broader re-imagining. The first case and fourth chapter will examine migration and xenophobia in South Africa. In 2008, communities across the nation were confronted with violence as xenophobic tension erupted throughout the nation. I explore the historical context for these incidents, with a focus on migration policies throughout much of South Africa's history, and the impact on conceptualizing inclusivity in South Africa.

The second case, and fifth chapter, examines Malta, a nation that has seen a close integration of a discourse related to migration in its broader identity narrative. As a nation that has historically been ruled by others, Malta's narrative is one where the identity of what it means to be Maltese has been central. This question of identity is one that in the early decades of the twenty-first century has grown in complexity due to Malta's joining the EU and questions of how to enhance the diversity resulting from an influx of migrants that began in 2002. As such, it is a locale from which critical questions around the EU's policies on migration have been considered. Malta's experiences with migration and some of the hostility expressed by certain segments of the population has a historic element that needs to consider the shifting rule by various parties over the years. It also must take into account Malta's challenge on what it means to be part of a broader set of intra-governmental relations—particularly driven by its role in the EU.

The third case, and sixth chapter, examines factors of migration in the United States. Here, I explore some of the trends of what is frequently referred to as the early age of immigration in the United States—that period from the late 1800s to the passage of the Immigration Act of 1924. Next, I focus on trends that evolved following the passage of the 1965 Immigration Act. I conclude with an exploration of more recent trends with a focus on matters related to children entering the country from Central American nations in the first two decades of the twenty-first century. This period was also coupled with waves of backlash against immigrants reflected in a political discourse that emphasized exclusion.

The seventh chapter will provide a conclusion, with an emphasis on how some of the themes explored in earlier sections relate to a broader discourse around matters of migration, xenophobia, and strategies for integration of new populations. It is in this chapter that I will revisit key themes from each of the cases presented as a way of comparing some of the lessons illustrated in the earlier cases. This last chapter will revisit concepts of national identity development, xenophobia, and hostility. Finally, it will examine in further detail how new instruments of the twenty-first century, in particular the Global Compact for Safe, Orderly and Regular Migration and the Global Compact on Refugees might be used to advance discourse and activity related to migration, addressing xenophobia, and enhancing integration in the nations examined in this book, as well as in other nations.

I conclude the book by presenting several of the documents that have framed the international discourse on migration from the mid-twentieth century and into the early twenty-first century. These documents range from the 1951 Convention Relating to the Status of Refugees to the 2018 Global Compact for Safe, Orderly, and Regular Migration. My hope is that these referenced documents will provide the reader with background on the policy discourse on a global level to better understand some of the national contexts for the cases provided as well as other cases that the reader might encounter.

CONCLUSION

According to the International Organization for Migration (IOM), by the middle of the twenty-first century, the number of migrants—many of whom will be fleeing adverse situations—could reach over 400 million people.[5] If these projections hold true, much of the first half of the twenty-first century, and perhaps longer, will be framed by policy discourse around the management of such migration. People will move, and in many cases, at a much faster pace than we have seen in earlier years. Sending and receiving nations will need to plan accordingly.

Communities around the world will receive people from parts of the globe that are not as stable—factors of safety, politics, economics, and other challenges that arise for various groups will drive much of the change. How these new arrivals are received will be critical for the development of local and national communities. The ability or willingness of receiving communities to integrate members of these new arrivals into a broader discourse of national belongingness, or purposeful marginalization, justified by local concepts of exclusion or xenophobia, will be critical points of reflection.

It is important that we spend time reflecting on why such movement occurs, what resistance to such movement looks like, and how we might ultimately assist both those migrating from one place to the next, and those situated in the communities where people are moving to adapt to the arrival of newcomers. This book aims to assist with such transitional reflections.

Ultimately, *Migration and Xenophobia* aims to redirect a discourse from one that further marginalizes migrants, refugees, and asylum seekers into a dialogue of how we might constructively leverage the human potential of these new arrivals for a broader society. For individuals who are refugees or migrants, their potential, if applied to the receiving nation is great. The challenge that individuals in the receiving communities face is one of managing how to shape such integration positively for the broader society.

NOTES

1. "Pope Francis visits Italy's Migrant Island of Lampedusa."
2. Trump, "Our Country Needs a Great Leader."
3. Anderson, *Imagined Communities*, 5.
4. Anderson, *Imagined Communities* 5–8.
5. *World Migration Report—2010*, 3.

Chapter Two

Theoretical Context for Racism(s) and Xenophobia

A critical undercurrent of much of human evolution has been framed by two vital questions. First, how do groups of people think about themselves in relation to others? Second, how do such conceptualizations in turn impact actions between groups of people? How we have answered these questions has varied throughout our journey as a human species—as interactions have differed depending on the sociological, political, and economic realities of a given time. Mobility, and the interaction it brings between new groups of people, has played a role in shaping such interactions. People from different groups, displaying different features, speaking different languages have met, and have responded sometimes positively, and sometimes negatively, to each other.

This chapter examines questions of how people's conceptualizations of other groups have impacted dynamics in communities and nations. Central to these questions are basic interrogations of why groups get along, why perceptions of difference might exist, and how such conceptualizations of difference shape the development of policies related to broader group dynamics.

Underscoring the chapter is a notion that difference in origin, ethnicity, race, and culture frequently shape public discourse and the conduct of people in roles framing such dialogue. Around the world, in our lead-up to the end of this first quarter of the twenty-first century, perspectives of superiority of one group over another prove to frame much human interaction—regardless of where people are situated. Ultimately, I seek to use this chapter to shape an overview of why some people feel a notion of disparagement toward others, and how race, nationality, and other differentiating factors lead—particularly in the lives faced by migrants—to such derision. I have divided the chapter into four sections.

The first section considers the emergence and development of theories of difference during the period stretching from 1400 to 1900. The period was shaped by increased movement of people, which in turn facilitated the development of theories of difference between populations around the world. Needing justifications for what would ultimately become patterns of domination and control, particularly as various European and Western nations expanded their reach, emergent scientific theories supported the enactment of patterns of domination of some groups over others.

Early to mid-twentieth-century natural and social scientific (and pseudoscientific) theories that developed from foundations established in the earlier periods provided various conceptualizations of race, ethnicity, and difference that were further galvanized. The work of scholars shaping such approaches allows for an understanding of the biases that underscored trends that evolved during a much earlier stage of escalated migration. The second section examines some of these approaches.

The middle of the twentieth century provides the foundation for the third section of this chapter. It was a period that witnessed a reversal of many of the theoretical trends of the previous two centuries. Having witnessed how scientific theory around race was used to justify exclusion, marginalization, and in some cases extermination, factors of difference between people were reconsidered. An interrogation of concepts of prejudice and difference during the postwar era led to a gradual change in perspective. The articulation of a postwar human rights framework led to the grounding in principles that helped to shape dialogue in several nations around rights related to difference. On one hand, reflection on concepts of prejudice and difference furthered activity in the area. On the other hand, further interaction by different groups of people, partially as a result of increasing postcolonial labor needs and migration trends, helped to scaffold many of the interactions of the era. Changes in relations between former colonial powers and their colonies or protectorates, as well as labor needs shifted the realities of where people lived and the dynamics through which they interacted with one another. In some cases, such new interaction was embraced. In other instances, it was rejected. The movement of and interaction between new groups of people who had previously been separated from one another, led to work by social scientists which explored differences in a new way. This work in turn shaped new theories around people's interactions with one another regardless of difference. In the third section of the chapter, I examine the work of several of the mid-twentieth-century scientists whose interrogation of difference helped to shape varied perspectives.

In the fourth and fifth sections, I examine some of the challenges pertaining to race and difference in the late twentieth and early twenty-first centuries. It is particularly in the years of this era that we saw scientific evidence that countered much of the science from a century earlier. Whereas in the early twentieth century, notions of difference were critical components in what we viewed as the foundational approaches to understanding human difference—we learned, beginning in the later twentieth century that we were more alike from a genetic perspective as a broad species than we had earlier thought.

This scientific base helped shape another discourse that emerged in the late twentieth and early twenty-first centuries. Increasingly, a human relations and human rights lens was used to provide a foundation for further comprehension of differences and the lens for understanding some of the ways of addressing tensions that might result from group differences. In the last section, I introduce some of these tensions and the opposition that the tensions provided for shaping policy frameworks grounded in notions of inclusivity.

Ultimately, the chapter frames an understanding of how members of groups might think about others unlike themselves and about whom formal policies might be framed. It is this understanding that in turn provides a foundation for subsequent chapters and their explorations of how people in societies where we have witnessed an influx of migrants have come to conceptualize, in some cases negatively and in some cases positively, the arrival and integration of people from other places.

DIFFERENCE IN THE AGE OF EXPLORATION, ENLIGHTENMENT, AND EARLY INDUSTRIALIZATION

While evidence of communities of people interacting with groups unlike themselves stretches far back in our history as a species, several important turning points occurred in the 1400s which shifted how these interactions would occur. This period witnessed an increase in the interactions with people who looked different than the explorers. As such interaction occurred, so did justifications of control, based on shifting social constructions of those who were ultimately conquered. Exploration in some ways made the world much smaller as interaction between people from different places became more common.

The age of exploration, aligned with an age of enlightenment, began a shift in conceptualizations of the centrality of science in Western foundations of knowledge. Seen as partially the result of the calls for empiricism as a basis of knowledge, and the development of scientific processes, the beginning of the era of enlightenment is frequently viewed as a point in time when scientific method became increasingly central to how Western societies would perceive and interact with other communities around the world.

Within the emerging importance of the sciences, came a process for engaging in categorization that would provide foundations for understanding the world. In the 1730s, the Swedish botanist and zoologist Carl Linnaeus published his *Systema Naturae*. Lineaus's work presented a theory of humans being divided into four races—each with a distinct set of physical and moral characteristics. They included Homo *Europaens albescens* (white European), Homo *Americanus rubescens* (red American), Homo *Asiaticus fuscus* (dark-colored Asian), and Homo *Africanus niger* (black African).[1]

In the mid-1800s Charles Darwin's *Origin of Species* and *The Descent of Man* shaped approaches to conceptualizing evolution and its role in the continual development of the species. It also provided a foundation for social theorists to apply concepts introduced in the natural sciences to the emergent social sciences. Darwin's work would ultimately impact perspectives of social scientists whose theories were growing to impact how different races and groups of people would be viewed in a broader societal context.

In 1883, Francis Galton's *Inquiries into Human Faculty and Development* introduced the term "eugenics" into a discourse that would eventually frame how some policy makers would shape their perceptions of others. Galton's work helped shape an interest in the field of eugenics as a mechanism for addressing various social issues pertaining to communities that were different from his own. Ultimately, many of the principles Galton articulated and explored shaped ideas on the racial basis of intelligence, development in sociological understandings, and some foundations of genetic engineering.

The perspectives of these theorists ultimately helped to galvanize arguments that had been evolving around racial superiority and justifications of why one racial group could subjugate itself over another. Emergent perspectives of racial difference, with what were perceived as scientifically bound notions, also crept into how various groups of immigrants were being perceived.

Coupled with rates of immigration in the later decades of the nineteenth century, theories of race and other differences helped to draw the lines between various groups of people at the time. With escalated rates of migration, many people working in policy arenas found themselves balancing their own perceptions of other groups with the development of new policies related to how nations would respond to the in-migration of such groups.

EARLY 1900s—MID-TWENTIETH CENTURY

The beginning of the twentieth century witnessed many social theorists adopting theories of human difference that were heavily impacted by the sciences of the late 1900s. In 1916, the United States author Madison Grant published *The Passing of the Great Race*. In the book, he bemoaned the decline of what he viewed as the superior Nordic races of Europe and the United States. For Grant, much of the history of humankind had been the product of the interactions of smaller groups of superior races of people with larger groups of inferior races. Such a history, according to him, was likely to be repeated in the early twentieth century, particularly in the United States, as people from Central and Eastern Europe increasingly interacted with Nordic and Anglo people who had been in the United States for a longer period. As he noted:

> We Americans must realize that the altruistic ideals which have controlled our social development during the past century, and the maudlin sentimentalism that has made America "an asylum for the oppressed," are sweeping the nation toward a racial abyss. If the Melting Pot is allowed to boil without control, and we continue to follow our national motto and deliberately blind ourselves to all "distinctions of race, creed, or color," the type of native American of Colonial descent will become as extinct as the Athenian of the age of Pericles, and the Viking of the days of Rollo.[2]

Grant's views, coupled with those of many of his contemporary writers, provided a basis for those who at the beginning of the twentieth century advocated against the arrival of people from Southern and Eastern Europe to the United States. Their writing framed much of the theoretical foundation for policies of the early twentieth century related to factors of race, nativism, exclusion, and ultimately xenophobia.

Grant's work echoed that of many social theorists in other parts of the world making observations at the time based on pseudo-scientific claims of racial superiority. In many cases, the perspectives of these individuals were integrated into policy positions that would shape the development of laws in nations around the world on migration trends.

By the 1920s and 1930s, social scientists were supporting ideas of racial superiority and in some cases, trying to make sense of such thinking as it was evolving in relation to matters of racial differences between people. One scholar whose work helped to challenge some of these evolving notions of racial superiority was historian Jacques Barzan. In the early 1930s, Barzan participated in a two-year fellowship with the support of the American Council of Learned Societies, to explore changing societal norms in Europe. At the time of his visit, Europe was undergoing rapid change in perceptions of different groups of people. Through his work, Barzan developed the concept "race-thinking" to describe much of what had been emerging on the continent pertaining to thought about different populations.

For Barzan, the emergence of race thinking was an outgrowth of the birth and evolution of anthropology:

> Race-thinking rests on abstractions—singling out certain traits that are observed, accurately or not, in one or more individuals, and making of these traits a composite character which is then assumed to be uniform, or at least prevailing, throughout the group. This product of thought is properly speaking a

superstition—literally, an idea that "stands over" the facts, presumably to explain them or make them coherent and memorable. All that is needed to make the superstition permanent and powerful is the presence of some easily noted feature—color of skin or hair, striking appearance of face or body, unusual mode of speech or dress. The fusion of the visual sign and the expected behavior is all the more rapid and unshakeable that it satisfies a need common in complex societies—the need to give body to vague hostility, to find excuses for what goes wrong, to fear aliens or neighbors and curse them, while enjoying self-approval from within the shelter of one's own group.[3]

Barzan was not alone in his interrogation of how race concepts were becoming integrated into different places in societies. Sociologist Robert Park was also engaged with how constructs around difference were shaping policy agendas. Park's work focused on the contact between races and the effect that association has on racial relations.

For Park, colonial expansion was central to the development of Western civilizations and the evolution of race relations. Colonialism influenced racial relations by enabling the exploitation of some groups of people by others. Relationships of exploitation centered on a technologically advanced culture seeking economic opportunity for expansion. Economic expansion, according to Park, leads to migration which results in a new distribution of population and division of labor. Park also attempted to challenge some of the sociological assumptions that had become popular in the nascent years of sociology related to Social Darwinism as linked to race.

POST-WWII THEORIES

Theories of racial superiority that shaped policies leading to World War II, helped frame the emergence of new postwar theories on difference between people. The years following the war provided a period for reflection on the fallacies of many of the theories of racial superiority that had led up to the war. Having witnessed the impact of misaligned race theories, a broad interrogation emerged on the intersections of human rights and differences between people. Grand principles of the universality of humankind became integrated in international discourse, particularly with the emergence of several institutions that would shape interactions between states.

The creation of the United Nations in 1945 provided a foundation from which conceptualizations of human rights shaped a global discourse on differences between people. The Charter of the United Nations played a central role in establishing norms of such universality. The Preamble to the Charter notes a determination, "to reaffirm faith in fundamental human rights, in the dignity and worth of the person, in the equal rights of men and women and nations large and small."[4]

Three years after the signing of the UN Charter, the Universal Declaration of Human Rights was adopted by the United Nations General Assembly, noting, ". . . the recognition of the inherent dignity and of equal and inalienable rights of all members of the human family is the foundation of freedom, justice and peace in the world."[5]

In 1949, the United Nations Commission on Human Rights Sub-Commission on Prevention of Discrimination and Protection of Minorities published a memorandum for the United Nations Secretary General which examined why factors of prejudice and discrimination had emerged over the years. According to the sub-commission, factors of race-based prejudice were relatively new phenomenon. As the commission noted:

> Some manifestations or instances of racial prejudice, in its most virulent form, are of relatively recent origin. Originated in the expansion of Europe following the Age of Discovery, they reached their full development after the Industrial Revolution. Traders sought tropical products, cheap labour, and slaves to work in the mines and plantations of the newly-discovered countries. Arguments to justify these conditions were drawn from imagination. Among these was a belief in the racial superiority of the exploiters and the racial inferiority of the colonized or controlled peoples. When slavery or political submission was abolished, the interest in considering people formerly subjugated as inferior did not disappear, but rather increased. If a man was a slave or a mere chattel, to be bought and sold, little attention was paid to the way he was treated. But when slavery was abolished, the desire remained to preserve, under another name, the humble condition of former servants, and to defend their inferior status on grounds other than those on which slavery had been based. Certain types of racial prejudices which were almost, if not entirely, unknown in antiquity, the middle ages and early modern ages, arose with the slave trade, and persisted after its abolition for economic reasons.[6]

The sub-commission saw several components related to conscious elements of group belonging that undergirded many of the prejudices that might exist between groups of people, noting:

> This consciousness induces the members of the group to regard their group as something special. In this way a sense of solidarity and unity is established. They feel themselves to be exclusive, and tend to regard others as outsiders, with foreign manners. To be with one's own group adds to one's sense of security. When the boundary between two or more groups is centered around racial differences, racial prejudice may, and usually does arise. The group which enjoys a higher status for any reason (economic, political, cultural, etc.) tends to consider itself superior to the other group.[7]

The emergence of both the institutions and the framing documents related to the United Nations helped shape a larger discourse on race norms and human interactions in societies.

In the years following World War II, a pattern emerged of rapid decolonization from colonial powers around the world. European nations that had been largely dependent on ideas of superiority to justify their colonial aspirations were beginning to explore strategies for disengaging from their colonies and protectorates. Speaking in South Africa in 1960, then-British Prime Minister Harold Macmillan reflecting on processes of independence, stated:

> Ever since the break-up of the Roman Empire one of the constant facts of political life in Europe has been the emergence of independent nations. They have come into existence over the centuries in different forms, different kinds of government, but all have been inspired by a deep, keen feeling of nationalism, which has grown as the nations have grown. . . . In the twentieth century, and especially since the end of the war, the processes which gave birth to the nation states of Europe have been repeated all over the world. We have seen the awakening of national consciousness in peoples who have for centuries lived in dependence upon some other power. Fifteen years ago, this movement spread through Asia. Many countries there, of different races and civilizations, pressed their claim to an independent national life. . . . Today the same thing is happening in Africa, and the most striking of all the impressions I have formed since I left London a month ago is of the strength of this African national consciousness. In different places it takes different forms, but it is happening everywhere.[8]

Macmillan's speech signaled a shifting trend in relations between many of the colonial powers and their protectorates. European nations, for reasons noted in Macmillan's speech, and for the mere costs associated with maintaining territories around the globe, were beginning to liberate their territories. One of the by-products of decolonization was the movement of people from one part of the world to other parts of the world.

In some cases, the movement of people in the postcolonial era helped to shape many of the dynamics that challenged assumptions about different groups of people. Postcolonial era labor needs triggered the movement of people into countries that had once served as colonial interest holders. In Britain, for example, large populations from nations in the Caribbean, West Africa, and the Indian subcontinent would move there and provide labor needed in many pockets in the nation. In France, a large influx of migrants also arrived from many of its former colonies. By the mid-1960s, France found itself home to over 500,000 Algerian nationals who had moved there following the war for Algerian independence. In West Germany, a labor recruitment agreement with Turkey in 1961 led to large numbers of immigrants from Turkey. Through this agreement, unskilled workers came to Germany to work for minimum wages and temporary work agreements lasting for one year. Between 1961 and the beginning of the recession in 1973, there were reportedly over 700,000 Turkish people who moved to Germany. In the United States, the Bracero program, which resulted from the 1942

Farm Labor Agreement between the United States and Mexico, brought an influx of laborers into the United States from Mexico. Over a twenty-two-year period, the program employed between four and five million Mexican workers in U.S. agriculture.

These population shifts established a new set of dynamics between migrants and people who had been in receiving nations. In some cases government encouraged these population movements to help address labor needs. In other cases, many of the people living in communities where many of these migrants would move, were not hospitable of people from new places. In some cases, the migrants were seen, particularly by long-term residents, as those who would take the jobs of locals.

Postwar Social Theorists on Difference

The recognition of changes in postwar perspectives on difference led to the emergence of social theorists wanting to understand intergroup hostilities and prejudices. One of the foundational works that emerged during the postwar era was Gordon Allport's 1954 *The Nature of Prejudice.* Allport spent most of his career at Harvard University where he ultimately influenced much of the then-nascent field of social psychology. His work quickly became one of the seminal publications on societal prejudice. It provides a foundation for considering means by which people categorize other groups. It also helps frame perspectives on group interactions with an emphasis on conceptualizations of prejudice.

Writing in the preface of the first edition of *The Nature of Prejudice*, Allport noted:

> At a time when the world as a whole suffers from panic induced by the rival ideologies of east and west, each corner of the earth has its own special burdens of animosity. Moslems distrust non-Moslems. Jews who escaped extermination in Central Europe find themselves in the new State of Israel surrounded by anti-Semitism. Refugees roam in inhospitable lands. Many of the colored people of the world suffer indignities at the hands of whites who invent a fanciful racist doctrine to justify their condescension. The checkerboard of prejudice in the United States is perhaps the most intricate of all. While some of this endless antagonism seems based upon a realistic conflict of interests, most of it, we suspect, is a product of the fears of the imagination. Yet imaginary fears can cause real suffering.[9]

Allport argues that, "the human mind needs to think with the aid of categories" as a foundation of pre-judgment that exists in different people. Orderly living, according to him "depends on it."[10] Such thought processes can be divided into rational and irrational categories.

Rational categories are backed up by experiences and have a high probability of predicting an outcome. Allport includes scientific laws as examples of rational categories and suggests rational pre-judgment as applied to a group of people requires "considerable knowledge of the characteristics of the group."[11]

Irrational categories by contrast are more easily formed than rational categories. They are framed without enough evidence. In some cases, the person is simply ignorant of the evidence, in which case a misconception is formed.

Allport's work provides a framework for comprehending prejudice, defining it as

> an aversive or hostile attitude toward a person who belongs to a group, simply because he belongs to that group, and is therefore presumed to have the objectionable qualities ascribed to the group.[12]

Allport also weighs in on the role of race as a distinguishing factor in thinking about prejudice, noting:

> When we speak of prejudice, we are likely to think of "race prejudice." This is an unfortunate association of ideas, for throughout history human prejudice has had little to do with race. The conception of race is recent, scarcely a century old. For the most part prejudice and persecution have rested on other grounds, often on religion. Until the recent past Jews have been persecuted chiefly for their religion, not for their race. Negroes were enslaved primarily because they were economic assets, but the rationale took a religious form; they were pagans by nature, the presumed descendants of Noah's son Ham, and cursed by Noah to be forever "the servants of servants." The concept of race so popular today is in reality an anachronism. Even if it were once applicable, it is scarcely so any longer, owing to the endless dilution of human stocks through cross-mating.[13]

Allport's theories of difference were important in the evolution of our understanding of group prejudices during the latter part of the twentieth century. Nations wrestled with questions of how to better comprehend prejudices between groups of people, particularly as it became increasingly evident that further interaction between different populations would progressively become the norm in societies.

In the last sections of *The Nature of Prejudice*, Allport presents strategies for reducing group tensions. First are approaches of developing law-making bodies and legislation engaged with civil rights matters. He notes three types of legislation that might focus on minority group protections—focusing on civil rights laws, employment laws and group libel laws.[14] These legal frameworks provide foundations for leveraging legal processes for structurally building opposition to institutional reinforcement of prejudice.

Critical in Allport's work is a roadmap he presented in *The Nature of Prejudice* for how to deal with tensions that exist between different populations. His approach has several important components that are useful for addressing these issues. The first of these recognizes that there is a basic human propensity toward prejudice. Recognizing this enables us to develop strategies for confronting such biases and minimalizing the impact of such prejudices on society.

Second is Allport's presentation of a contact hypothesis, which suggested that under the proper conditions, group interaction enhances relations and reduces prejudice between communities of people. These conditions include equal group status and common goals within the situation. They also include intergroup cooperation, often with the support of authorities, law, or custom.

Third is developing processes for challenging the roles of demagoguery in society. As Allport warns of demagogues, they, "play up false issues to divert public attention from true issues. Not all of them select the alleged misconduct of minority groups as their false issue—but a great many do so."[15] Allport's concerns regarding demagogues, and their impact on the broader societies in which they are situated, can be found articulated by other writers and social observers over the years. In the mid-1800s, James Fenimore Cooper, for example, the U.S. author probably best known for *Last of the Mohicans*, published a book of essays on observations of U.S. society, entitled *The American Democrat*. Included in the book is his essay "Of Demagogues," in which, he defined a demagogue in the following manner:

> The peculiar office of a demagogue is to advance his own interests, by affecting a deep devotion to the interests of the people. Sometimes the object is to indulge malignancy, unprincipled and selfish men submitting but to two governing motives, that of doing good to themselves, and that of doing harm to others. The true theatre of a demagogue is a democracy, for the body of the community possessing the power, the master he pretends to serve is best able to reward his efforts.[16]

Throughout history, humankind has witnessed the rise of political figures later to be characterized as demagogues. Following the definition provided by Cooper and the cautions provided by Allport on the potential roles that such individuals might play in facilitating prejudicial notions, a strategy around minimizing the impact of such individuals in a society is a point of critical reflection for stakeholders.

Early Twenty-First-Century Approaches

In late August and early September 2001, delegates from around the world gathered in Durban, South Africa, for the *World Conference on Racism and Xenophobia*. Conference attendees adopted a definition of the term xenophobia as, "attitudes, prejudices and behavior that reject, exclude and often vilify persons, based on the perception that they are outsiders or foreigners to the community, society or national identity."[17] The summit built upon earlier proclamations such as the Vienna Declaration and Program of Action, adopted by the World Conference on Human Rights in June 1993, and called for an elimination of racism and discrimination of any nature.

Despite the advance in human relations, an awareness of similarities, and new language around difference, the later twentieth and early twenty-first centuries witnessed the emergence of various groups that continued to maintain and promote separation. In the United States, according to the Southern Poverty Law Center, there has been a dramatic rise in the number of hate crimes in 2016–2017.[18] In Europe, increases in xenophobic activity has been reportedly on the rise during the first two decades of the twenty-first century.[19] In parts of Africa, Asia, and South and Central America, there have also been increases in xenophobia against groups of "others." Globally, we have not been able to fully address human nature tendencies to categorize, alienate, and marginalize those who might be unlike the groups in which one might identify the most.

CONCLUSION: A NOTE ON THE PLURAL

As we approach the end of the first quarter of the twentieth century, we have an opportunity to reflect on how we have demonstrated our ability to live with difference. Our results in being able to find solutions for addressing the challenges of difference have been mixed. We are beginning to see in many parts of the world an increased level of hostility aimed at populations that are deemed different from groups considered mainstream or a historic majority.

I have attempted throughout this chapter to present several frameworks for considering how our considerations of difference between people has evolved. In the next chapters, part of the goal will be to review strategies for applying some of these theoretical constructs to institutional approaches for considering such frameworks and explore how perspectives have risen over time against populations—particularly those viewed as "outsiders." Prior to exploring specific cases however, some discussion will be provided on the contexts for migrations that have brought different groups of people together, and the evolution of institutional frameworks to manage such migration.

NOTES

1. Skott, "Linnaeus and the Troglodyte," 144.
2. Grant, *The Passing of the Great Race*, 263.
3. Barzun, *Race*, x.
4. Preamble to the Charter of the United Nations.

5. Preamble to the Universal Declaration of Human Rights.
6. United Nations Commission on Human Rights, *The Main Types and Causes of Discrimination*, 20.
7. United Nations Commission on Human Rights, *The Main Types and Causes of Discrimination*, 19.
8. Boddy-Evans, "Harold Macmillan's 'Wind of Change' Speech."
9. Allport, *The Nature of Race Prejudice*, xv.
10. Allport, *The Nature of Race Prejudice*, 20.
11. Allport, *The Nature of Race Prejudice*, 22.
12. Allport, *The Nature of Race Prejudice*, 7.
13. Allport, *The Nature of Race Prejudice*, xvii.
14. Allport, *The Nature of Race Prejudice*, 464.
15. Allport, *The Nature of Race Prejudice*, 410.
16. Cooper, *The American Democrat*, 99.
17. International Labour Office, et al., *International Migration, Racism, Discrimination and Xenophobia*, 2.
18. Beirich and Buchanan, "2017: The Year in Hate and Extremism."
19. Horn, "Is Eastern Europe Any More Xenophobic than Western Europe" and Ford, "In the Wake of Xenophobia."

Chapter Three

Migration and Conceptualizations

People have migrated from one place to another for as long as humans have been in existence. Driven by changing realities of conflict, food security, and environmental change, people have moved for numerous reasons. Normally, those moving have done so under the assumption that the next place will provide an easier life and, in many instances, one safer than the place from which they are moving. Our conceptualizations related to migration stem from several abstract factors that shape most of the parameters of society today. Concepts such as state, nationhood, and citizenship, provide the foundation for much of the discourse related to people's mobility. The evolution of these factors has impacted how we consider people's migration as well as how we characterize displacement due to violence, economic realities, or environmental factors.

This chapter explores some of the conceptualizations related to migration and related subareas of refugee policies. I begin the chapter with an overview of modern state systems and their evolution. The acknowledgment of such systems enables us to ask questions around how membership occurs and what the means are for determining who is and who is not a member of such a system. A basic examination of what makes a state also provides a point of departure for examining state failures—and ultimately how such failures have increased the flow of displaced people over the years.

Next, I examine historical evolutions that help lead to the current discourse on migration. I begin in the late 1800s, an era framed by mass migration driven by economic and social realities of the time. This period also occurred at a point when nations were actively drawing and redrawing borders as they shaped colonial empires—thus impacting the development of interactions between groups of people for at least a century.

Much of the historical context focuses on the development of the institutional framework that evolved in the middle of the twentieth century, when many of the organizations engaged in refugee matters were established. Much of this relates to the development of a refugee regime infrastructure, which consists of the institutions that are involved in the management of refugee affairs. The creation of the UN High Commission for Refugees and the scores of nongovernmental agencies working in the refugee arena have played important roles building this field. In the early twenty-first century, shifting realities in the refugee arena ultimately led to new frameworks for future directions of the field.

I conclude by synthesizing the concepts explored around state institutions, non-state actors, and the development of processes related to refugee migration patterns and institutional roles in responding to such patterns. It is in this final section that I suggest, partially due to the challenges faced by the systems and institutions that have emerged, that there is a place for exploration on rebuilding institutional processes on the management of refugee migration and settlement.

STATES MATTER

The signing of the Treaty of Westphalia in 1648 facilitated the creation of the nation-state as a foundation for our comprehension of international systems. The nation became a place with boundaries made up of people with a common heritage. Concepts of nationhood framed through the Westphalian system set the groundwork for how much of the world has been conceptualizing states. As nations were contextualized under the Westphalian framework, people were able to identify with nations and their forms of government. Nations had citizens, and processes through which citizenship was established. They also had measures by which they could marginalize those who they did not want to claim as citizens.

As national boundaries were established during the Westphalian era, so were mechanisms for national expansion, as it occurred during the 1700s, 1800s, and 1900s when some nations sought to expand their territorial boundaries and their claims of ownership of foreign lands. The development of a post-Westphalian framework for the colonial expansion permitted the evolution of discourse around what would make a state, what would make a protectorate, how citizens of states (and those of protectorates) would be conceptualized, and how to define those individuals who cannot claim citizenship of the state. The Westphalian era also would frame a discourse around the responsibilities of nation-states to their citizens. In the centuries following the signing of the Treaty, different models emerged for thinking about the nation-state's broader responsibilities to its citizens. Over time, as concepts of the non-citizen emerged, so did questions of the role of the state to this category of individual as well.

MASS MIGRATION AND MOVEMENTS

The middle of the 1800s saw the beginning of what would later be referred to as the age of mass migration. During this period, which lasted until the early 1920s, millions of people moved across the Atlantic Ocean from Europe to the United States. The magnets that drew many people away from their homes included those of economic betterment and safety from local strife. This wave was characterized by rapid industrialization and large-scale economic migration. People were being drawn to perceived work in receiving centers. Cities like New York, Philadelphia, Baltimore, Pittsburgh, and other areas of urban industrialization became the locales to which many migrants of the era were moving.

World War I triggered some of the widespread violence that would result in the mass movement of people throughout Europe. In the years following the war, many people found themselves wandering across the landscape of Europe, trying to find a place that they could ultimately consider home. The international system that began to emerge in the period immediately following the war shaped possibilities for addressing some of the broader challenges between nations in a world that was growing in its interconnectivity.

In 1921, as a result of the outflow of Russian refugees in the wake of the Russian Revolution, the International Red Cross Committee approached the League of Nations, on behalf of several nongovernmental organizations (NGOs), to assist with managing the growing refugee population. According to the Committee, the League was, "the only super national political authority capable of solving a problem which is beyond the power of exclusively humanitarian organizations."[1]

The Committee proposed the creation of a High Commissioner for Russian Refugees. Selected to lead the organization was Fridtjof Nansen, who had been a famous polar explorer. Nansen's role focused on issues of defining legal status for the refugees, identifying employment opportunities, and working on matters of repatriation. To address issues of legal protection, Nansen created an identity document that ultimately became known as a Nansen passport. He also negotiated a series of arrangements that facilitated legal protections for Russian refugees in their host nations. In 1922, the issue of two million refugees from the Greco-Turkish war surfaced as an area of pressing concern for the international community. Nansen stepped into the issue by traveling to the conflict region. There he helped coordinate relief efforts, and ultimately was assigned a role with the League of Nations to assist with refugee resettlement.

Nansen's efforts with the Russian refugees and those from the Greco-Turkish war shaped a context for international institutional approaches for working with refugee matters. The efforts he conducted with these League of Nations-supported initiatives would provide a foundation for later work in constructing international refugee responses.

Fascism's Rise and Impact on Migration

The rise of fascism in Europe following World War I created a need for activity on the growing populations marginalized by their governments. Under fascism, the state was perceived to have absolute power and authority. Those proclaimed enemies of the state were often persecuted with the full powers of state authority. In countries such as Italy, Portugal, Germany, and Spain, where fascist regimes were established during the interwar period, increasing persecution of designated groups and individuals deemed as such enemies of the state became a relative normality. Accounts of persecution of many individuals who politically fell on the wrong side of the authoritarian leaders of the era became commonplace.

In the early 1930s, with the rise of National Socialism in Germany and the accession of Adolf Hitler into the role of the nation's chancellor in 1933, a wave of refugees began to flee the country. Initially, those leaving consisted of intellectuals and others deemed by the government as problematic to Hitler and his allies. Over time, they included larger population segments. In time, the proportion of Jewish migrants increased as signs of rising anti-Semitism began to surface throughout Germany. With the passage of the Nuremberg laws of 1935, which stripped German Jews of their citizenship and further marginalized them, the number of German Jews seeking to leave the nation increased.

In a speech delivered at London's Chatham House in June of 1938, Sir John Hope Simpson, former member of the British Parliament and chronicler of refugee affairs, noted the climate in Germany that had been developing since the early 1930s:

> The assumption of power by the National-Socialists in the early months of 1933 introduced new elements of domestic and international policy in Germany. The particular matter with which we are concerned is the treatment of the Jews, of those whom they term non-Aryans and of the political antagonists of the Nazi Party. The domestic policy which they have adopted is to render impossible any decent life for those people in Germany. They persecute them spiritually and physically. They treat them in a way no self-respecting person can support, and in practice they compel those who can do so to escape from the country, while at the same time they take steps to see that they do not take any property with them. In effect what they are saying to the rest of the world is this: "We do not like these people. We are going to render their life intoler-

able if they remain in the country. We are willing that you should take them, but without their property. If, in these circumstances, you are not willing to take them, we shall keep them and treat them in any way that we think fit." In other words, the German Government is placing the other governments of the world in a dilemma. Either they have got to open their doors to hundreds of thousands of poverty-stricken Jews, non-Aryans and political refugees, or they have got to close their doors and to share the responsibility, as they undoubtedly will feel they do, with the German Government for the way these people are treated in Germany. That is not a fair dilemma in which to place the world.[2]

In 1938, upon the suggestion of Franklin Roosevelt, leaders gathered in Evian, France, to discuss Germany's threatened populations. The gathering aimed to assist with the departure and resettlement of refugees from Germany and Austria. Despite the gathering of emissaries from thirty-two nations, and the lingering question of whether or not countries represented would take in any refugees, only the Dominican Republic offered to host people fleeing the Nazi regime.

For Hitler and his representatives attending the conference, the unwillingness of governments from around the world to take in much of Germany's Jewish population provided an example of what the German government saw as the hypocrisy of other nations. World leaders, in Hitler's opinion, were willing to criticize his policies around Germany's Jewish population, but they were unwilling to absorb Jewish migrants looking to leave Germany. Such perceived hypocrisy was interpreted by Hitler as approval to move forward with Nazi designs for populations his government viewed as being undesirable.

WORLD WAR II—MIGRATION AND REFUGEE TRENDS

During World War II, the movement of millions of people around the world, driven by conflict and the atrocities of the era, set into question a tone for how the global community would respond to people in flight. In 1943, the Allied Powers established the United Nations Relief and Rehabilitation Agency (UNRRA) to aid those likely to flee the Axis powers. UNRRA was established by a group of forty-four states to assist displaced people in the years following the war.

In 1947, UNRRA was replaced by the International Refugee Organization (IRO), an entity focused largely on the repatriation of refugees. IRO's mandate enabled it to enter into agreements with governments and occupation authorities to ensure such repatriation.

Two years following the creation of the IRO, in December 1949, the United Nations General Assembly voted to create the Office of the United Nations High Commissioner for Refugees (UNHCR). The initial mandate for

UNHCR was for the organization to come into existence on January 1, 1951, for an initial period of three years. Critical to the organization's framing statute was Chapter 1(2), which notes that the High Commissioner's work, "shall be of an entirely non-political character; it shall be humanitarian and social and shall relate, as a rule, to groups and categories of refugees."[3] This helped to ensure the organization's ability to function over the years in a global political climate that was enhanced in its complexity by the realities of a Cold War environment.

1951 Convention on the Status of Refugees

A year following the creation of UNHCR, the United Nations adopted the 1951 Convention Relating to the Status of Refugees (1951 Convention). This set the stage for much of the global refugee policy for the remainder of the twentieth century and the first part of the twenty-first century.

The 1951 Convention entered into force on April 22, 1954. It established several important terminologies related to the broader scope of refugee matters. Central was Article 1A (2), which defined a refugee as any person who:

> As a result of events occurring before 1 January 1951 and owing to well-founded fear of being persecuted for reasons of race, religion, nationality, membership of a particular social group or political opinion, is outside the country of his (or her) nationality and is unable, or owing to such fear, is unwilling to avail him [or her]self of the protection of that country, or who, not having a nationality and being outside of the country of his [or her] former habitual residence as a result of such events, is unable or, owing to such fear, is unwilling to return to it.[4]

The cornerstone of the 1951 Convention, and subsequent refugee policies, is the principle of non-refoulment. Defined in Article 33, this principle states that a refugee should not be returned to a country where he or she faces serious threats to his or her life or freedom. This notion of non-refoulment is viewed as being binding in all States, regardless of whether parties have acceded to the 1951 Convention.

An important stipulation in the Convention is that subject to specific exceptions, refugees should not be penalized for their illegal entry or stay. This recognizes that asylum-seeking can require refugees to breach immigration rules. Prohibited penalties might include being charged with immigration or criminal offences relating to the seeking of asylum or being arbitrarily detained purely based on seeking asylum.

A critical function of the Convention is its introduction of durable solutions. This concept refers to the processes through which nation-states and organizations working with such states should be engaged with refugees.

Three types of durable solutions are presented in the Convention: repatriation, integration, and resettlement.

The first of these, *repatriation*, is presently the most preferred of the three types of durable solutions. It also often carries the most risk. It consists of finding ways to re-integrate refugees and members of other uprooted populations back into their home nations. The assumption where repatriation occurs is that the situation in the home nation is stable enough to facilitate a return for those who had been displaced. The acknowledged risk with repatriation cases is that situations in home nations, particularly after conflict, take some time to stabilize.

The second durable solution, *integration*, entails the establishment of processes in host nations that engage the refugees in local settings. Factors of language acquisition, employment, and accessing educational opportunities are important components of integration.

The third durable solution, *resettlement,* entails the development of a pathway to citizenship for the refugee as he or she enters his or her new country. Often resettlement occurs when a migrant or refugee is relocated from temporary placement to a permanent location.

The decision making around which durable solution to implement has several stakeholders involved. The receiving governments have various policies around the number of people who might be settled. Numerous agencies serving as protecting entities—such as UNHCR, and growing numbers of nongovernmental agencies partnered with UNHCR and governments, are engaged in durable solution selection and implementation. Finally, sending nations, particularly in the rare instances when repatriation is an option, will impact the feasibility of that option.

1967 Protocol Relating to the Status of Refugees, 1969 OAU Convention, and 1984 Cartagena Declaration

The 1951 Convention was originally limited in scope to situations that had occurred before January 1, 1951, and those geographically limited to Europe. Sixteen years following the adoption of the 1951 Convention, its applicability was expanded by the 1967 Protocol Relating to the Status of Refugees (1967 Protocol), which removed the geographical and time limits that were part of the 1951 Convention.

Two years following the adoption of the 1967 Protocol, the Organization of African Unity (OAU) adopted its Convention Governing the Specific Aspects of the Refugee Problem in Africa (OAU Convention). The Convention was developed due to concerns of Heads of State and Government over an increasing number of refugees in Africa. The drafters of the document recognized that much of the refugee flow stemmed from various wars of liberation, the aftermath of colonial occupation, and the presence of Apartheid and quasi-Apartheid governments in place at the time, such as South Africa and then-Rhodesia. The OAU Convention provided the following two-part definition for refugees:

1. ... every person who, owing to a well-founded fear of being persecuted for reasons of race, religion, nationality, membership of a particular social group or political opinion, is outside the country of his nationality and is unable or, owing to such fear, is unwilling to avail himself of the protection of that country, or who, not having a nationality and being outside the country of his former habitual residence as a result of such events, is unable or, owing to such fear, is unwilling to return to it.
2. The term "refugee" shall also apply to every person who, owing to external aggression, occupation, foreign domination or events seriously disturbing public order in either part of the whole of his country of origin or nationality, is compelled to leave his place of habitual residence in order to seek refuge in another place outside his country or origin of nationality.[5]

While the OAU framework was being developed, dynamics related to displacement were about to surface in Central America. By the mid-1980s, civil wars in El Salvador, Guatemala, and Nicaragua would cause thousands of people to flee the conflict in their nations. In 1984, leaders from several nations in South and Central America signed the Cartagena Declaration on Refugees, a non-binding agreement addressing growing challenges pertaining to refugees in the region.

The Cartagena Declaration was also drafted in recognition of the fact that people were fleeing dictatorships in South America at the time the declaration was drafted. The countries involved in framing and ultimately signing the declaration were Belize, Colombia, Costa Rica, El Salvador, Guatemala, Honduras, Mexico, Nicaragua, Panama and Venezuela.

Like the 1967 protocol and the OAU Convention, the Cartagena Declaration expanded the definition of "refugee." Its definition included "... persons who have fled their country because their lives, safety or freedom have been threatened by generalized violence, foreign aggression, internal conflicts, massive violation of human rights or other circumstances which have seriously disturbed public order."[6]

Ultimately, in the last half of the twentieth century, the emergence of the 1951 Convention on the Status of Refugees, the 1967 Protocol, the 1969 OAU Refugee Convention, and the 1984 Cartagena Declaration formed the framework of protection systems for refugees, asylum seekers, and at-risk migrants.

EVOLVING ROLE OF UNHCR

Initially begun with the goal of being a temporary organization meant to address the needs of European refugees from World War II, UNHCR has adapted over the years to shifting global dynamics of increasingly diverse and geographically distributed global refugee populations.

During the Cold War, the emergence of refugees from nations fleeing communist regimes during the 1950s, such as Hungary, placed many nations in positions of resettling people. In the case of Hungary, the exodus of nearly 200,000 people shaped several questions around how the world would address matters pertaining to refugees from that nation.

The flow of refugees in Africa and Asia during the 1960s and 1970s differed from those envisioned in the 1951 Refugee Convention. In these cases, mass flows of refugees were leaving because of war and violence, not the persecution feared by some of the populations that were of concern to the organizations in the 1950s. UNHCR had to adapt in terms of widening its scope of services to newer populations. In many cases, refugees from sending nations were not interested in resettling for the long term. Instead, they were interested in repatriating to their home nations—once such nations were stabilized and rebuilding.

The 1970s began to see a role emerging for UNHCR in Southeast Asia as more people from Cambodia, Vietnam, and Laos found themselves outside of their home nations due to regional conflict—and increasingly found themselves in camps. Many of the refugees that had arrived in some of the initial areas of receipt, such as Thailand or the Philippines, would find themselves languishing in refugee camps for years. Camps, operated by UNHCR and various NGOs, were locations of concern regarding refugee warehousing, as an increasing number of countries were keeping refugees in camps where they would stay for long time periods.

Post-Cold War Era and Refugees

The post-Cold War era, beginning in the 1990s, witnessed the evolution of a series of regional shifts, encouraging a reconfiguration of the refugee infrastructure. The thawing of cold-war tensions enabled regional conflicts that had been held in place by preexisting balances of power to emerge. This ultimately led to the development of new conflicts between groups of people, which in turn led to new refugee flows.

One of the major shifts experienced at the time involved repatriation processes. Due to the end of many of the cold-war era conflicts, hundreds of thousands of refugees returned to their home nations. The process of such returns engaged intermediaries to assist in the management of resettlement and repatriation.

Conflicts such as those in former Yugoslavia, Iraq, and in the Great Lakes Region of Africa, brought about numerous questions of the role of UNHCR. In the Great Lakes region of Africa, over 3 million people were forced from their homes. In 1999, over 850,000 Kosovar Albanians were driven from Kosovo. UNHCR found itself having to adapt to a world with a variety of conflict types generating large numbers of displaced people around the world.

In 1993, the United Nations General Assembly passed Resolution 48/116, which brought the issue of internal displacement to the forefront of discussions related to uprooted populations. The resolution included language that designated UNHCR to become engaged with internal displacement upon the request of the UN General Secretary.

Twenty-First Century

Conflicts, including those in Syria, Iraq, Libya, and South Sudan have shaped much of the discourse thus far in the twenty-first century on the movement of uprooted populations. This century has also witnessed factors beyond the scope of the war and conflict that have traditionally triggered the flow of refugees. Environmental crises and natural disasters, such as the 2004 Indian Ocean tsunami and the 2010 Haitian earthquake have played a role in displacing populations in ways that are new in their degree of intensity. Finally, economic challenges such as Venezuela's financial destabilization that began in 2010, have caused waves of movement from one region to the next.

The beginning of the twenty-first century saw the adoption of the Millennial Development Goals (MDGs). These development benchmarks ultimately helped frame discussions on more governmental and nongovernmental focused efforts for addressing human advancement in the new century. A criticism that emerged of the MDGs was around the lack of discussion on migration, including migration related to the movement of refugees and asylum seekers. The adoption of the Sustainable Development Goals (SDGs) in 2015 provided an opportunity for the integration of refugee matters into broader discourse. Several sections of the SDGs include language directly relating to migration patterns.

Kofi Annan's Declaration on Migration

The new century provided an opportunity for the United Nations to reflect upon its role in a rapidly shifting world. In 2003, the Office of the Secretary General released its strategy for internal transformation. One of the areas of concern was ensuring that the actions and goals of the UN would reflect changes in the world at the time.

A central theme in the work was on matters of migration. Noting in the policy document *Strengthening of the United Nations: An Agenda for Further Change*, then-Secretary General Kofi Annan articulated a need for developing new policy responses to global migration. He wrote:

> We need to understand better the causes of international flows of people and their complex interrelationship with development. We must also prepare for the shift that has already started in the relative proportions of young people and the aged in most parts of the world and its implications for the labour force, social services and political processes.[7]

Shortly following the release of *Strengthening of the United Nations*, Annan asked Peter Sutherland, former Attorney General of Ireland, to serve as the UN Special Representative for International Migration. In September 2016, Sutherland presented a report to Secretary General Ban Ki Moon on the subject of migration. The Sutherland Report, as it came to be known, presented several recommendations on responding to migration trends. According to the report, comprehensive, international cooperation involving all sectors of society will ultimately help states gain better control over the increasing movement of people across borders, ". . . thereby facilitating safe and legal migration, which is greatly preferable to migration forced underground."[8]

The report established five policy priorities for how states might respond to areas of particular need in migration. The first of these five policy priorities focused on the management of crisis movements and protecting migrants in vulnerable situations. The second was on building opportunities for labor and skills mobility. The third was on ensuring orderly migration, including return of migrants. The fourth focused on fostering migrant inclusion and development benefits. The fifth focused on strengthening governance capacities. To Sutherland and his team, implementation of these priority areas meant that three sets of commitments would be established—those between states and migrants, those among states, and those between states and other stakeholders.[9]

TOWARD A GLOBAL COMPACT ON MIGRATION

The release of the Sutherland report coincided with the United Nations General Assembly's adoption of The New York Declaration for Refugees and Migrants in September of 2016. The Declaration endorsed a set of commitments for refugees and migrants. In its introduction, the Declaration observes:

> We are witnessing in today's world an unprecedented level of human mobility. More people than ever before live in a country other than the one in which they were born. Migrants are present in all countries in the world. Most of them move without incident. In 2015, their numbers surpassed 244 million, growing

at a rate faster than the world's population. However, there are roughly 65 million forcibly displaced persons, including over 21 million refugees, 3 million asylum seekers and over 40 million internally displaced persons.[10]

The Declaration established a set of aspirational goals for the international community to consider as it reflects on the realities of migration in the first quarter of the twenty-first century. Among the commitments in the Declaration is on the matter of combating xenophobia. It notes:

> We commit to combating xenophobia, racism and discrimination in our societies against refugees and migrants. We will take measures to improve their integration and inclusion, as appropriate, and with particular reference to access to education, health care, justice and language training. We recognize that these measures will reduce the risks of marginalization and radicalization. National policies relating to integration and inclusion will be developed, as appropriate, in conjunction with relevant civil society organizations, including faith-based organizations, the private sector, employers' and workers' organizations and other stakeholders. We also note the obligation for refugees and migrants to observe the laws and regulations of their host countries.[11]

In its message countering xenophobia and its broader support for those engaged in migratory processes, the Declaration is an aspirational document that aims to build a consensus among governments, civil society actors, and other parties related to managing the flow of migrants (including refugees)—and ensuring purposeful integration into their new societies.

CONCLUSION

Migration is a component of the human experience. Our means of conceptualizing various groups moving from one place to another have grown more complex as the reasons for such movement have become more diverse. The twentieth century witnessed the evolution of a system for the management of flows of uprooted people, as well as processes for defining those who are uprooted.

In the aftermath of World War II, a series of institutions evolved to manage the flow of populations. The most constant of these organizations has been the United Nations High Commission for Refugees. Over its development, UNHCR has had to adapt as an institution to reflect the shifting realities impacting the flow of refugees and other migrant populations. The twenty-first century is witnessing a new set of realities linked to the movement of people. Factors of war and conflict continue to provide reason for flight. We are, however, now witnessing a greater level of movement due to environmental and economic reasons.

The first two decades of the twenty-first century have seen movement toward a new set of frameworks for responding to migration trends, including the flow of refugees. The framework established by the New York Declaration in 2016, the 2018 Global Compact for Safe, Orderly, and Regular Migration, and the 2018 Global Compact on Refugees have all framed a context for engagement in the reformulation of policy discourse related to the movement of people.

The next chapters will explore three specific cases of migration trends and some of the resistance that has emerged in relation to such migration, as well as some of the shifting dynamics that have arisen as state and other actors have engaged with refugees and other displaced populations.

NOTES

1. Holborn, "The League of Nations and the Refugee Problem," 124.
2. Simpson, "The Refugee Problem," 616.
3. General Assembly Resolution 428 (V) of 14 December 1950, Chapter I (2).
4. Convention Relating to the Status of Refugees, art. 1 § A(2).
5. OAU Convention Governing the Specific Aspects of Refugee Problems in Africa, art. I § 1–2.
6. Cartagena Declaration on Refugees.
7. UN General Assembly, "Strengthening of the United Nations: an agenda for further change," 10.
8. UN General Assembly, "Report of the Special Representative of the Secretary General on Migration," 2.
9. UN General Assembly, "Report of the Special Representative of the Secretary General on Migration," 2.
10. UN General Assembly, Resolution 71/1.
11. UN General Assembly, Resolution 71/1 § 8.

Chapter Four

South Africa

Aspiration Meets Human Condition

Like many other migrants, Ernesto Alfabeto Nhamuave left his country to provide a better life for his family. The thirty-five-year-old departed his village of Vuca, in the Inhambane region of Mozambique, and after some time was able to legally settle in South Africa, where ultimately, he and his brother-in-law, Francisco, rented a shack in the Ramaphosa settlement near Johannesburg.

Ernesto was one of thousands of people who moved to South Africa in the late twentieth and early twenty-first centuries, partially driven by the economic realities in their home countries. Mozambique's financial instability resulted from years of civil war and postwar rebuilding that had yet to yield positive results for many of its citizens. Due to the war and the instability of the postwar era, thousands of Mozambicans had moved to South Africa in search of a better life. For many of them, South Africa—shed of its Apartheid-era realities—created a space of perceived enhanced economic opportunity.

While in Ramaphosa, Ernesto regularly sent money to his wife and children, helping where he could. At one point, he felt he would be able to save enough from the sporadic work he found as a bricklayer to build a concrete house for his family to replace the reed hut in which they lived. His dreams for what he might ultimately be able to provide included a home where his family would not have to walk a half kilometer for water, and where there would be adequate sewage removal.

Many of the people from other countries who had settled in Ramaphosa were aware that they were not welcomed by many of their South African neighbors. Ernesto and Francisco knew they were outsiders. Like many outsiders, they were aware that at times, they would face hostilities from communities where they lived. Over the years, such concerns had been reinforced with stories of growing violence targeting foreigners living in different parts of South Africa. Nine years earlier in an area known as Ivory Park in Johannesburg, six men from Mozambique were accused of rape, theft, and terrorizing residents. Acting as its own jury, a mob of nearly 400 locals caught two of the men, placed tires doused in gasoline around their necks, and set them on fire. In 2000, a refugee from Sudan had been thrown from a train by a group of armed men.[1] The next year, in the Zandspruit settlement, near Johannesburg, attacks against Zimbabweans by local South Africans led to over 150 shacks being looted or destroyed by fire and the displacement of several hundred mostly Zimbabweans who lived there.[2] There were scores of other cases where incidents of violence targeting foreigners were occurring.

On May 11, 2008, a riot erupted in Alexandra, a township not far from Ramaphosa. Like Ramaphosa, Alexandra had been struggling with high rates of poverty and unemployment for many years. Both communities had inadequate housing for many of their residents. Both had witnessed their own share of violence since the early 1990s. Both townships also had significant populations of people like Ernesto—those from other places on the continent whose outsider status was a characteristic upon which locals would seize as they sought people to blame for their social and economic circumstances. To many of the unemployed in Alexandra, Ramaphosa, and communities like them, it was frequently believed that foreigners like Ernesto and Francisco were taking their jobs and causing the dire economic circumstances in which local South Africans found themselves. As news spread of the violence in Alexandra, Ernesto and other foreigners living near him sensed that Ramaphosa would be next.

A few days following the Alexandra outbreak, Ernesto phoned home and shared with his wife some of his fears regarding the hostilities that he was sensing. He told her that he thought the tensions would pass. He also noted, however, that if things did not get better, he would find a way to return home. Over the following days, Ernesto and Francisco watched and listened for any signals of increased danger that they might face.

A week later, Ernesto and Francisco walked to the nearest taxi stand. Earlier that day, Francisco had been robbed by a roving group targeting foreigners living in the community. Neither of the two men were certain where that mob was, or if there were other mobs roaming the area, searching for foreigners. Near the taxis, Ernesto and Francisco were spotted by some of the members of one of the roving mobs and pursued. When the crowd caught them, members began to attack the men with iron bars and machetes. At one point, after some time of beating Francisco to a point of near death, the crowd turned its wrath onto Ernesto.

Through a hazed consciousness from several meters away, Francisco watched as members of the crowd beat Ernesto, threw blankets and old clothes on top of him and set him on fire. Ernesto tried to stand a few times, only to fall as he was beaten further and increasingly smothered by the flames that enveloped his body. Finally, the police arrived, dispersed the crowd, and extinguished the flames that had consumed Ernesto. By then however, it was too late. Ernesto Nhamuave was dead.

Over the next several weeks, photographs of Ernesto's last moments spread through the national and international media. Articles that appeared about him would refer to him as the "burning man," as pictures of his body engulfed in flames circulated in the press. In time, he became for many people the representational image of the violence that surfaced in several communities throughout South Africa during a few short weeks in 2008, when over sixty people were killed and roughly 100,000 people were displaced during attacks on foreigners.

The story of Ernesto Nhamuave was noted for the violence and because it countered the narrative that had been building about South Africa in the years prior to the incident. Recognizing a past which included the brutal and oppressive years of Apartheid, and clashes between rival parties in the years following Apartheid, policy makers and civil society leaders were working on shaping a very different story about their nation. This new account was based on reconciliation and harmony between people of the various groups that made up the nation.

The violence encountered by the scores of people driven out of their communities during the outbreaks of attacks in Ramaphosa, Alexandra, and similar communities, raised several questions about why such attacks on foreign-born individuals had occurred and what could be done to prevent them from being repeated. Were there things that government could do to minimize violence between South Africans living in a nation where a concept of mutuality was being promoted? What was the role of civil society? For many people at the time promoting the idea of inclusivity that Nelson Mandela, Archbishop Desmond Tutu, and others articulated in their language of a *new South Africa*, based in a "reality that will reinforce humanity's belief in justice, strengthen its confidence in the nobility of the human soul, and sustain all our hopes for a glorious life for all,"[3] ran counter to what the nation was experiencing in its outbreaks.

This chapter examines patterns of migration and xenophobia in South Africa around the time of these incidents in 2008 and in the years since. In the wake of the 2008 outbreaks, several analyses surfaced relating to why such incidents occurred and how they fit into the broader legacies of the nation. Could the incidents be viewed as isolated occurrences, or were they indicative of a broader set of political, economic, and social challenges of the time?

I begin this chapter with a review that considers the numerous periods of reinvention that the nation experienced with a focus on some of the processes of purposeful exclusion that have underscored much of South Africa's development. Underlining this exploration of the outbreaks in 2008, and the years since, is a complex narrative that incorporates much of the nation's history of inclusion, exclusion, and transition. This historical framework is critical as migration policies have evolved alongside South African conceptualizations of who should be included within government's facilitated marginal populations. Issues of state-enabled marginality were applied to non-white populations born in South Africa and those who in time would move there as migrants.

Between the early twentieth and early twenty-first centuries, several legislative and policy documents stretching from the 1913 Immigration and Regulation Act to the 2017 White Paper on International Migration to South Africa helped to frame government's narrative around migration. The history that emerged during the century that separated these policy provisions illustrates the perspectives at the time on different groups of migrants. For much of the period, policies were built on strategies to control population movement as part of a broader tactic of racial separation in South Africa through most of the twentieth century. In their own way, these approaches shaped much of the evolution that led to some of the currents underlying the xenophobic tensions that emerged in the early twenty-first century.

Next, I examine the outbreaks of xenophobic incidents in 2008. I use a specific case of a community impacted directly by the xenophobic outbreaks, that of Alexandra Township in 2008. As a community that has a historical role in the nation's broader patterns of segregated communities, the outbreaks in Alexandra provide a context for comprehending how factors of historic economic exclusion interfaces with outbreaks of xenophobic tension. I explore approaches that shape how patterns have evolved, and are shaped by broader spatial issues.

After a review of incidents that emerged in Alexandra and other communities over the years, I focus on questions of response to these incidents by government, NGOs, and other entities. Part of the reaction was the development of new policies related to the enhancement of integration strategies for migrants and refugees.

I conclude the chapter with an examination of three of the specific causes of the xenophobic outbreaks that have surfaced in South Africa: pre-1994 legacies, economic challenges, and enhanced ethnic nationalism. While these factors do not stand alone as sources for violence aimed at many of the third country nationals at the time, they do allow for a better understanding of the tension related to cycles of xenophobia in South Africa.

HISTORICAL REVIEW OF IMMIGRATION POLICY

Fifty years prior to the formation of the Union of South Africa in 1910, British colonialists of the Natal Province began importing indentured servants from the Indian subcontinent to work on sugar plantations. As a result of the labor importation, the Indian population in the province grew from being practically nonexistent in 1860 to one with over 150,000 people fifty years later. As the population grew, many government officials and members of the business community, began to perceive this growing Indian population as a threat to the social and economic stability that they had come to know in the province and the broader nation.

In 1913, to address these concerns around the size of the Indian population, the government passed the Admission of Persons to the Union Regulation Act, also known as the Immigration and Regulation Act of 1913. The Act defined immigrants as those who were "prohibited" and those who were "desired." Some of the differentiating characteristics that determined who was prohibited and desired included the ability to read and write a European language and contribute to the labor needs of the region. Ultimately, prohibited immigrants were perceived as people who were undesirable for political reasons, carried criminal records, were mentally or physically disabled, or who carried a contagious disease.

The Act also provided immigration and police officers with discretion in arresting and detaining prohibited immigrants (or those suspected of being prohibited immigrants), without a warrant of arrest. It also gave them the right to deport immigrants under warrant.

To assist with the administrative components, the Act created a Department of Immigration, which in turn established the Immigration Board. This board served to hear appeals by people who had been declared prohibited immigrants. The powers given to the Board posed a challenge to the rights of prospective immigrants and prohibited persons and established a precedent which exists to the present.

Section 4 of the Act placed restrictions on who could and who could not enter South Africa. The Act in effect created a two-tier system which also denied access to immigrant status to black Africans from the rest of the continent while ensuring the supply of labor to the mining industry and commercial agriculture.

Further Foundations of Migrant Exclusion

While the 1913 Act was targeted to limit the migration of Indians and blacks, it occurred during a point in time when growing rates of anti-Semitism shaped the evolution of migration policy in South Africa.[4] Seven years following the passage of the 1913 Act, the South African Minister of the Interior, Patrick Duncan, introduced the first measure to curtail Jewish migration into the country. Over subsequent years, Duncan would issue a series of directives that indicated the hesitation related to the increase of Jewish migrants entering the Union. In one confidential instruction issued to a staff member, he noted that, "these special cases should of course be very sparingly dealt with as the Ministerial policy is against any migration of fresh Jews from Russia."[5]

Two years later, in April 1922, Duncan issued a notification that aspects of the 1913 Immigration Regulation Act that were used to keep out non-white immigrants, would now be applied to Eastern Europeans.[6] Duncan's term as Minister of the Interior coincided with the years of the Bolshevik Revolution, when concerns around the potential in-flow of Russian Jewish migrants were being articulated in many nations. During those years, Duncan noted in one of his correspondences regarding the events in Russia:

> The victims are of course all Jews. . . . I am very doubtful if much can really be done to stop the stream . . . but they are really coming in much faster than we can assimilate them and the present Bolshevik scare which is nothing but a scare—gives a good opportunity for trying a little restriction.[7]

Duncan's perspectives provided evidence that public officials and members of the general public in South Africa were not immune to the anti-Semitism that was emerging in different corners of the world in the 1920s and 1930s. In 1926, a Census Department document entitled, "Notes on Immigration of Hebrews into South Africa," noted:

> The fact that one person in every four who has entered the Union this year is a Hebrew, generally of a low type, is a matter which requires some attention from the Government. . . . The existing conditions under which . . . the better class of the European section is being depleted, cannot be allowed to continue indefinitely without seriously affecting the standing of the European population as a whole.[8]

In 1930, largely with the support of officials such as Patrick Duncan, the South African Parliament passed its Immigrant Quota Act. This Act established a framework for separating migrant groups into those deemed desirable and undesirable. Much of this distinction was established by differentiating individuals from preferred countries and those from less preferred countries. The scheduled countries included many of those identified in the 1913 Act such as those in Northern and Southern Europe (excluding Greece) and the United States.

Less desired countries were provided a quota of fifty immigrants per year. A further 1,000 places were allotted to immigrants from non-scheduled countries (primarily wives, children and other dependents of people already resident in South Africa). The Act stated that nationality would be decided by country of birth, not citizenship. The purpose of this section was to exclude eastern Europeans who could otherwise have claimed German nationality.

While members of Parliament and others advocating for the passage of the 1930 Act noted that the act did not specifically target Jewish immigrants to South Africa, there were several undertones to discussions related to Jewish migrants that underscored some of the conversations related to exclusion. Such debate rested on four basic assertions: (1) Jewish migrants were not part of the original stock of settlers of the Union (English or Afrikaaners); (2) the differences perceived with Jewish migrants posed a threat to the quality of the white community and therefore the political control of the then black population by the white population; (3) because they were seen as innately different, Jews were not seen as assimilable or willing to assimilate with the white population; and (4) Jews did not contribute to the production capacity of South Africa.[9]

Data related to the numbers of Jewish immigrants arriving into South Africa illustrated the impact of the act. In 1929, the number of Jewish immigrants was 2,788. A year later, the number dropped to 1,881. In 1931, there were 885 Jewish immigrants who entered the nation.[10]

Aliens Act of 1937

Seven years following the Immigration Quota Act of 1930, Parliament passed the Aliens Act of 1937. Much of this Act was further aimed at determining how South Africa would address its influx of Jewish migrants. Some of the government's justification for the 1937 Act was the realization that it limited the entry of citizens who may have been better educated German-Jewish citizens who wished to reside in South Africa. Section 4(3)(b) of the Act stated that all applicants should be, "likely to become readily assimilated" with the European inhabitants of the Union and that they should not represent a threat to "European culture."

Almost immediately upon its enactment, the 1937 Act was used to deny the applications of German Jews to South Africa. As was the case with the 1930 Act, the impact on Jewish migration of the 1937 Act was felt immediately. The year before the Act was passed, there were 2,549 Jewish immigrants admitted from Germany. The year the Act was passed, that number dropped to 481, and in 1938, the number fell to 236.[11]

1940s — Nationalist Party and Immigration

The Nationalist Party's assumption of control of government in 1948 provided an opportunity for many of the leaders of the government to define characteristics that they felt were critical in shaping South African identity and establish a model for shaping the policies that impacted the movement of people.

A central figure in shaping the Nationalist Party and its policies during the 1950s and 1960s was Hendrick Verwoerd. In 1950, Verwoerd was appointed Minister of Native Affairs and held that position until 1958. Then, from 1958 to 1966, he served as Prime Minister. Verwoerd focused largely on protecting the white minority in South Africa, as well as developed policy frameworks and legislation that would support notions underscoring Apartheid systems.

One law which helped to frame much of the activity of the Nationalist Party, was the 1950 Population Registration Act, which provided the foundation upon which most of the population was classified. This Act ultimately added to the racial division in the nation by facilitating the segregation of the population and the further separation of communities. The Act legalized a racial classification system that would come to serve as a cornerstone for the Apartheid era.

1960 Census and Referendum

The 1960 South African census indicated that black South Africans outnumbered white South Africans by approximately 7 million citizens.[12] This prompted the South African government to seek ways of increasing the white population to further retain political control. The government sought to specifically encourage migration from England and Germany.

In October 1960, a referendum for the nation to become a republic was voted upon by white South Africans (non-whites were not permitted to vote). Voters elected a new government that would ultimately articulate the position of many of the Afrikaner Nationalists who sought to build a stronger sense of identity.

The years following the referendum witnessed the further implementation of policies aimed at promoting racial separation. It also saw deepening isolation of South Africa from much of the world, as policies of racial exclusion set it on a very different course than many countries that were beginning to actively promote strategies for racial inclusion. South Africa sought to implement further policies that would ensure minimal inflow of additional black Africans.

The 1970s and 1980s witnessed a period of turbulence for the Nationalist Party. Enhanced decolonization on the African continent left South Africa increasingly surrounded by nations hostile to the Apartheid government. Increased urbanization by black South Africans added pressure in the white government for transformation that would ultimately occur in the 1990s. Immigration strategies during the Apartheid era focused on strengthening the government's positions of reinforced policies of black immigration primarily for labor needs and enhancing white migration as a strategy for helping control the black population. Increased anti-Apartheid activity, both with internal opposition and through external pressure, isolated the country and made government more resistant to policies of migration.

In 1990, the government made several policy determinations that would ultimately create dramatic changes in the governance of South African society. First government permitted the existence of the ANC and ultimately the release of Nelson Mandela and scores of other political prisoners. These actions led to long-term political reform, which would, in time, shape immigration policy in South Africa.

Aliens Control Act of 1991

One of the final pieces of legislation adopted by the Apartheid-era Parliament was the Aliens Control Act of 1991. Building upon the government's immigration policy of control and deportation, the Act established what would be the government's transitional policy and coalesced Apartheid-era legislation linked to migration.

Central to the Act were factors of discretionary authority by immigration officers—thus limiting courts' abilities to check the decisions of immigration officers who had determined a person's legality or prohibited status. Section 55 of the Act was central in shaping this authority. It noted:

> no court of law shall have any jurisdiction to review, quash, reverse, interdict or otherwise interfere with any act, order or warrant of the Minister, an immigration officer, or master of a ship performed or issued under this Act and which relates to the restriction of determination, or the removal from the Republic, of a person who is being dealt with as a prohibited person.[13]

As a result of this authority, the immigration officers were emboldened in making decisions that would ultimately impact the fate of migrants.

While the 1991 Act was one of the last acts of the Apartheid era, it also provided a transition to some of the approaches related to migration patterns and strategies of the transition years that would follow. It would, in time, become the piece of legislation that would be criticized and ultimately adjusted with future policy.

Refugee Convention and Norms

In 1993, the South African government and the United Nations High Commissioner for Refugees (UNHCR) signed a memorandum that permitted refugees to enter the country. This action signaled an engagement of South Africa in global migration frameworks. Within three years, South Africa had become party to several of the international conventions related to refugees, including the 1951 United Nations Convention Relating to the Status of Refugees, the 1967 Protocol Relating to the Status of Refugees, as well as the 1969 Organization of African Union Convention Governing the Specific Aspects of Refugee Problems in Africa. These advancements signaled a willingness within South Africa to engage in strategies related to the broader global refugee discourse.

South Africa also witnessed a shift in inward migration. For years, South Africa was perceived as a place where non-white migrants could not settle (except for those who entered for work in fields such as mining). Eventually, it became a place where people could enter. Increasingly, people from countries throughout the African continent began to see South Africa as a destination.

THE REPUBLIC OF SOUTH AFRICA: 1994 ELECTIONS AND 1996 CONSTITUTIONAL FRAMEWORK FOR CONSIDERING MIGRATION

Celebrated as signifying the end of the Apartheid years, South Africa's 1994 elections promoted a period of magnified expectations in areas of human rights and broad inclusion in South African society. The transition to a new government established a framework that would make its way into the discourse on migration policy. The expectation was that the new South Africa would create opportunities for those who had been prohibited from fully participating in the economic and civic fabric of the nation. Many people from groups historically marginalized had numerous expectations around how they would ultimately be able to participate in the broader society.

Two years following the 1994 elections, South Africa adopted its 1996 Constitution. Since its adoption, the Constitution has been lauded as one of the more progressive and human rights-focused constitutions in the world. A critical element of the Constitution is South Africa's Bill of Rights, which includes several components that can be applied to the rights of migrants and refugees.

One of these sections that stands out is Section 9 of the Bill of Rights. It focuses on concepts of equality. It notes:

1. Everyone is equal before the law and has the right to equal protection and benefit of the law.
2. Equality includes the full and equal enjoyment of all rights and freedoms. To promote the achievement of equality, legislative and other measures designed to protect or advance persons, or categories of persons, disadvantaged by unfair discrimination may be taken.
3. The state may not unfairly discriminate directly or indirectly against anyone on one or more grounds, including race, gender, sex, pregnan-

cy, marital status, ethnic or social origin, colour, sexual orientation, age, disability, religion, conscience, belief, culture, language and birth.
4. No person may unfairly discriminate directly or indirectly against anyone on one or more grounds in terms of subsection (3). National legislation must be enacted to prevent or prohibit unfair discrimination.
5. Discrimination on one or more of the grounds listed in subsection (3) is unfair unless it is established that the discrimination is fair.[14]

Another component of note is Section 10, which focuses on issues of human dignity. It argues, "Everyone has inherent dignity and the right to have their dignity respected and protected."[15]

A third component, Section 12(1) of the Bill of Rights, focuses on issues of freedom and security of the person. This section notes:

1. Everyone has the right to freedom and security of the person, which includes the right
   a. not to be deprived of freedom arbitrarily or without just cause;
   b. not to be detained without trial;
   c. to be free from all forms of violence from either public or private sources;
   d. not to be tortured in any way; and
   e. not to be treated or punished in a cruel, inhumane or degrading way.[16]

Since the adoption of the 1996 Constitution, several cases have emerged which have established a broader understanding of how the courts would consider issues pertaining to migrants, refugees, and asylum seekers in South Africa. Three cases provide examples of the deliberative processes and facts underscoring court determinations in relation to these populations.

The first of these is the 2003 South African Supreme Court of Appeal case *Minister of Home Affairs v. Watchenuka*. In Watchenuka, a challenge to a decision was made under the Refugee Act No 130 of 1998 that focused on the right of asylum seekers to work and obtain an education while they await finalization of an asylum application.

The case came about after Muriel Watchenuka, an asylum seeker, and her son contested elements of the Refugee Act No 130 of 1988 that prohibited her and her son from working and studying while waiting to be recognized as refugees.

The Court held that the prohibition of employment and study by the asylum seekers presented in the case was in direct conflict with the right of dignity as presented in the Bill of Rights. As Judge Robert Nugent, writing for the majority noted:

> Human dignity has no nationality. It is inherent in all people—citizens and non-citizens alike—simply because they are human. And while that person happens to be in this country—for whatever reason—it must be respected and is protected by s. 10 of the Bill of Rights.[17]

The notion of dignity underscoring this case is a concept that proved central in other judicial reviews of rights of migrants and asylum seekers in South Africa.

In a case the following year, *Lawyers for Human Rights v. Minister of Home Affairs*, the Constitutional Court provided another example of the intersection of rights as articulated in the Bill of Rights and circumstances impacting migrants. In this case, questions pertaining to how illegal foreigners were to be removed from South Africa in accordance with section 34 of the Immigration Act were of concern.

According to the government, foreign nationals at a port of entry, unable to formally enter South Africa, were not protected by the nation's Bill of Rights. The government argued that Section 7(1) of the Constitution applied rights to people "in our country." According to the government's position, people at ports of entry were not technically in South Africa.

The determination of this question of applicability of rights to illegal foreigners at ports of entry could adversely affect the freedom of the people concerned as well as their dignity as human beings. As Judge Zac Yacoob, writing for the majority noted:

> The only relevant question in this case therefore is whether these rights are applicable to foreign nationals who are physically in our country but who have not been granted permission to enter the country formally. These rights are integral to the values of human dignity, equality, and freedom that are fundamental to our constitutional order. The denial of these rights to human beings who are physically inside the country at sea- or airports merely because they have not entered South Africa formally would constitute a restriction of the values underlying our Constitution. It could hardly be suggested that persons who are being unlawfully detained on a ship in South African waters cannot turn to South African courts for protection, or that a person who commits murder on board a ship in South African waters is not liable to prosecution in a South African court.[18]

Ultimately the case reaffirmed the importance of the concept of "everyone" in the Constitution's Bill of Rights as a component of a constitution that "enshrines the rights of all people in our country and affirms the democratic values of human dignity, equality, and freedom."[19]

Finally, in the case *Khosa v Minister of Social Development*, the Constitutional Court held that the principle of "[e]quality in respect of access to socio-economic right is implicit in the reference to 'everyone' being entitled to have access to such rights in Section 27."[20] In Khosa, the applicants were Mozambican citizens who had fled Mozambique due to the civil war in the 1980s and were living in South Africa as permanent residents. They challenged sections of the Social Assistance Act 59 of 1992, which disqualified people who were not South African citizens from receiving social grants, child support grants, and dependency grants.

The applicants contested that they were eligible for social assistance and child support grants, however, were being prohibited from accessing the assistance because they lacked South African citizenship. According to them, the exclusion of non-citizens from the welfare scheme is inconsistent with the state's obligations under section 27(1)(c) of S.A. Constitution to provide access to social security to "everyone."

The Court's majority held that the exclusion of permanent residents from the welfare scheme infringed on the right to equality, and were discriminatory. Writing for the majority opinion, Judge Yvonne Mokgoro noted the unfairness would not be justifiable under the constitution. As she noted, "the exclusion of permanent residents from the scheme is likely to have a severe impact on the dignity of the persons concerned, who, unable to sustain themselves, have to turn to others to enable them to meet the necessities of life and are thus cast in the role of supplicants."[21]

These cases demonstrate that all individuals in South Africa, regardless of legal status, have all of the rights indicated in Section 7(1) of the Bill of Rights, which notes that the Bill of Rights is a "cornerstone of democracy in South Africa." Accordingly the Bill of Rights "affirms the democratic values of human dignity, equality, and freedom."[22]

Shifting Approaches: 1997 Green Paper on Migration

In 1997, the Ministry of Home Affairs published its Green Paper on International Migration. This document reconceptualized what were increasingly being perceived as limitations of the 1991 Aliens Control Act and reflected some of the tension related to migration within South African society. The authors of the Green Paper shifted the dialogue to focus on the benefits that planned and efficient immigration would bring for South Africa.

The Green Paper helped define three main categories of people who were entering South Africa at the time: immigrants, refugees and migrants. It suggested that an immigrant who wanted to move to South Africa should participate in a labor market-based point system, an immigration policy focusing on skills and abilities of the immigrants to contribute to the economy.

This approach implies that immigration policy should be socially and economically oriented.

The second focus of the Green Paper was on refugees. Here, the paper advocated for burden sharing with other nations in the Southern African Development Community (SADC). This implied that every SADC member should take responsibility to also assist those who are vulnerable or develop their economies to help reduce the risk of cross-border migration.

The third focus was on migrants. Here the paper argues that the South African government, using the planned immigration system or skill-based system to determine who should be allowed in the country, should specifically prioritize those foreigners who do not plan to stay in the country long-term.

Refugee Policy in South Africa

In June of 1998, the South African government published its Refugee White Paper. The paper argued that South Africa's refugee policy was based in both international and constitutional obligations around migration control objectives, security interests, economic interests, and relations with other nations.

The paper noted that the ratification of the 1951 UN Convention Relating to the Status of Refugees, the 1967 UN Protocol, and the 1969 OAU Convention Governing the Specific Aspects of Refugee Problems in Africa had legitimized the role of refugee policy in South Africa. As a result of South Africa's ratification of these documents, definitions of refugees presented in them were used as the foundations upon which refugee status was determined.

Shortly following the publication of the 1998 Refugee White Paper, Parliament passed The Refugees Act 130. This act provided the South African government with the relevant international legal instruments, principles and standards relating to refugees. It provided for the reception of asylum seekers into South Africa and a regulation of applications for recognition of refugee status. As a result of the White Paper and subsequently, the Refugee Act 130, South Africa finally had a refugee policy in place that was in alignment with international standards.

Toward the Immigration Act of 2002

Two years following the release of the 1997 Green Paper on International Migration, and a year following the publication of the 1998 Refugee White Paper, the South African government published its 1999 White Paper on International Migration. This paper reconciled stringent migration control and the fight on illegal migrants with mechanisms for a new and more open skills-based system. Because the 1998 Refugee White Paper addressed matters pertaining to refugee concerns, the 1999 migration paper focused on broad matters pertaining to migration.

The 1999 White Paper on International Migration provided the foundation for a bill in 2000 that would ultimately become the Immigration Act of 2002 and a replacement of the 1991 Aliens Control Act.

Xenophobic Outbreaks and Policy Responses: A Case of Alexandra

While South Africa was undergoing its various transitions in the last decade of the twentieth century and first decade of the twenty-first century, one of the pressing concerns was the economic and social disparity that remained in existence. The disparity was particularly of concern comparing the lives of those living in township communities throughout the nation.

The community of Alexandra is one of the settings where achieving post-1994 economic transformations has been elusive. Established in 1912 near Johannesburg as one of the primarily black townships in the nation, Alexandra had long been a site for social tension, protest, and general unrest. In the 1970s, as student protests in nearby Soweto began to lead to community mobilization, Alexandra saw members of its community engaged in many of the activities focused on civil protest around educational opportunity.

In the early 1990s, Alexandra erupted due to political and ethnic divisions that separated the community, with violence igniting between the primarily Xhosa-supported ANC controlled areas and the primarily Zulu-supported Inkatha Freedom Party controlled areas. These tensions reflected the underscoring political challenges of the time.

In the decades since the 1994 elections, a growing tension related to unrealized expectations in service delivery and high levels of poverty were still prevalent in many communities. Alexandra was one of these communities. Over the years, with slow rates of service delivery in Alexandra, tensions continued to mount due to social and economic realities. In addition to concerns about crime levels, there were complaints that newcomers were stealing the jobs of native South Africans who had been in the community longer.

On May 11, 2008, a group of community leaders met with police in Alexandra Township regarding concerns about rising crime and service delivery in the community. Central in the claims of many of the people gathered were concerns that the lack of opportunity, the levels of crime, and other general challenges in the community were the result of actions by foreigners. Not receiving the guarantees that they wanted, meeting attendees decided to forcefully evict foreigners from their neighborhoods. They later converged that evening with various weapons in hand. With cries of, "Khipha ikwerekwere" (kick out the foreigners), mobs attacked certain enclaves of shacks known to be inhabited by foreign nationals.

More than 3,000 people fled that night from their homes for refuge at the police stations. An estimated 500 people remained in the township under the protection of police. The attacks in Alexandra continued for four days and quickly spread to other communities throughout the nation. In each instance, the situations were similar. Tensions would mount in some gathering where groups of South Africans in poor communities would complain about the presence of foreigners and the opportunities they were perceived to have. At some point a call would be made to kick the foreigners out of communities. In many instances groups ranging in size would begin roving the communities, looking for foreign-born people or people from outside of the immediate areas to attack.

Immediate Aftermath

Many of the pressing questions in 2008 following the attacks focused on how the violence targeting foreign-born populations escalated as quickly as they did. For Thabo Mbeki, then-President, the incidents were not acts of xenophobia, but merely incidents of violence. As he noted at a memorial gathering for victims:

> When I heard some accuse my people of xenophobia, of hatred of foreigners, I wondered what the accusers knew about my people, which I did not know.... The dark days of May which have brought us here today were visited on our country by people who acted with criminal intent. What happened during these days was not inspired by a perverse nationalism, or extreme chauvinism, resulting in our communities violently expressing the hitherto unknown sentiment of mass and mindless hatred of foreigners—xenophobia . . . and this I must also say—none in our society has any right to encourage or incite xenophobia by trying to explain naked criminal activity by cloaking it in the garb of xenophobia.[23]

Mbeki's criticisms paralleled those of others who refused to consider the outbreaks of May 2008 as reflective of xenophobic tensions—versus issues of simply community-based violence that stemmed from years of frustration due to economic uncertainty. Government and civil society reflected on what had happened in the country, and how to respond to the outbreaks, ensuring that they would not occur in the future.

In several instances, people were reminding one another of South Africa's inequities—and the conditions in many of the communities where tensions were escalating. Several observers noted that while the attackers in communities like Alexandra, and Ramaphosa were to blame for the direct violence, the fact that an economic, political, and civic framework that further enabled levels of poverty to persist helped provide a framework for the broader community tensions as well.

Changes in Migration Approaches

Eight years following the 2008 outbreaks, government released a 2016 Green Paper on migration. The paper pointed to limitations in South Africa's then-existing migration policy as inadequately embracing opportunities linked to migration, while safeguarding sovereignty, public safety, and national security. The paper went on to note that the debate at the time reflected a tension between stricter immigration control advocates and advocates supporting relaxed immigration policies.

The Green Paper proposed the development of a managed migration approach that would achieve common goals toward the development and implementation of new migration policies. It also sought to educate the public at large concerning the rights of foreigners, illegal immigrants, and refugees through the Department of Home Affairs. Lastly, the government proposed placing a legal requirement on the government to actively contest xenophobia in public service, leading to the creation of departments focused on countering incidents of xenophobia. One year following the release of the Green Paper, in July of 2017, the Department of Home Affairs released its White Paper on International Migration.

The White Paper noted various limitations of the 1999 paper and signaled shifting frameworks for policies related to migration. For example, the 2017 paper noted that the previous paper had significant gaps in areas such as the management of migrant integration, management of emigration, and the management of asylum seekers and refugees.

The 2017 White Paper based its framework around holistic approaches to international migration that appreciated the interconnectedness of migration matters and a link to South Africa's broader National Development Plan, which had become the guiding document for much of South Africa's national strategic planning processes.

Ultimately, the White Paper signaled a shift to policies that reflected on awareness of a fuller set of complexities on matters of migration that had been evidenced in previous approaches established. It also placed South Africa in stronger alignment with evolving global norms related to migration.

SOUTH AFRICA, MIGRATION, AND XENOPHOBIA: SOME UNDERLYING ISSUES

The evolution of South African migration policies over a century provide a framework for comprehending some of the complexities that correlate with growing rates of xenophobia and linked violence. Racial and ethnic divisions connected to the history of the nation, the evolving social dynamics between different groups of people, the government policies on the separation and control of populations that were a part of the nation's development over the years, and continued economic disparities between groups, provide a logical conclusion that there might be a persistence of tensions between populations. Three areas stand out regarding possible causes for the emergence of tensions.

Underlying Issue I: Pre-1994 Legacies

South Africa's pre-1994 legacies included the implementation of policies of purposeful exclusion. Much of South Africa's colonial history long before the formation of the Union in 1910 was focused on controlling for labor needs and managing migration flows so as to not rebalance a political system that favored a white minority. As these measures of control were developed over time, questions of how to continue policy practices of controlling immigration rates, and ensuring retention of wealth and land in the hands of a limited few framed ongoing goals.

The 1913 Immigration Regulation Act emerged as a strategy for managing the inflow of large numbers of immigrants from India. The Land Act of the same year set in motion policies that helped ensure the unequal distribution of wealth. Years of purposeful segregation and exclusion of specific population groups, supported by these pieces of legislation and other acts of law, helped facilitate economic imbalances that would underscore some of the group tensions that existed in Alexandra, Ramaphosa, and other communities.

Ultimately, population control mechanisms of the Apartheid era helped to galvanize efforts aimed at further marginalizing segments of South Africa's black population. The legacies prior to 1994 focused on keeping segments of South Africa's populations in specific places and minimizing opportunities outside of prescribed roles in society. The pre-1994 legacies framed the economic and political foundations of marginalization that shaped much of the tension that would lead to some of the community-level frustrations that surfaced in May of 2008, and other periods where foreigners were viewed as a cause of some of the continued challenges in communities.

Decades of purposeful exclusion and the long-term economic consequences of such exclusion set in place a framework for tensions that would impact communities. The shift to a new government in 1994 did not result in economic and social change for as many of the people as had been imagined during the early years of transition. The xenophobic tensions surfaced at the time, largely linked to a broad set of community-level frustrations, and helped to illustrate some of the then existing fault lines that would need to be addressed in South African society.

Underlying Issue II: Economic Challenges

South Africa's economic challenges have been among some of the larger issues that the nation has encountered in its years following the mid-1990s transitions. With one of the world's largest Gini coefficients, the nation's economic divide has been central to its multiple challenges in the years since the transitions of the 1990s. Often, when large segments of a population sit on the economic margins, a tendency to scapegoat for their own economic situations occur. Perceptions of both personal and national economic situations tend to correlate strongly with general population attitudes toward foreigners.

> In 2015, an Inter-Ministerial Committee on Migration Report noted:
> ... the primary cause of the violence against foreign nationals is the increased competition arising from the socio-economic circumstance in South Africa.[24]

Economic marginalization often breeds jealousy and concerns among those who may end up in positions less well off than others. The existence of several of the divisions in South Africa that have been supported and encouraged by previous governments have helped to exacerbate present-day tensions. As people who have lived in communities watch as others move into the communities, and comparatively succeeded, the resulting tension can impact broader incidents of intergroup violence. Many of the communities that experienced conflicts in 2008 saw some of them as a direct result of the intergroup economic tensions.

Underlying Issue III: Enhanced Ethnic Nationalism

According to Human Rights Watch, there have been several statements by South African public officials that have supported anti-foreigner violence. As Human Rights Watch noted in 1998, a decade prior to the attacks noted in Ramaphosa and Alexandra:

> South Africa's public culture has become increasingly xenophobic, and politicians often make inflammatory statements that the 'deluge' of migrants is responsible for the current crime wave, rising unemployment, or even the spread of diseases. As the unfounded perception that migrants are responsible for a variety of social ills grows, migrants have increasingly become the targets of abuse at the hands of the police, the army, and the Department of Home Affairs, refugees and asylum seekers with distinctive features from far-away countries are especially targeted for abuse.[25]

Public officials have promoted ideas on social dangers associated with foreign or non-native members of South Africa's immigrant population. Migrants have been depicted as the source of crime and other social ills in South Africa. A decade before the 2008 outbreaks in Alexandra, Ramaphosa, and other communities, South African Defense Minister Joe Modise noted:

> As for crime, the army is helping the police get rid of crime and violence in the country. However, what can we do? We have one million illegal immigrants in our country who commit crimes and who are mistaken by some people for South African citizens. That is the real problem. We have adopted a strict policy and have banned illegal immigration in order to combat the criminals coming from neighboring states so that we can round up the criminals residing in South Africa.[26]

Modise's comments mirror those of other public officials who over the decades have placed members of migrant groups in unfavorable positions in the public eye.

In 2015, Zulu King Goodwill Zwelithini called for the deportation of foreign nationals living in the country. The King reportedly said it was unacceptable that locals were being made to compete with people from other countries for the few economic opportunities available, noting:

> Most government leaders do not want to speak out on this matter because they are scared of losing votes. . . . As the king of the Zulu nation, I cannot tolerate a situation where we are being led by leaders with no views whatsoever. . . . We are requesting those who come from outside to please go back to their countries. . . . The fact that there were countries that played a role in the country's struggle for liberation should not be used as an excuse to create a situation where foreigners are allowed to inconvenience locals. . . . I know you were in their countries during the struggle for liberation. But the fact of the matter is you did not set up businesses in their countries.[27]

King Zwelithini's comments reflect the feelings of many people who are looking at members of migrant communities with some level of suspicion and as an economic threat to local communities. That he plays a role as a public figure raises questions on the legitimacy that his voice provides for members of a broader public with various degrees of concern about foreigners it might choose to view as a threat.

CONCLUSION

In February of 2017, protesters marched through the streets of Pretoria in opposition to many of the newcomers who had come into the area in recent years. Their protests were focused on the number of migrants from other nations and perceptions of economic competition that these migrants were presenting to South Africans. The complaints against the migrants echoed many of the same sentiments heard several years prior. Concerns about migrants taking their jobs, bringing crime into communities, and competing for housing and other resources were among the many issues voiced.

South Africa is a nation of potential and achievement. Unfortunately for many people who are still awaiting the promises of post-Apartheid opportunity, it is also a nation where there has been a great deal of frustration. The protests against many migrants is a sign of frustrations of dreams that have remained elusive in many communities where the anticipated changes of 1994 are still far from being realized.

Despite its challenges, South Africa is also a nation where processes of re-imagining have been consistent components of the nation's history. The 1996 Constitution is the product of a new imagination that swept through South Africa in the early to mid-1990s. It represents a vision of a nation building itself as one that would be inclusive and one that would promote a level of respect for human rights, and notions of equality. Part of the challenge in realizing that vision is one of determining how to address continued inequalities in economic, civic, and social inclusion. Balancing the realities of frustrations of those still at the economic and social margins with the realities of a nation that has and will have new people arriving to its borders, will be one of the ongoing challenges of South Africa's future.

NOTES

1. Crush, *The Perfect Storm*, 47–48.
2. Smith, "Zimbabweans Flee Shanty Town Attacks in South Africa."
3. Mandela, "Statement of the President of the African National Congress."
4. The same year that the Immigration and Regulation Act was passed, South Africa passed the 1913 Land Act, which would play a central role in framing wealth inequalities that would shape South African society. The Land Act established the boundaries of land ownership for black South Africans, and prohibited them from buying, leasing or acquiring land outside of the reserves. Such economic disparities would impact tensions between black South Africans who faced the effect of such policies, and newer arrivals.
5. Peberdy, *Selecting Immigrants*, 59.
6. Peberdy, *Selecting Immigrants*, 59.
7. Peberdy, *Selecting Immigrants*, 60.
8. Peberdy, *Selecting Immigrants*, 75.
9. Peberdy, *Selecting Immigrants*, 58.
10. Peberdy, *Selecting Immigrants*, 65.
11. Peberdy, *Selecting Immigrants*, 69.
12. McGlashan, "White Immigration into South Africa," 383.
13. Aliens Control Act 96 of 1991 § 55.
14. South African Const. ch 2 § 9.
15. South African Const. ch 2 § 10.
16. South African Const. ch 2 § 12(1).
17. *Minister of Home Affairs v. Watchenuka*, 25.
18. *Lawyers for Human Rights v. Minister of Home Affairs*, 26.
19. South African Const. ch 2 § 7(1).
20. *Khosa v. Minister of Social Development*, 42. Section 27(1)c of the South African Constitution notes that everyone has the right to have access to social security if they are unable to support themselves or their dependents.
21. *Khosa v. Minister of Social Development*, 80.
22. South African Const. ch 2 § 7(1).
23. Mbeki, "Address of the President of South Africa."

24. Carciotto and Mavura, "The Evolution of Migration Policy in Post-Apartheid South Africa," 48.
25. Human Rights Watch, *"Prohibited Persons,"* 4.
26. Human Rights Watch, *"Prohibited Persons,"* 185. Quote of Defense Minister Joe Modise, 1997.
27. Ndou, "Foreigners Must Go Home—King Zwelithini."

Chapter Five

Malta

Toward an Integrative Strategy

On October 9, 2016, roughly one hundred members of the Moviment Patrijotti, a group claiming to represent more than 20,000 people, gathered in the Maltese town of Bugibba to protest the building of a new mosque. Earlier in the year, the Malta Muslim Council had applied to the local town hall requesting permission to convert a room in one of its buildings into a prayer room. With chants of "Malta is ours only," and "Malta for Maltese and not for foreigners," the demonstrators expressed their frustrations around accepting those who had recently moved to the country as migrants, asylum seekers, or refugees. Among the concerns raised by Henry Battistino, leader of the group, was that small prayer rooms such as the one proposed, were breeding grounds for extremism.[1]

This was not the first time that members of Moviment Patrijotti had risen in opposition to the increasing presence of migrants in Malta. Over the years, they had gathered, protested, and made very public statements against the newcomers. Some members of the group had even suggested that Malta needed a national registry for members of the nation's Muslim community.[2] In their opposition to the migrants, the members of the Moviment Patrijotti found that they were not alone in their opposition to Malta's growing migrant population. Claims of Malta having been "invaded" and at risk of losing much of its identity due to the rising number of migrants were central arguments from individuals who opposed the growing number of people coming to Malta from elsewhere.

Despite the presence of organizations such as the Moviment Patrijotti, there were groups and individuals sympathetic to the plights of many of the migrants who had arrived in this small nation in recent years. For them, there was a recognition that many of the newest arrivals had come to Malta as refugees and asylum seekers in search of a better life. For those proving themselves to be more sympathetic, there was a simple desire to be supportive of the plight of people who had moved there. There was an awareness that refugees and asylum seekers would, if possible, move back to their home countries if not for the political, social, or economic realities, which caused concerns for safety, and protection of their lives.

Many supporters of the demographic changes under way in Malta understand that the discourse on migration has been based on the transition that the nation is undergoing. As a country with a population of under a half-million people that has received a disproportionate number of migrants over the years, Malta has found itself in a position of framing policies in relation to both a small population and a rapid rate of growth in its migrant population. At a point in time when questions of the right blend of migration policies have been framing discourse in Europe, Malta provides a locale for conceptualizing how nations might develop strategies on migration, integration, and the recognition or dismissal of some of the more xenophobic perspectives in a society. It also however provides a setting for understanding policy adaptation for responding to rapid demographic change.

This chapter examines patterns of migration in Malta and resultant policy development over the years. I have divided the chapter into three sections. First, I explore the historical context for migration to Malta. For most of its history, Malta has been a place where outsiders have come for periods of time, ruled, and often left their influences on the broader society. Today, in looking at such cultural clues as language, architecture, and religion, we find evidence of the broader impacts of outside cultures on the evolution of the nation. As a result of this history, there are communities that articulate a notion of Malta having been "invaded" throughout its history as the justification for some of the xenophobic perspectives that exist among some segments of the population.

Next, I explore patterns of migration in the early years of the twenty-first century. In 2002, Malta began to receive an influx of people coming from nations on the African continent, supplementing numerous arrivals who had been coming from the Middle East, and Central and Eastern Europe. Questions related to patterns for these new arrivals initially led to the development of policies focused on exclusion and marginalization of migrants and asylum seekers. Approaches at the time to managing the inflow of migrants initially placed Malta in a position where it was criticized by members of the international community for policies which were defended by government officials as merely those of deterrence.

This initial influx occurred several months before Malta experienced a political shift that would impact Maltese identity and its various policies related to migration. In 2003, Maltese voters decided through a public referendum to become members of the European Union (EU). The vote and EU membership led to policies that would shape a broader discourse related to shifting policies on migrants and a tension related to EU migration.

More recently, the nation has incorporated policies that have focused on the development of integration strategies to proactively engage members of its migrant populations. In 2005, the Maltese government launched its first integration framework. Since then, the nation has been actively exploring efforts around managing the realities of changing populations, culminating in the formal adoption of a national integration strategy in late 2017. This shift toward a position where Malta has been exploring strategies for enhancing integration tactics, as opposed to promoting anti-migrant policies, provides both a critical part of the narrative and a component that may, in time, provide valuable lessons for other nations exploring integration strategies. Such a movement has occurred in the face of mixed public opinion on migration and an altering social and civic landscape with a rapidly changing group of stakeholders in the migration discourse. This has been a critical part of the narrative around migration in Malta.

I suggest in this chapter that Malta has navigated a transition that has moved from that of a nation opposed to migration to one that has become more accepting of processes of migration. This transition has several policies pertaining to acceptance and integration which have supplanted perspectives opposing such transition. Because of the rapid demographic changes and the realization of policy makers that such changes will continue to occur, the decision of assuming a proactive stance on migration, are central elements of Malta's experiences around migration in the first two decades of the twenty-first century.

HISTORICAL FRAMEWORK AND IDENTITY

Geographically situated in the middle of the Mediterranean, Malta has been positioned in the center of sea routes that have been important to human migration for centuries. The early history of the islands Gozo, Comino, and Malta, that we now jointly refer to as Malta, is one that saw Phoenicians, Carthaginians, and Romans occupying the land and bringing their own cultural influences on people living there. Much of the modern context for tensions related to Maltese policy on patterns of migration can be viewed based on the interplay of history and culture over several centuries.

Narratives of migration to and from Malta often begin with a New Testament story of a shipwreck in roughly 60 AD. On board the ship was a group of prisoners being transported to Rome, where they were due to be tried as political rebels. According to the story, among the prisoners who swam to shore following the wreck was a prisoner known as Paul of Tarsus. One evening, shortly after reaching the shore, Paul was bitten by a poisonous viper. The island natives watched as Paul shook the creature from his hand and remained unaffected by its venom. For the islanders, this display of not being affected by the snake's poison was an indication of Paul's connection to some level of divine power.

During the rest of his three month stay on the island, Paul continued to be welcomed warmly by the local inhabitants, who remained fascinated by the spiritual connection they viewed him as having. While he was there, Paul taught the natives of the island about his religion. Over the years, the teachings of Paul of Tarsus spread, and he would become viewed as the person responsible for introducing this new religion of Christianity to Malta. St. Paul, as he later came to be known, would play a critical role in the overall narrative of the Christian faith in Malta. He would also come to serve in Maltese lore as a depiction of the treatment of the refugee or newcomer to Malta. The image that spread widely over time was of the shipwrecked individual, who was warmly welcomed by the people of the island and bestowed upon them the gift of a faith that would carry forward throughout the country's history.

By the fourth century AD, Malta had become part of the Byzantine Empire. As such, upon Emperor Constantine's making the official religion of the Empire Christianity, the people of the archipelago found themselves adopting the Christian faith. Constantine's processes for ensuring conversion included beheading if one refused to convert, thus leading many who otherwise may not have done so to adopt the Christianity.

In 870 AD, after several battles between the Byzantine Empire and the North African Aghlabids, Malta fell under Aghlabid rule. This period has little known about it, as many of the historical records were abolished by subsequent rulers. During this period, as the religion of the Aghlabids, Islam became more prominent throughout Malta. There are also some indicators that suggest further areas of impact by these rulers on Malta during this period. The Maltese language, for example, is heavily influenced by Arabic, and parts of Malta have architecture which demonstrates the impact of Islamic cultural influences under Aghlabid rule.

The period of rule under the Aghlabids is considered the beginning of a several hundred-year tension between Christian and Muslim rulers that some suggest is the cause of much of the xenophobia expressed toward many of today's migrant populations in Malta, particularly those who are Muslim. Indeed, today as groups such as the Moviment Patrijotti express their concerns about the presence of Malta's migrant communities, they occasionally do so with arguments of past Muslim invasions and periods of Islamic rule such as those under the Aghlabids as providing historic justification for their opposition to the arrival of further Muslims. Their movement is one that is, in their opinions, protecting Malta from future conquest.

Slightly two hundred years following Malta's fall under the Aghlabid rule, forces under Count Roger of Normandy invaded Malta in 1091. This invasion was welcomed by Christians in Malta who saw it as an opportunity to permit a resurgence of Christianity there and an expulsion of Islamic rulers. The Norman period represents a re-emergence of Christianity in Malta in place of Islamic rule.

The Knights Hospitaller and the Great Siege

By the 1500s, much of Europe was a milieu for battles between empires, with a predominant set of conflicts between European populations and the Ottoman Empire. In 1522 the battle of Rhoades left one of the forces—the Knights Hospitaller—without a base of operations. In 1530, Charles V, then head of the Holy Roman Empire of St. John of Jerusalem, ceded Malta to the Knights Hospitaller. The Knights had been given control of the islands so that they could maintain their religion and protect the Christian nations of Europe against enemies of their faith.

One of the enemies of the Hospitaller was Mustafa Pasha a military commander in the Ottoman Empire. Pasha saw Malta as a critical gateway into Europe. He also held a long-term animosity against the Knights, and particularly against their leader, Grand Master Jean Parot de Valette.

In 1565, Mustafa Pasha sailed a force of 38,000 soldiers to Malta, with the intent of conquering the island and ridding it of the Knights. Over what became a three-month campaign, Pasha's forces made incursions onto the land, yet found the much smaller forces of the Knights to be formidable opponents. What ultimately became a successful effort of the Knights to repel the forces of Pasha has become intertwined in Maltese national legend.

Metaphorically, the Great Siege can be seen as a representation of the tensions that are capitalized upon by those opposed to migration. That Malta, under the Knights Hospitaller, was able to repel invading forces of the Ottoman Empire in the 1500s is understood as a role that Malta can replay, according to some opposed to modern migration trends.

The Siege of Malta also contributes to a narrative of Malta being seen as an outpost for broader Christian Europe during the sixteenth century. As such, it was viewed as an outpost that was critical in protecting the continent from the Ottoman Empire and other Islamic forces against which much of Christian Europe was battling at the time.

French and British Rule, and Independence

In the late 1700s, Napoleon Bonaparte's forces entered Malta upon a negotiated granting of power by then-Grand Master Ferdinand von Hompesh, who recognized that any resistance to Napoleon's desires to acquire Maltese territories would result in his taking the country by force. Hompesh's capitulation resulted in the Knights Hospitaller's departure from Malta, as Napoleon had long held opposition to them, viewing the Knights as a reflection of the aristocracy that he abhorred. As a result, with French control over Malta, Napoleon launched an effort to eradicate evidence of Hospitaller presence on the islands.

While his actual stay in Malta was brief, Napoleon placed French lieutenants in key roles overseeing elements of Malta's government. Shortly after his departure, Napoleon set out for Egypt, where at the mouth of the Nile, his forces were defeated by the British. With this defeat, Napoleon's control over Malta, along with many of his other territories fell to the British. While Malta's existence under Napoleonic rule was brief, it continued a narrative of the country being ruled by outsiders.

As a protectorate under the British Crown, following the defeat of Napoleon, Malta was ruled by a Governor, who was a representative of the British monarch. During the 160 years of rule in Malta, the British used the territory for its strategic location during the Crimean War, World War I, and World War II. This time under the British rule served as a continuation of Malta's being under the governance of a foreign power.

Independence and Constitutionalism

In 1964, as Britain became involved with its global decolonization process, Malta was granted its independence. This provided for the first time in the nation's long history, opportunities for the Maltese to shape their own set of laws as well as develop their own sense of identity without undue influence from external powers. Factors of how the nation constitutionally shaped its identity would play a central role in the evolution of Malta's contemporary relationship with migrants and asylum seekers.

Malta's constitutional era of the mid-to-late 1960s enabled the nation to reflect on the foundations that would shape the laws and identity of Maltese society. One of the constitutional elements that had a central role in shaping matters of identity in Malta relates to the Constitution's second article, which denotes Roman Catholicism as the official religion of Malta. Religion has played a critical role in framing Maltese national identity.

Citizenship Act

Malta's Citizenship Act outlines who is eligible for citizenship in the nation and provides the steps necessary to acquire it. According to the Act, several factors impact the determination of citizenship in Malta. Among these are residency and language requirements. Also, citizenship has to be determined through an assessment if the applicant is "of good character" and "would be a suitable citizen of Malta." Part V of the Citizenship Act inserts a degree of ministerial discretion in determining who is to become a citizen of Malta by noting that "aliens" and stateless persons can be naturalized if it "satisfies the Minister." This ministerial determination is normally made after five years of residency.

Citizenship has traditionally been acquired through one of two means. The first is through the bloodline—a citizenship route known as "ius sanguine." The second is through something referred to as "ius soli," which refers to one being born on the land.

In November 2013, in a decision made with some degree of controversy, Malta approved amendments to its Citizenship Act to establish a new means of obtaining citizenship; one that would allow high-net-worth applicants to gain a Maltese passport in return for € 650,000. Under this initiative, many of the requirements that ordinarily apply to those seeking naturalization, such as language competency, extended residency periods or renunciation of another citizenship, are waived.

Immigration Act and Refugee Act

Malta's Immigration Act, originally passed in 1970, established much of the legal framework regarding migration. It established a "prohibited immigrant" label which facilitated language around those who might be deemed to threaten public interest in Malta. As a result, it helped shape a division between the prohibited immigrant and the "suitable citizen," pointing to specific actors who are involved in protecting "public interest" through means of deportation or detention. Prohibited immigrants are politically constructed by the act as criminals *to be feared*. Dehumanizing security means, such as detention and deportation, are justified because they purportedly protect the public from dangerous outsiders.

The adoption of Malta's Refugee Act thirty years following the Immigration Act provided a pivotal moment in the evolution of refugee matters in Malta. Prior to this, there were five characteristics that framed the strategies through which Malta treated refugees: (1) limiting legal responsibility for asylum seekers and refugees, (2) giving discretionary benefits to some of the refugees instead of enforceable rights to all, (3) refusing to create procedures for status determination, (4) differentiating refugees into distinct categories that were usually not implemented in practice, and (5) detaining asylum seekers for long periods.[3]

The Act led to the adaption of the definition of refugee influenced by the 1951 Convention and the 1967 Protocol, specifically defining a refugee as a person, (1) outside of his/her country of origin, (2) with a well-founded fear, (3) of persecution, (4) due to one of the specified grounds, and 5) who is unable to seek protection from their country of origin. By officially enacting the 1951 Convention and the 1967 Protocol in the Refugee Act, Maltese law acknowledged the vulnerability of refugees and fear of persecution that they may have experienced before flight.

The Refugee Act, in shaping a long, complicated asylum determination process, failed to protect asylum applicants from being labeled as "prohibited" during this waiting period. In other words, they were still subjected to *being feared*, as designed by the Immigration Act. The law envisioned a formal and unitary procedure for status determination which would be adjudicated by the Refugee Commissioner in the first instance and from which appeals could be made to the Appeals Board. These were both new administrative offices established by the Act.

MALTA AND THE EUROPEAN UNION

In 2003, Maltese citizens voted for the nation to join the European Union. Despite the vote to join, there was a great deal of concern about becoming part of the EU, largely because of concern about how much the EU would influence Malta's policies and sense of independence now that it was no longer ruled by foreign powers.

Membership in the European Union would mean a degree of adherence to European Union policies in several areas, including policies related to migration. One of the central arenas of policy focus would be in adherence to the Dublin II regulation which establishes the processes by which member states are assigned responsibility for asylum seekers. Under Dublin II, the nation where an asylum seeker first makes an asylum claim is responsible for the asylum process that the person undergoes.

Irregular Arrivals in Malta

In the early evening of March 7, 2002, police on the Maltese island Gozo were alerted that a small boat had drifted into Xlendi Bay, on the island's southwest coast. Aboard the forty foot boat were 250 people from several countries who had left the Turkish coast a few days earlier. Police officials gathered all of the boat's passengers and placed them in custody for medical examinations and processing, and moved them to two of the country's centers for illegal immigrants.[4]

Over the next several months, Malta would receive several other boats of irregular migrants—leading officials to increasingly recognize that they would need to manage the several challenges with the arrivals of their boats. By October, reflecting on the new arrivals that Malta encountered, Tony Borg, Minister of Home Affairs noted, "the 800 illegal immigrants arriving in Malta this year are an unbearable strain on our law enforcement and infrastructure."[5]

Borg's comments raised a number of concerns that were beginning to surface in Malta around how to effectively manage what was being perceived as an early crisis for the government. One of the major concerns focused on questions of how should Maltese officials deal with shifting public opinion related to migrants. As Borg noted in September of 2002:

> . . . as representatives of European governments, we can never ignore public opinion on the problems which migration, if left uncontrolled, may give rise to. If we do, attitudes will take longer to evolve, fomenting the extremist feelings which are already thriving in certain countries. [6]

As he added,

> we cannot ignore the legitimate concerns and anxieties of ordinary people, and we cannot project ourselves as being detached from them. A balanced approach toward this delicate manner will ensure that our common values will be put in practice in a way which is accepted by the majority of the people we represent. [7]

While this question of how to ensure government responded to articulated public interest on migration was being raised, a second, pressing challenge focused on how to manage the inflow of irregular migrants. As migration increased with the rising instability of Libya and other nations in the Middle East and North Africa during the Arab Spring these questions grew. In the decade and a half following the arrival of the boat in Xlendi Bay, Malta wrestled with challenges related to balancing its strategies and pressures between international expectations and domestic pressures related to irregular migration and the flow of refugees.

Detention

One of the central policy issues that Malta wrestled with in the early phase of this wave of migration focused on detention. During the early years of this migration cycle, Malta had a standard period of detention of eighteen months. The facilities used for such detention were often former military barracks that were overcrowded. The facilities were also in conflict with various internationally recognized human rights norms. Because of both the length of the detention and the conditions of the facilities, detention became a central component of tensions between Malta and the European Union.

According to Maltese officials, their detention policies were central to the nation's broader deterrence strategies, yet they also raised questions on how to balance human rights of asylum seekers with the country's needs. In a 2005 document published by the Ministry for Justice and Home Affairs and the Ministry for the Family and Social Solidarity, Malta's processes were justified as protecting a "vulnerable" nation from groups of irregular migrants that threaten the nation's stability. The document noted several groups within categories of migrants. They included

> those who enter the country legally but remain beyond their authorized stay, there are others who arrive in Malta without the proper documentation and others who arrive in an irregular manner either voluntarily or after finding themselves in distress at sea and are saved by the Maltese coast guard authorities. Most of these irregular immigrants eventually apply for refugee status. All such immigrants, with the exception of those who are still minors, pregnant women and those who have some form of disability, or condition are kept in detention in terms of the Immigration Act until such time as their request for refugee status is determined . . . for reasons concerning employment, accommodation and maintenance of public order, that a detention policy be adopted in cases concerning the arrival of irregular immigrants. Such a policy has actually been in force since the enactment of the Immigration Act in 1970.[8]

In 2011, the International Commission of Jurists sent a delegation to Malta to examine its detention facilities and other processes related to the treatment of migrants. One of the primary concerns in the document focused on issues of overcrowding, noting:

> The ICJ delegation found the conditions of Warehouse One of the Safi Barracks to be overcrowded. Even without the possibility of counting the number of detainees held there, the delegation was readily struck by its plain unsuitability in respect of the number of detainees it held. The distance between the lines of bunk beds was just enough for one person to stand in. There were no cells or bedrooms, the detention centre being constituted of a single open space. There was absolutely no space for even a minimal level of privacy. A lesser, though still worrisome, situation of overcrowding existed in B-Block of the Safi Barracks at the time of the ICJ visit. While this centre was provided with open cells, these were overcrowded with bunk beds, and the only privacy was that which had been tentatively achieved through hanging blankets from the top of the bunks.[9]

A second concern focused on addressing the hygienic conditions of the facilities. As the report noted:

> In the Warehouse One, the ICJ delegation noted that hygienic needs of the detainees were provided for only by a couple of basins, located in the external recreation yard. These basins were the main source of water for the detainees, which they used to clean, wash items and drink. There were also plastic showers without hot water. In the same external space were located plastic chemical toilets, which appeared unsanitary despite the fact that one of the detainees volunteers to clean them. The numbers of toilets and showers appeared to the delegation to be insufficient in comparison to the number of people detained. In B-Block, the kitchen and the bathroom, in this case located at the interior of the

detention yard, appeared rather dirty. By contrast, the Lyster Barracks facility visited did not appear to present serious problems of hygienic maintenance.[10]

In 2016, after pressures from international agencies, and domestic NGOs, the Maltese government adjusted its detention policies. Under its new approach, detention cases would be examined on a case-by-case basis, instead of on a basis through which anyone arriving through irregular means would automatically be placed in detention.

Shifting Discourse

In April 2015, an overcrowded boat carrying people of various nationalities departed from Tripoli, attempting to cross the Mediterranean to Italy. Somewhere between the point of departure and its intended destination, the ship capsized. At least 800 people drowned. Twenty-eight people survived.[11]

This sinking changed much of the global conversation about migration. Italy criticized the EU for not responding to the disaster quickly enough. The International Organization for Migration representative, Flavio Di Giacomo of IOM Italy, noted that it had been the "deadliest disaster in the Mediterranean."[12]

Coupled with other sinkings to date and an awareness of challenges, this tragedy led to a discourse on how Malta and other nations of the EU would address the growing numbers of irregular migrants arriving in the nation. Under pressure from the European Union, countries in the Central Mediterranean would identify strategies for addressing the growing challenge in the region of irregular migrants arriving by boat.

Approaches to Migration Management

In November of 2015, heads of state from countries in Europe and Africa gathered in Malta's capital Valetta, to discuss strategies to address the expanding crisis on migration in Europe. The Valetta Summit focused on how European and African nations could collaboratively respond to many of the issues of movement that were occurring at the time. The Summit provided some strategies for responding to some of the challenges related to migration, including encouraging migrants to remain in their home nations.

The Valetta Summit resulted in the development of the Valetta Action Plan, a plan with five priority areas related to migration. These areas included considering the development-related elements linked to the root causes of irregular migration and forced displacement; the promotion of legal means of migration and promotion of mobility; a focus on matters of protection and asylum; strategies for addressing irregular migration, migrant smuggling, and human trafficking and issues pertaining to return, readmission and reintegration. In addition to the Valetta Action Plan, the summit resulted in the adoption of an EU Emergency Trust Fund, a 1.8 billion Euro fund aimed at curbing the number of migrants aiming to come to Europe, particularly from North Africa, the Lake Chad area, the Horn of Africa, and other regions.

The Valetta Summit helped leverage a discourse related to strategies for managing the path and speed of migration. More importantly, it helped with the navigation of a roadmap for participant countries to cooperatively work between Africa and Europe to address the challenges related to irregular migration in the early twenty-first century.

Integration Strategy

While international discussions were taking place around the challenges related to migration, there was domestic activity developing in Malta on matters of migration. In 2012, the Ministry for Social Dialogue, Consumer Affairs, and Civil Liberties was created in the Maltese Cabinet to partially implement integration strategies.

In 2015, the Ministry published a document entitled *Toward a National Migrant Integration Strategy 2015–2020*, which in turn aimed to facilitate integration approaches. The goal of this strategy was to identify ways to combine proposals from citizens, government, and NGOs for Malta's broader integration strategy.

Two years following, on December 15, 2017, the Ministry for Social Dialogue and European Affairs officially launched Malta's integration strategy, and placed its implementation largely under the control of the Directorate for Human Rights and Integration. Malta's Minister of Social Dialogue and European Affairs, Helena Dalli noted, "with the Migrant Integration Strategy and Action Plan (Vision 2020), Government is now setting-up a stronger framework for integration of migrants who are already working, living and sending their children to school in Malta." She also noted, "Malta was always at the crossroads, and our culture and language reflect this. For Government, it is important that no individual or community feels isolated from those around them."[13]

The establishment of the Ministry and Directorate and launch of a formal integration strategy was an acceptance by the Maltese government of the broader value of diversity in the nation.

MALTA, MIGRATION, AND XENOPHOBIA: SOME UNDERLYING ISSUES

The protesters against the Bugibba mosque in October 2016 encountered a group of counter-protesters who wanted to signal that there was support for the growing communities of migrants in the nation. The tensions of the day reflected a broader debate in Malta related to the demographic changes that the nation was undergoing and its place in global activity related to migration. Several themes arise related to Malta's evolving challenges and opportunities related to migration.

Underlying Issue I: Question of Identity

Malta's location and size place it in a unique position for contemporary discussions about migration. The nation has experienced an inflow of different people, from a range of places in the Mediterranean region, and other parts of the world for much of the history of the archipelago. Because of the historic inflow of different populations, there has also been opportunity for reflection on the make-up of Maltese identity.

Since the nation's independence in 1964, questions of Maltese identity have found further elements of complexity. As the drafters of Malta's constitution developed the laws of their nation, questions of national identity became codified and integrated into the various frameworks of the political, economic, and social fabrics of the nation. The decision to become part of the European Union in 2003, and the integration that occurred in 2004, furthered the challenges around identity formation. Malta was both its own nation and an actor in a larger body of nations with a guiding set of international norms and principles.

Malta has witnessed the arrival of populations from other lands throughout its history. These arrivals have provided the foundation for differing narratives on migration. The first narrative focuses on openness and receptivity to the migrant. Here, the story of Paul of Tarsus provides a metaphor on the contributions that migrants might bring to the broader population. Because of such benefits, populations are encouraged to be receptive of the new arrivals. The other narrative is one of opposition to the migrant. At times, this narrative integrates an argument of today's anti-migrant protests being an example of needed protection from outsiders. Malta's history, including its years under the rule of other nations, is central to comprehending the multiple layers in place in this narrative.

The constitutional definition of Maltese citizenship helps to frame some of these perspectives on what it means to be Maltese. With a rapidly changing demographic profile, a central question is how might Malta revisit some of the factors underlying this definition? How might the definition apply to those who are in the nation temporarily?

The inflow of refugees and asylum seekers in the early part of the twenty-first century has forced Malta to explore its limitations around how "others" are accepted into the broader civic discourse. How would it balance areas of religious diversity and tolerance with a constitutionally embedded religion? In several ways, the tensions in Malta reflect the tensions in Europe around factors of migration. Government has begun assuming a much more pro-migrant stance than many of the anti-migrant forces would like. In its 2017 integration policies, Malta has begun to lay out strategies for positively addressing integration. With some of these strategies come questions of migrant identity as integrated with notions of Maltese identity.

Underlying Issue II: Role of Government

Government in Malta has several roles that it must play in relation to factors of migration. The first has been in the development of policies related to irregular migrants. At the center of these approaches have been the implementation of policies aimed at both deterrence and encouraging other European nations to accept a greater proportion of migrants.

A second position has seen government identify ways that it might facilitate integration strategies. Consideration of the role of government in addressing the flow of irregular migrants, has become an increasingly important part of the discourse on migration beginning with the early arrivals of boats of irregular migrants in 2002.

Malta has found itself in a position of joining with the countries where geography places them at the front line of receiving influxes of migrants. Maltese sovereignty—a notion that was a long time forthcoming—is one of the issues that is central to how government responds to some of these issues pertaining to migration. The complexities of ensuring national sovereignty at a time of EU integration and a period of EU regulation around migration in an area in which government is actively engaged.

Underlying Issue III: Evolving Civil Society Role

Following the Valetta Summit, there has been an elevated discussion on the role of civil society organizations in addressing the challenges related to migration. In some instances, the energy of Valetta assisted with the elevation of these organizations and their work on behalf of groups of migrants.

The evolving role of civil society organizations has included creating entities to assist with integration. In several cases, third sector organizations have also engaged in rescue operations and other activities to assist with the broad management of these issues on migration.

Civil society entities have also assumed a greater role in assisting with the integration of migrants, provision of shelter, and advocacy for enhanced opportunities. The role of these actors is one that is rapidly evolving as the voices on migration are becoming more diverse and more involved in segments of Malta's national discourse on migration.

CONCLUSION

Malta has seen a large influx of migrants during the initial years of the twenty-first century. Some of these have entered through what the country deems as regular means of entry. Others have entered through what are referred to as irregular channels. The conversations in the public spheres on how to manage the challenges of migration have been increasing in regularity as the nation has witnessed increases in the inflow of people.

There has been a policy tension related to the movement of people—and how to manage such movement. On the one hand, have been individuals engaged in identifying obstacles for further migration. On the other hand, are individuals interested in enhancing broader integration strategies. Malta's process of navigating policy between these positions will provide an example for balancing conflicting migration policy in other nations.

The process of national imagining in Malta must take into account that it has undergone several periods of creation and re-creation throughout its history. There is a question on the role of imagination in coming up with solutions that will be implementable as Malta continues to wrestle with matters of migration over the years. Some of the imaginative processes will result from issues pertaining to the challenges of migration. In some cases, these dynamics will not be able to be achieved without the broader set of actors from multiple perspectives being involved in Malta's broader national discourse on migration.

NOTOES

1. Schembri and Bonnici, "Update:You're All Dirty."
2. Schembri and Bonnici.
3. Zammit, "Vernacularizing Asylum Law in Malta," 81.
4. Grech, "Illegal Immigrants Drift into Xlandi Bay," 1.
5. Walker-Leigh, "Tunis Declaration 'will help Malta cope with illegal immigrants,'" 8.
6. "Malta and European Migration," 35.
7. "Malta and European Migration," 35.
8. "Irregular Immigrants, Refugees and Integration," 6.
9. "Not Here to Stay," 29.
10. "Not Here to Stay," 29.
11. "Italian Navy Recovers Ship That Sank with Over 800 People on Board."
12. "Italian Navy Recovers Ship That Sank with Over 800 People on Board."
13. Ministry for European Affairs and Equality, "Integration =Belonging," 1.

Chapter Six

The United States

History Repeats

On January 1, 1892, fifteen-year-old Annie Moore celebrated her birthday in a location she wouldn't have dreamt of years prior, on the deck of the steamship *Nevada* as it docked in New York Harbor. After a journey across the Atlantic, she would become on that day, the first immigrant to disembark at Ellis Island. Over the years, she would be followed by twelve million people who would arrive as migrants into the United States under the shadow of the Statue of Liberty. Moore's arrival was ultimately greeted with a great deal of fanfare. The *New York Times* printed a story documenting Moore's entry to the nation and the opening of the island, noting:

> As soon as the gangplank was run ashore, Annie tripped across it and was hurried into the big building that almost covers the entire island. By a prearranged plan she was escorted to a registry desk which was temporarily occupied by Mr. Charles M. Hendley, the former private secretary of Secretary Windom. He asked a special favor the privilege of registering the first immigrant, and Col. Weber granted the request. . . . When the little voyager had been registered Col. Weber presented her with a ten-dollar gold piece and made a short address of congratulation and welcome. It was the first United States coin she had ever possessed. She says she will never part with it but will always keep it as a pleasant memento of the occasion. She was accompanied by her two younger brothers. The trio came to join their parents, who live at 32 Monroe Street, this city.[1]

Like the stories of many of the migrants who passed through Ellis Island over the years, Annie Moore's story would become part of U.S. historical legend, as a recognition of the role of migration in our broader narrative of national identity. Over the years, tales of migrants from Europe would frame a story that would be deeply integrated with the country's history at the dawn of the twentieth century. The stories of many of these groups would become the legend of urban America as immigrant enclaves formed the foundation of many cities across the nation.

Nearly a century and a quarter following Annie Moore's arrival, hundreds of protesters met busses as they pulled into Murrieta, California, in early July of 2014. On board were primarily unaccompanied children and youth from El Salvador, Honduras, and Guatemala. For those on the bus, the arrival to the United States filled them with hope of a better life than the ones they left behind. The welcome they received differed greatly from the welcome Annie Moore had received. There were no public officials waiting to welcome them. There were no gold pieces to be presented, or newsmen celebrating their arrival. Instead, Murrieta had dozens of people screaming at the children and youth that in no uncertain terms, they were not welcome.

The protests of the busses, while met with shock in some areas, reflected some of the patterns that have arisen over the decades in the United States around the treatment of youth attempting to migrate from countries in Central America. For those at the front lines of the protests, it was a sign of their concerns about those who were on the bus—youth who they believed would bring numerous problems to their communities. For others, the protests were a sign of growing hostility, nativism, and xenophobia that had surfaced over the past several decades in communities across the country. In the years following the arrival of the Murrieta youth, the receptivity faced by young people (along with their accompanying families) in similar circumstances grew in hostility.

The decades between Annie Moore's arrival and that of the youth in Murrieta witnessed a cycle of migration in the United States with varied waves of support. Some of the phases were characterized by an acceptance of the immigrants. Others were characterized by resentment displayed toward them. Intertwined with the cycles were issues of legitimacy of experience, debated scope of legality, factors of race, and other broad contextual elements. Between the two perspectives is a widening debate on matters of migration in the United States and perceptions that have emerged pertaining to various groups of migrants.

This chapter explores migration and xenophobia in the United States. It focuses primarily on the stretch of time between the arrival of Annie Moore and the years immediately following the children on the busses pulling into Murrieta. I have divided the chapter into five sections. The first examines cycles of migration from the late 1800s to the mid-1920s with the passage of the 1924 Johnson-Reed Act. It was during this period that many of the foundations for later-day arguments would be laid against future immigrants from abroad. The language and the justification of policies against immigrants, particularly those who were from nations in Southern, Central, and Eastern Europe at the time, framed limitations to the entry of people from nations in these regions. Policies implemented during this era shaped perspectives on migration patterns for decades following.

Next, I examine the period between the Johnson-Reed Act and the 1965 Hart-Celler Immigration and Nationality Act. The forty-year period between these pieces of legislation witnessed the closing of points of entry to the United States. As a result, the period witnessed the moral debates on the limitations to closing borders.

Changes brought about by the 1965 Act have resulted in tremendous demographic shifts in the United States. They also brought backlash in political arenas to such changes. For the latter half of the twentieth century, political and social debates emerged related to such change, particularly around the make-up of migrants coming into the United States. The country also witnessed justification for hostility targeting migrants. The third section reflects these transitions.

Next, I explore some of the cycles of migration pertaining to young migrants with an emphasis on children and youth arriving around the time of, and under circumstances like the Murrieta arrivals. Here in particular, I explore the challenges encountered by the youth and the impact of such circumstances. This last section examines how the modern arrivals are conceptualized in a discourse on immigration in the first decades of the twenty-first century.

I conclude the chapter with several factors that underscore some of the outbreaks related to xenophobia in the United States: changing demographics following the 1965 Hart-Celler Immigration Act, shifting trends in political rhetoric, changing roles of the media, and circular trends of nativism.

HISTORICAL FRAMEWORK: 1800s–1920s

Nine years before Annie Moore's landing in New York, poet Emma Lazarus' *The New Colossus* first appeared at an auction where she had donated it to raise funds to build the pedestal that would support the Statue of Liberty. In 1903, a plaque with the text of the poem was placed at the statue's base. Largely known for its words that are inscribed on the plaque, the poem has come to symbolize much of what people have grown to appreciate about the stories of the immigrant experience in the United States. As what has become the most famous stanza of the poem reads:

> "Keep ancient lands, your storied pomp!" cries she
> With silent lips. "Give me your tired, your poor,
> Your huddled masses yearning to breathe free,
> The wretched refuse of your teeming shore.

Send these, the homeless, tempest-lost to me.
I lift my lamp beside the golden door!"[2]

The story of the immigrant who landed at Ellis Island and then went on to help populate some of the growing cities of the United States has come to play a major narrative of the overall American experience. While the period when Lazarus wrote *New Colossus* is often viewed as one when the arrival of immigrants is celebrated, it is also seen as a time of resistance to the growing number of newcomers to the United States. Underneath the story of the turn of the late eighteenth and early nineteenth century immigrant to the United States are tales of communities demonstrating hostility to new arrivals as well as a shifting policy discourse around migration in the United States.

In 1882, a year before the *New Colossus* was published, President Chester Arthur signed the Chinese Exclusion Act. This act had been passed in response to increasing public outcry over the large influx of Chinese immigrants over the previous two decades. For years, Chinese labor had been imported to work on the building of the railroads, and in other low-wage manual jobs. In time, however, the displacement of local sources of labor by the incoming Chinese bred resentment from many non-Chinese working-class laborers.

The Chinese Exclusion Act suspended the influx of Chinese laborers into the United States and designated anyone who was responsible for bringing Chinese laborers into the country guilty of a misdemeanor punishable by a fine and possible imprisonment. It was the first law implemented to prevent a specific ethnic group from immigrating to the United States. It was initially intended to last for ten years, but was renewed in 1892, and was made permanent in 1902 with the passage of the Geary Act.

By the early 1890s, it became clear that the outcry against the Chinese was only a small part of the rising wave of anti-foreign sentiment surfacing across the nation. Anti-migrant discussion was beginning to emerge and shape perspectives on the hostilities against various groups of migrants. In 1892, the Republican and Democratic party platforms demonstrated the levels of hostility around migrants at the time. The 1892 Republican Party platform called for the creation of further legal protections against increased immigration, noting, "We favor the enactment of more stringent laws and regulations for the restriction of criminal, pauper and contract immigration."[3]

The Democratic Party meanwhile noted in its 1892 platform:

> We heartily approve all legitimate efforts to prevent the United States from being used as the dumping ground for the known criminals and professional paupers of Europe; and we demand the rigid enforcement of the laws against Chinese immigration and the importation of foreign workmen under contract, to degrade American labor and lessen its wages; but we condemn and de-

nounce any and all attempts to restrict the immigration of the industrious and worthy of foreign lands.[4]

A year following the publication of the positions of the Democratic and Republican platforms, the historian Frederick Jackson Turner published his 1893 essay, "The Significance of the Frontier in American History," which warned about an exhaustion of free lands in the western United States. Turner suggested that this limitation of land would alter the makeup of immigrant communities in the country. According to him, the United States would find itself facing a change in the stock of immigrants, from the older group (primarily from Western and Northern Europe) who had the sense of independence and moved into these expanding areas, to the newer groups, who would not have the same sense of rugged independence and thus would remain in congested cities.

In New England, Charles Warren, Robert Ward, and Prescott Hall, all recent graduates of Harvard University echoed some of Turner's concerns around the rising number of immigrants entering the United States and formed the Immigration Restriction League in 1894. The group eventually included such figures as Senator Henry Cabot Lodge, Madison Grant, and Harvard President A. Lawrence Lowell. The Immigration Restriction League sought to limit the number of immigrants, particularly from nations in Central, Eastern, and Southern Europe who came to the United States. This group came to ultimately articulate positions greatly opposed to the trends of increasing immigration of the era.

Two years following the founding of the Immigration Restriction League, Francis Walker, who had served as Director of the 1880 Census and would later serve as President of the Massachusetts Institute of Technology (MIT), published an article in *The Atlantic Monthly* entitled "The Restriction of Immigration." In it, Walker depicted the newer immigrant as being of a lesser quality than the immigrants of the past:

> Fifty, even thirty years ago, there was a rightful presumption regarding the average immigrant that he was among the most enterprising, thrifty, alert, adventurous, and courageous of the community from which he came. It required no small energy, prudence, forethought, and pains to conduct the inquiries related to his migration, to accumulate the necessary means, and to find his way across the Atlantic. Today the presumption is completely reversed. So thoroughly has the continent of Europe been crossed by railways, so effectively has the business of emigration there been exploited, so much have the rates of railroad fares and ocean passage been reduced, that it is now among the least thrifty and prosperous members of any European community that the emigration agent finds his best recruiting ground.[5]

In several cases, Walker used American exceptionalism to argue against the increase of immigrants during the progressive era. As he further noted:

> For nearly two generations, great numbers of persons utterly unable to earn their living, by reason of one or another form of physical or mental disability, and others who were, from widely different causes, unfit to be members of any decent community, were admitted to our ports without challenge or question.... The question today is, not of preventing the wards of our almshouses, our insane asylums, and our jails from being stuffed to repletion by new arrivals from Europe; but of protecting the American rates of wages, the American standard of living, and the quality of American citizenship from degradation through the tumultuous access of vast throngs of ignorant and brutalized peasantry from countries of eastern and southern Europe.[6]

In 1907, Congress formed the United States Immigration Commission, also known as the Dillingham Commission, named after its chair, Vermont Republican Senator William Paul Dillingham. Over the next four years, The Dillingham Commission gathered extensive research on immigration. The Commission's final report, released in 1911, comprised forty-two volumes that examined various components of immigration. Much of the work in the report helped to advance theories of the superiority of some groups over others. In time, these philosophies became part of the legislative discourse and helped to shape subsequent immigration policy.

The Commission's final report concluded that immigration from southern and eastern Europe posed a serious threat to U.S. society and culture and should be greatly reduced in the future. The Commission made only one recommendation: that Congress enact a literacy test as a method of restricting immigration. The Commission's overall findings were also used a decade later to support a decrease in immigration levels through the use of quotas.

Johnson-Reed Immigration Act

Thirteen years following the publication of the Dillingham Commission report, Congress passed the Immigration Quota Act of 1924, also known as the Johnson-Reed Act. The Act introduced a system of immigrant quotas determined by the estimated national origins distribution of the white population in the 1920 census. This Act replaced the "emergency" quota system by changing the reference census to 1890 instead of 1910 and lowering the quota to two percent of the nationality-linked population in the United States at that time (down from 3 percent). This reduced potential immigrants from southern and eastern European nations. It also lowered the nationwide numerical limit to 165,000 immigrants.

The law was aimed at further restricting immigration of Southern and Eastern Europeans. It also restricted the immigration of Africans and banned the immigration of Arabs and Asians. Despite the Act's aim at preserving U.S.'s racial homogeneity, it set no limits on immigration from other countries of the Americas. The Johnson-Reed Act made permanent the basic limitations on immigration into the United States established in 1921 and modified the National Origins formula that had been established.

The Act established preferences under the quota system for certain relatives of U.S. residents, including their unmarried children under 21, their parents, and spouses aged 21 and over. It also preferred immigrants aged 21 and over who were skilled in agriculture, as well as their wives and dependent children under age 16. Non-quota status was accorded to wives and unmarried children under 18 of U.S. citizens, natives of Western Hemisphere countries with their families, and non-immigrants.

The 1924 Act also established the consular control system of immigration, which divided responsibility for immigration between the State Department and the Immigration and Naturalization Service. It mandated that no "alien" should be allowed to enter the United States without a valid immigration visa issued by an American consular officer abroad.

1920s–1960s

The Johnson-Reed Act went into effect in 1929, the same year that the stock market crash triggered the Great Depression. As a result, the employment magnet no longer served as a foundation for attracting immigrants to the United States. The years following the passage of Johnson-Reed witnessed a steady decline in the number of people immigrating to the United States, particularly from nations in Central and Eastern Europe.

Immigration and the Second World War

As the political landscape in Europe in the 1920s and 1930s increasingly pointed to rising fascism, questions began to surface of what the United States might do to assist people encountering increasing hostilities in their own nations. Would the United States be willing to adjust its policies related to immigrants and allow people into the country?

In February 1939, shortly after the Kristallnacht attacks in Germany signaled the looming crisis facing Jewish communities in much of Europe, Senator Robert F. Wagner (D-NY) and Representative Edith Rogers (R-Mass) introduced legislation to authorize granting of 10,000 immigrant visas to children in Germany or German annexed territories. In the introduction to the legislation, Senator Wagner noted:

> Millions of innocent and defenseless men, women and children of every race and creed, are suffering from conditions which compel them to seek refuge in

other lands. Our hearts go out especially to the children of tender years, who are the most pitiful and helpless sufferers. The admission of a limited number of these children into the United States would release them from the prospect of a life without hope and without recourse, and enable them to grow up in an environment where human spirit may survive and prosper.[7]

The bill had widespread support among religious and labor groups but was opposed by nationalist organizations. Noted one opponent, Francis H. Kinnicutt, president of the Allied Patriotic Societies, an organization representing several groups opposed to the legislation,

we must recognize that this is just part of a drive to break down the whole quota system—to go back to the condition when we were flooded with foreigners who tried to run the country on different lines from those laid down by the old stock.... Strictly speaking, it is not a refugee bill at all, for by the nature of the case most of those to be admitted would be of the Jewish race. And in the last two years we already have admitted eighty thousand Jewish refugees.[8]

Another person opposed to the Wagner-Rogers Bill noted:

I am the daughter of generations of patriots.... This nation will be helpless to guarantee to our children their rights, under the Constitution, to life, liberty, and the pursuit of happiness if this country is to become the dumping ground for the persecuted minorities of Europe. The refugees have a strong heritage of hate. They could never become loyal Americans.[9]

After several weeks of testimony, on July 1, 1939, the Child Refugee Bill was re-introduced with a modification that the youth migrants would be counted against the quota from Germany. Because this was not as a supplement to the quota, a fear set in that it would ultimately replace adults who could use visas due to the threats that they were under. As a result, Senator Wagner withdrew the bill from consideration.

Several months following the introduction of the Wagner-Rogers Bill on May 13, 1939, the *St. Louis*, a trans-Atlantic ocean liner left Hamburg, Germany, for Havana, Cuba, with 937 passengers on board. Most of the passengers were Jewish, and many of them were fleeing the conditions they faced in Europe. Most were German citizens, some were from Eastern Europe, and a few were officially "stateless." Most of the Jewish passengers had applied for US visas and had planned to stay in Cuba only until they could enter the United States.

On May 27, the *St. Louis* arrived in Havana harbor. The Cuban government only admitted 29 passengers. The government prohibited the remaining 908 passengers from disembarking. After Cuba denied entry to the passengers on the *St. Louis*, press throughout Europe and the United States brought the story to millions of readers throughout the world. Though US newspapers generally portrayed the plight of the passengers with great sympathy, only a few journalists and editors suggested that the refugees should be admitted into the United States.

A *New York Times* editorial noted of the incident:

> It is hard to imagine the bitterness of exile when it takes place over a faraway frontier. Helpless families driven from their homes to a barren island in the Danube, thrust over the Polish frontier, escaping in terror of their lives to Switzerland or France, are hard for us in a free country to visualize. But these exiles floated by our own shores. Some of them are on the American quota list and can later be admitted here. What is to happen to them in the interval has remained uncertain from hour to hour. We can only hope that some hearts will soften somewhere, and some refuge be found. The cruise of the St. Louis cries to high heaven of man's inhumanity to man.[10]

The passengers on board were ultimately denied entry into the United States. A telegram sent to passengers from the State Department stated that they must "await their turns on the waiting list and qualify for and obtain immigration visas before they may be admissible into the United States."[11] U.S. diplomats in Havana unsuccessfully tried to intervene once more with the Cuban government to admit the passengers on a humanitarian basis. Their interventions were also denied.

Following the U.S. government's refusal to permit the *St. Louis*'s passengers to disembark, the ship sailed back to Europe on June 6, 1939. Negotiations by the Jewish Joint Distribution Committee and other NGOs helped to secure entry visas into Great Britain, the Netherlands, Belgium, and France. Of the passengers admitted by Great Britain, all except for one survived World War II. Of the 620 passengers who returned to continental Europe, 87 managed to emigrate before the German invasion of its neighboring countries. Only 278 of the *St. Louis*'s passengers survived the Holocaust.

As the defeat of the Wagner-Rogers Bill and the denial of entry of the *St. Louis* confirmed, there was minimal interest in supporting the entry of European Jewish migrants into the United States.

postwar II

In the years following World War II, Congress debated what, if any, role the United States should play in serving as a place of relocation for those who had become displaced by the war. In 1948, it passed the Displaced Person Act. This Act enabled 400,000 individuals who had lost homes during the war to immigrate to the United States from Europe.

Four years after passing the Displaced Person Act, Congress passed the Immigration and Nationality Act of 1952. This Act upheld the national origins quota system established by the Immigration Act of 1924. The law repealed the last of the existing measures to exclude Asian immigration, allotted each Asian nation a minimum quota of 100 visas each year, and eliminated laws preventing Asians from becoming naturalized U.S. citizens. At the same time, however, the law only allotted new Asian quotas based on race instead of nationality. An individual with one or more Asian parents, born anywhere in the world and possessing the citizenship of any nation, would be counted under the national quota of the Asian nation of his or her ethnicity or against a generic quota for Asia. Low quota numbers and a uniquely racial construction for how to apply them ensured that total Asian immigration rates after 1952 would be minimized.

There were other changes to immigration policy implementation in the 1952 Act. One was the creation of a system of preferences which helped U.S. consulates prioritize visa applicants in countries with heavily oversubscribed quotas. Under the preference system, individuals with special skills or families already resident in the United States received precedence. Moreover, the Act gave non-quota status to "alien" husbands of U.S. citizens, and created a labor certification system, designed to prevent new immigrants from becoming unwanted competition for U.S. laborers.

President Truman was concerned about maintaining the national origins quota system and the racially constructed quotas for Asian nations. He thought the new law was discriminatory, and noted, "the idea behind this discriminatory policy was, to put it boldly, that Americans with English or Irish names were better people and better citizens than Americans with Italian or Greek or Polish names. . . . Such a concept is utterly unworthy of our traditions and our ideals."[12] Despite Truman's opposition, the Act had enough support in Congress to pass over his veto.

Toward the Immigration and Nationality Act of 1965

In 1958, John Kennedy, then serving as a Senator from Massachusetts, published his book *A Nation of Immigrants*. In it, he presented the contributions of immigrants to U.S. life. Kennedy noted various demographic trends related to immigration, and cited the legacies of various immigrants since the early years of the United States.

As he shifted from being a Senator to the United States President, Kennedy's agenda focused largely on immigration. In July of 1963, Kennedy proposed a series of immigration reforms to end the quota system that had been established in the 1920s. In a speech to Congress, outlining these perspectives, he noted:

> The enactment of this legislation will not resolve all our important problems in the field of immigration law. It will, however, provide a sound basis upon

which we can build in developing an immigration law that serves the national interest and reflects in every detail the principles of equality and human dignity to which our nation subscribes.[13]

Unfortunately, despite his enthusiasm for such immigration reform, Kennedy did not live to see new immigration policies implemented, as his November 1963 assassination curtailed the possibility of such change occurring during his administration.

IMMIGRATION AND NATIONALITY ACT OF 1965

Shortly after assuming the presidency, Lyndon Johnson opted to continue the agenda that Kennedy had initiated related to immigration. As a result, he decided to make immigration a major component of his presidential agenda by promoting The Immigration and Nationality Services Act of 1965. The Act, also known as the Hart-Celler Act abolished the national-origin quotas that had been in place in the United States since the Immigration Act of 1924.

Much of the strategy for gaining Congressional support for the Act was to emphasize that it would not have a long-term impact on the percentages of people migrating into the United States. At the signing ceremony for the 1965 Act on Liberty Island, President Johnson noted his belief that the legislation had more symbolic than real importance, stating, "This bill that we will sign today is not a revolutionary bill. It does not affect the lives of millions. It will not reshape the structure of our daily lives, or really add importantly to either our wealth or our power."[14]

The Act substituted the nationality quotas by limiting total immigration by hemisphere with total limits (20,000) per country. For the eastern hemisphere, immigration was capped at 170,000, while 120,000 was the limit for the western hemisphere.

Post Hart-Cellar

In 1968, the Hart-Cellar Act was implemented. Over time, its impact did, despite the assurances from President Johnson, change the demographic make-up of the nation, in terms of groups of people that relocated to the United States. In the 1950s, for example, immigrants from Germany made up the largest number of new arrivals (followed by Mexico and Canada). By 1972, the largest numbers of migrants were from Mexico, the Philippines, and Italy.[15] Ultimately, the pattern of migration would dramatically change the make-up of communities across the nation.

REFUGEE ACT OF 1980

War continued to be a major factor in forcing the displacement of people. In 1975, the United States resettled 130,000 refugees who escaped Vietnam as Saigon fell. Three years later, as large commercial ships bearing thousands of refugees fleeing Vietnam appeared in the South China Sea, the United States allowed the admission of 25,000 Indochinese refugees. In addition, refugees from other regions of the world were beginning to appear, increasing the pressure on U.S. policy makers to address the challenges of the snowballing numbers of refugees.

In March of 1980, President Carter signed the Refugee Act of 1980 into law. This Act aligned the federal government's definition of refugee with that of international practice and defined a refugee as anyone with a fear of persecution or physical harm. The Act also raised the annual allotment for refugees from 17,400 to 50,000, created a process for reviewing and adjusting the refugee ceiling to meet emergencies, and required annual consultation between Congress and the President and refugee matters. The Act also funded the new Office of U.S. Coordinator for Refugee Affairs and the Office of Refugee Resettlement.

PLYLER V. DOE:
EDUCATION AND REFUGEE/MIGRANT YOUTH

Five years before the passage of the 1980 Refugee Act, the Texas legislature passed Education Code Section 21.03 (Section 21.03), which permitted education districts to withhold funds for the education of undocumented children. This law also authorized local school districts in the state to deny entry to these children.

Two years following the passage of Section 21.03, the Tyler Independent School District implemented a new policy based on the law. The district historically only had a few dozen undocumented children, who it let attend. In 1977, under Superintendent James Plyler, the district expelled children who didn't have a U.S. birth certificate and then said children could return to class only if the impacted families paid a fee of $1,000 per child.

In 1978, a federal district judge ruled that Section 21.03 violated the 14th Amendment of the U.S. Constitution, and barred the school district from enforcing it in Tyler. The district appealed, and the case of *Plyler v. Doe* landed in the Supreme Court. The high court heard arguments in 1981.

In 1982 the Supreme Court issued its decision in *Plyler v. Doe*, and held that states cannot constitutionally deny students a free public education due to their immigration status. By a 5–4 vote, the Court found that any resources which might be saved from excluding undocumented children from public schools were outweighed by the harms imposed from denying them an education.

Plyler v. Doe would ultimately shape the discourse related to educational opportunities for refugee, asylum seeking, and migrant youth in the United States. For those youth whose migrant status made them vulnerable, they now had legal protection for educational access.

GROWING RESISTANCE: 1986 ACT AND BEYOND

By the mid-1980s, concerns surfaced on the impact of immigration policies in the United States in the years since the 1965 Act. Policy debates became increasingly pronounced between those who were supportive of the changing demographics in the United States and those who articulated concern about how the nation was changing its general make-up.

In 1986, Congress passed the Immigration Reform Control Act (IRCA) to control and deter illegal immigration to the United States. Its major provisions stipulated legalization of undocumented "aliens" who had been continuously unlawfully present since 1982, legalization of certain agricultural workers, sanctions for employers who knowingly hire undocumented workers, and increased enforcement at U.S. borders. The IRCA allowed millions of unauthorized immigrants to apply for legal status and granted amnesty to 3.2 million illegal immigrants living in the United States.

Four years following the passage of the 1986 Immigration Reform and Control Act, President George H. W. Bush signed the Immigration Act of 1990 into law. First introduced by Senator Ted Kennedy in 1989, the 1990 Act increased overall immigration to allow 700,000 immigrants to come to the United States per year for the fiscal years 1992–1994, and 675,000 per year after that. It also provided family-based immigration visas, created five distinct employment-based visas (categorized by occupation), and developed a diversity visa program that created a lottery to admit immigrants from countries underrepresented in the United States.

Post-1990 Opposition and Rising Anti-Migrant Sentiment

In the years following the passage of the 1990 Act, resistance to the changing demographics around the country grew. In California, reaction to the waves of immigrants, particularly from Mexico, led to the passage of California's Proposition 187 in 1994. Referred to as the "Save Our State" proposal, Proposition 187 aimed to establish a state-run citizenship screening system and prohibit illegal migrants from accessing non-emergency health care, public education, and other services in the State of California.

The mid-1990s also witnessed the emergence of several publications that supported the growing anti-migrant sentiment of the era. Peter Brimelow, a

British-born author whose 1995 book *Alien Nation: Common Sense About America's Immigration Disaster*, emerged to make him one of the anti-immigrant voices at the time. Much of Brimelow's work attacked the 1965 Immigration Act. Brimelow was particularly concerned with Hispanic immigrants, upon whom he focused many of his arguments about immigration's negative impact on health care, education, and crime in the United States.

Brimelow's concern about immigration in the United States was echoed nearly ten years following the publication of *Alien Nation*. In 2004, Harvard scholar Samuel Huntington's book *Who Are We?* examined what he perceived as impending threats to U.S. identity. According to Huntington, the foundation of the United States' Anglo-Protestant culture was crumbling due to a rapid influx of Mexican immigrants. He argued that U.S. citizens should

> recommit themselves to the Anglo-Protestant culture, traditions and values that for three and a half centuries have been embraced by Americans of all races, ethnicities, and religions and that have been the source of their liberty, unity, power, prosperity, and moral leadership as a force for good in the world.[16]

Huntington went as far in his arguments as to depict a threat of "Hispanization" of U.S. culture as a result of Mexican immigration. He painted this process as a reconquest of territories which the United States claimed from Mexico during the Mexican-American Wars of 1835–1836 and 1846–1848. He argues that Mexico is taking these lands back through demographic shifts that he portrayed as a unique form of conquest.

Huntington pointed out the demographic image of many U.S. border cities as being overwhelmingly Hispanic. This change, he argued leads to further difficulty in assimilating Mexican-Americans with the Anglo-Protestant roots of U.S. culture.

Such attempts to normalize and intellectualize anti-migrant sentiment, by authors such as Brimelow and Huntington, have ultimately supported the development of a discourse in the United States that has been opposed to the demographic changes that the nation is experiencing. They have become part of the late twentieth and early twenty-first century narrative that has pressed against the demographic changes relating to migration.

UNDOCUMENTED YOUTH: SECOND DECADE OF TWENTY-FIRST CENTURY TRENDS

Ten years following the appearance of Huntington's work, Mayeli Hernandez, a twelve-year-old from Honduras found herself testifying in front of a Congressional committee on migrant issues. During the hearing, Hernandez made a plea for children like her, stating, "please help protect children like me and my little sister. We cannot go back to our country because they are very dangerous and poor. For the first time, I am happy living in the United States because my mom is not sad all the time. I love to go to school and have the best grades in my class."[17] Hernandez is one of dozens of youth whose stories were shared during that period. For many, their lives in their home communities reflected incredible dangers. Mayeli's story would be echoed many times over by youth from the Northern Triangle nations of El Salvador, Guatemala, and Honduras.

In 2016, a report by UNHCR examined some of the reasons and background related to the growth in numbers of youth migrating north. UNHCR noted that approximately 56 percent of the four hundred children interviewed for the report from El Salvador, Guatemala, and Honduras had potential international protection needs. The UNHCR study found that not all unaccompanied children in their population sample were seeking their parents or other family reunification or looking for better economic opportunities. A greater number were fleeing violence from organized criminal groups or family violence.[18]

Three years before Mayeli Hernandez testified before the Congressional committee, the United States Border Control (USBC) noted an increase in the number of unaccompanied alien children who were entering the United States. In FY 2011, USBC apprehended 16,067 accompanied children at the Southwest border. Three years later, in FY 2014, more than 68,500 unaccompanied children were apprehended. During the first two months of FY2017 (October and November 2016), USBP apprehended 14,128 unaccompanied children.[19]

To address this crisis at its peak in 2014, the Obama administration developed a working group to coordinate the efforts of federal agencies involved. In June 2014, the administration announced plans to provide funding to the affected Central American countries for a variety of programs and security-related initiatives to mitigate the flow of unaccompanied migrant children. In July 2014, the administration requested $3.7 billion in supplemental appropriations to address the crisis. Congress denied the request.[20]

New Policies

Five days into his term as President of the United States, Donald Trump signed Executive Order 13767: Border Security and Immigration Enforcement Improvements. This executive order established a foundation for the implementation of the new president's vision for management of migration issues, and his means of differentiating his policies from those of his predecessor. Trump had campaigned on the notion of making new immigration policies central to his administration. The new executive order focused particularly on enhancing border security, particularly along the southern borders of the United States, enhancing detention facilities near the border with Mexico, and reinforcing procedures to return illegal migrants, particularly those coming in along southern borders, to their home nations.

The implementation of EO 13767 was one of a number of initiatives advanced by the new administration to implement its policies related to migration.

On April 6, 2018, the Department of Justice issued a memorandum calling for the criminal prosecution of anyone who enters the United States unlawfully. Five days later Attorney General Sessions delivered remarks to attendees of a conference on immigration enforcement. In the speech he provided a depiction of the dangers of the border regions, noting:

> A 2,000 mile border leaves this country vulnerable to transnational criminal organizations like drug cartels, violent street gangs like MS-13, human traffickers, and other criminals who bring drugs, guns, and gang violence into our communities. . . . Most of the heroin, cocaine, methamphetamine, and fentanyl in this country was not made here. It came here across the border. These are the deadliest drugs this country has ever seen—and they are killing more Americans than ever before. From coast to coast, people are dying from drugs that were brought over this border. [21]

In early May of 2018, the Department of Homeland Security determined that the "zero tolerance" approach would cover alien adults arriving illegally with migrant children. By late May 2018, the impact of these policies upon families was widely felt. Reports began to come from the border of families who had been separated as a result of the policies.

The implementation of the separation policies resultantly caused a great deal of public outcry as stories circulated through the media of widescale separation and trauma experienced by the children impacted by these policies.

On June 20, 2018, in response to the outcry, President Trump issued Executive Order 13841, directing DHS to detain alien families together "whenever appropriate and consistent with the law and available resources." Six days later San Diego-based U.S. District Judge Dana Sabraw issued a preliminary injunction barring family separation from continuing.

By mid-summer 2018 it was estimated that nearly 3,000 children had been separated from their parents as a result of family separation procedures that resulted from the implementation of the zero tolerance policies promulgated by the Trump administration. In January 2019, however the Office of the Inspector General of the U.S. Department of Health and Human Services indicated that thousands of additional children may have been separated from their parents as a result of the implementation of the policies.[22]

THE UNITED STATES, MIGRATION, AND XENOPHOBIA: SOME UNDERLYING ISSUES

In a televised speech from the Oval Office on January 8, 2018, President Trump presented his arguments for a wall on the border between the United States and Mexico, a promise he had made during his campaign and during the first two years of his presidency. The speech was laden with illustrations of the crime and violence that the President argued resulted from illegal aliens entering through the southern border of the United States. He claimed:

> Day after day, precious lives are cut short by those who have violated our borders. In California, an Air Force veteran was raped, murdered and beaten to death with a hammer by an illegal alien with a long criminal history. In Georgia, an illegal alien was recently charged with murder for killing, beheading and dismembering his neighbor. In Maryland, MS-13 gang members who arrived in the United States as unaccompanied minors were arrested and charged last year after viciously stabbing and beating a 16-year old girl. Over the last several years, I have met with dozens of families whose loved ones were stolen by illegal immigration. I've held the hands of the weeping mothers and embraced the grief-stricken fathers. So sad. So terrible. I will never forget the pain in their eyes, the tremble in their voices and the sadness gripping their souls. How much more American blood must be shed before Congress does its job.[23]

Trump's speech incorporated a number of references that echoed imagery that had been used to frame arguments for closing borders and supporting anti-migrant sentiment for over a century. The language echoed a series of depictions that advanced a series of arguments for expanding upon systems that worked off of depictions of the immigrant "other" that reinforced the need to many for a degree of severity in deterrence and penalization strategies.

Debates around migration have been a recurring theme for much of the history of the United States and have been framed by a number of factors. Several of these that have surfaced in recent years are worth exploring in further detail.

Underlying Issue I: Post-1965 Realities

If one were to have listened to the language of the promoters of the 1965 Immigration Act, it would have been difficult to anticipate the changing demographics that would result from the legislation that ultimately passed. We are, demographically speaking a much different nation than we likely would have been had that piece of legislation not been enacted. Consensus among most demographers points to the fact that we will continue to change in our make-up as a nation.

For some, the changing demographic realities are perceived as a threat to the nation. Articulated in the writings of Brimelow, Huntington, and others, there is a perceived threat with these changes. Some parts of the nation have embraced the changing demographics, other places are still processing what the changes mean for their specific communities. Regardless of level of acceptance, change has come and it will continue to do so.

In his 2014 book *The Diversity Explosion*, demographer William Frey suggests that by 2040, the shifting demographics in the United States will lead the nation to being one that won't have a single majority group. Referring to this dynamic as a "diversity explosion," Frey notes:

> The diversity explosion that the United States is now experiencing is ushering in the most demographically turbulent period in the country's recent history. By "turbulent" I do not mean that the nation is about to experience sharp conflicts over its growing diversity. In fact, I believe just the opposite. As the United States comes to understand the magnitude and significance of this new diversity for its economic future and for its interconnectedness in an increasingly global village, it will seek to find ways to both embrace and nurture its diversity.[24]

The shifting dynamics ultimately means that the nation will need to prepare for how to adapt to and manage its new demographic realities. Constructive conversations on anticipating and managing the realities of the migration will be critical as citizens consider what the country will look like in the middle of the century and how it will navigate its path for getting there.

Underlying Issue II: Political Rhetoric

In the late 1800s and early 1900s, language about different migrant groups painted imagery of threats that they would bring to the broader nation. Rhetoric in the political sphere played a central role in shaping much of the anti-migrant perspectives that have driven political discourse. Late twentieth- and early twenty-first-century rhetoric has also promoted anti-migrant perspectives in the broader political discourse. The increasing prevalence of twenty-four-hour news cycles and the substitution of opinion and agenda-based news, focused on the repositioning of fact has shaped many of the questions of news processes. The advent of online sources has also framed vehicles for communicating a wide range of messages about who these various groups of immigrants are.

An issue for exploration is around the shared responsibility in interrogating the political language around migrant groups. In such interrogation are questions of the roles of actors in the discourse—whether actors in the media, political sphere, or other areas—in shaping the rhetoric. Media choice is frequently driven by market approaches, shaped by factors on what drives ratings. How to hold media accountable for the promotion of various perspectives as trends is one of the critical factors that will need further consideration as we look at future trends.

Underlying Issue III: Sending Country Challenges

Migration has push and pull elements at its core. In the case of Mayeli Hernandez and others fleeing the challenges in the Northern Triangle, there are experiences that they are encountering in their day-to-day lives that encouraged them to ultimately leave their homes. Stories of criminal activity in communities are often central to many of the studies recounted.

Much of the debate around migration in the United States in recent years has focused on issues of migration by youth entering from the Southern border of the country. An emphasis of the debates has focused on identifying strategies for keeping the youth out of the country. There is minimal focus on understanding reasons that the youth are leaving their home nations in the first place. Considerations of the root causes for flight—with a focus on sending country challenges are important components of the debate. This identification of challenges in the Northern Triangle provides indication of the reasons for migration in the early decades of the twenty-first century.

Ensuring the development of strategies for better understanding, and where possible for helping to address, the push factors that encourage movement provides a useful means for addressing some of the challenges. Causes of youth migrant movement will be critical as the United States considers comprehensive strategies for managing waves of youth migration in the future.

CONCLUSION

In the decades since Annie Moore arrived at Ellis Island, the United States has experienced several waves of migration. Many of these waves were accompanied with corresponding resistance to the arrival of the new migrants. An often created threat of people who may have looked different, or spoken a different language has been an ongoing element related to migration trends in political discourse. The past century's alternating support for and opposition to the inflows of migrant populations has been a constant part of the narrative.

It is widely anticipated that in the years ahead, an increasing number of migrants will attempt to enter the United States—with many of them continuing to be children. Several questions stand out in terms of the management of the challenges that these youth encountered. First are questions of the largest impact of policy perspectives on their well-being as migrants settling into the United States. Are there policies in place that will ultimately influence and shape how these individuals are received, detained, and potentially resettled? As the experiences during the years of policy evolution in the United States regarding migration have demonstrated, there are numerous lessons related to the management of migration trends.

The United States has had a continual process of re-imagining that has been central to its evolution as a nation. In the 1770s and 1780s, the process of re-imagining led to the framing of a Constitution that has been tested and adapted for nearly two and a half centuries. Over time, the United States has engaged a broader diversity of voices than the limited few that assembled to draft and ultimately press for the ratification of the Constitution. The nation has, through various stages of development, broadened its base of who could be included in the broader U.S. polity.

In the late 1800s and early 1900s, despite opposition to their arrival, people from nations far away migrated to the United States. Their arrival was ultimately confronted with legislative acts that sought to limit their entry into the nation. The 1960s witnessed the passage of legislation that reopened opportunities for people from different parts of the world to migrate. This shift ultimately had a tremendous impact on the demographic make-up of the nation.

As the United States entered the latter decades of the twentieth century and the first years of the twenty-first century, the nation has witnessed increasing tensions around migrant populations and the extent of inclusive processes for engaging members of such populations in the national discourse around U.S. identity. The meaning of such identity will shift as the nation increases in its diversity. Migrants, including those with stories similar to the children on the Murietta bus will play a role in the evolving narrative. As the nation moves into the middle decades of the twenty-first century it will have opportunities for further national reflection on the meaning of its demographic shifts and how to factor in diversity resulting from migration into the continued discourse on the make-up of future generations.

NOTES

1. "Landed on Ellis Island."
2. Lazarus, "The New Colossus," 233.
3. Hall, *Immigration and Its Effects Upon the United States*, 310.
4. Hall, *Immigration and Its Effects Upon the United States*, 310.
5. Walker, "The Restriction of Immigration," 822.
6. Walker, "The Restriction of Immigration," 823.
7. Forbes and Fagnin, *Unaccompanied Refugee Children*, 3–4.
8. Morse, *While Six Million Died: A Chronicle of American Apathy*, 259.
9. Morse, *While Six Million Died: A Chronicle of American Apathy*, 260.
10. "Man's Inhumanity," 20.
11. Wang, "A Ship Full of Refugees Fleeing the Nazis."
12. Kennedy, *A Nation of Immigrants*, 78.

13. Kennedy, *A Nation of* Immigrants, 102.
14. Public Papers of the Presidents of the United States: Lyndon B. Johnson, 1965.
15. Higham, *Politics of Immigration* Restriction, 36.
16. Huntington, *Who Are We? The Challenges to America's National Identity*, xvii.
17. Friedman,"Congress Hears from the Children that Fled Violence at Home for the U.S. Border"—July 30, 2014—*New York Daily News*.
18. *Children on the Run.*
19. Kandel, "Unaccompanied Alien Children: An Overview," i.
20. Kandel, "Unaccompanied Alien Children: An Overview," i.
21. Sessions, "Remarks on Immigration Enforcement."
22. *Separated Children Placed in Office of Refugee Resettlement Care.*
23. Trump, "Address to the Nation on the Crisis at the Border."
24. Frey, *The Diversity Explosion*, 239.

Chapter Seven

Conclusion

In late October 2016, the French government declared that it would dismantle the Calais refugee camp in Northern France. Commonly referred to as "the Jungle," the squatter camp at one time provided refuge for over 6,000 refugees. At the time government was planning the camp's demolition, many feared that there were more than 1,000 children living in shipping containers at the site.[1]

Several weeks before the Calais clearance, leaders from around the world gathered in New York for the UN Summit for Refugees and Migrants. At the meeting, representatives made several pledges pertaining to the status of refugees globally. On September 19 they agreed upon the New York Declaration for Refugees and Migrants signaling the recognition by world leaders of the changing realities around migration in the early years of the twenty-first century. Their signatures also signaled an acknowledgment by these world leaders of the need for a different discourse around migration.

One of the commitments in the New York Declaration was toward the development of two compacts that would be developed over a two-year period and ultimately shape a broader global discourse on migration trends. Two years following the signing of the New York Declaration, delegates met in Marrakech, Morocco, on December 9 and 10, 2018, for the signing of the Global Compact for Safe, Orderly, and Regular Migration (Global Compact for Migration) and in New York on December 17, 2018, for the adoption of the Global Compact on Refugees.

The Global Compact for Migration is built around twenty-three objectives for safe, orderly and regular migration. Each objective has a set of goals which help establish a framework for how the international community might address changing realities related to migration. The Global Compact on Refugees is built around four goals: (1) ease pressures on host countries; (2)

enhance refugee self-reliance; (3) expand access to third country solutions; (4) support conditions in countries of origin for return in safety and dignity. The majority of the Compact was written as a plan for achieving the goals noted. The Compact was also written with an awareness that the process of achieving the goals meant identifying needs to be undertaken alongside efforts to address some of the root causes for the flow of refugees.

Demographers predict that the twenty-first century, will witness large numbers of people who will move from their place of birth to other locations. Some of this movement will be voluntary. Much of it however will be involuntary and at times, forced. Factors of conflict, climate change, and increasing human populations, will encourage additional people to move from one locale to another. Management of migration will be one of the critical legacies of the twenty-first century.

INSTITUTIONAL REFORM AND DEVELOPMENT

The twentieth century witnessed the emergence of organizations for addressing the shifting geopolitical population movements that made up much of the century. The late 1940s and 1950s saw the emergence of institutions engaged in the development and promotion of an international order. In the areas of migration and refugee affairs, organizations such as the United Nations High Commission for Refugees (UNHCR) and the International Organization for Migration (IOM) emerged as two of the major entities. As the century continued, other institutions were launched from governmental sectors, nongovernmental sectors, and in the international sphere, to respond to the general movement of people.

The organizations that emerged in the twentieth century came into existence in a very different world than the world that exists today. At times they have reflected the needs and environments of the broader international settings, full of the turbulence that made up different periods.

Strengthening institutions working in migration and refugee affairs, particularly as they adapt to the new realities of migration in the twenty-first century, are central elements to addressing challenges related to migration today. In addition to strengthening preexisting institutions, there are questions around developing new institutions that might be able to leverage their unique positions to support governmental and intragovernmental entities that have been engaged in migration efforts. In each of the cases examined in this book, there are institutional development questions that relate to preexisting agencies and the roles of these agencies in responding to more recent migration issues.

South African institutions have focused largely on issues of socioeconomic transformation, with an emphasis on reversing many of the inequalities that have been in place for much of the nation's history. Internal policies that have enabled activity related to refugees and migrants have adjusted accordingly. Today, there is a need for institutional engagement in addressing requirements of institutions involved in addressing xenophobia in various settings. A need for NGOs to effectively step in to address some of the challenges encountered in Alexandra and other communities has been an important development—particularly in the absence of other institutions that might be have been able to respond to community-level tensions. The years since the 2008 violence have witnessed varied roles for NGOs as institutions that can be involved where state limitations are present.

In Malta, the emergent integration focused work of the Ministry of European Affairs and Equality provides an emphasis on strategies for the facilitation of integration. It focuses on a commitment by some branches in government to identifying strategies for addressing the integration challenges that have arisen with the influx of new arrivals. Such positions have countered questions of how far Malta should stretch its resources as it explores the acceptance of new arrivals. The nation has also, and perhaps more importantly, witnessed a rise in nongovernmental organizational efforts related to emergent third sector responses to migration issues and needs. Several third sector organizations have come to the forefront on migration needs. Several are led by migrants and refugees themselves—thus helping to ensure factors of refugee engagement and enhancing matters of refugee voice in responding to several of the issues at hand.

Finally, in the United States, an extensive network of agencies has evolved over the decades—particularly in the years following both the 1965 Immigration Act and more recently the passage of the 1980 Refugee Act. These networks of organizations provide a foundation for engagement by NGOs in resettlement and integration processes. One of the pressing lessons that emerged with new policies related to migration policies under the Trump administration—and shifting degrees of support has been around how these entities might shift to engage. Institutional roles, in sum can be considered at a broad level, and on an individual level for the broader engagement of sustainable approaches.

UNDERSTANDING THE COMPLEXITIES OF XENOPHOBIA AND STEPS TOWARD INTEGRATION

A critical theme in the New York Declaration focused on issues pertaining to xenophobia and discrimination confronted by migrants and refugees. It noted:

> We strongly condemn acts and manifestations of racism, racial discrimination, xenophobia and related intolerance against refugees and migrants, and the

stereotypes often applied to them, including on the basis of religion or belief. Diversity enriches every society and contributes to social cohesion. Demonizing refugees or migrants offends profoundly against the values of dignity and equality for every human being, to which we have committed ourselves.[2]

Cycles of hostility and antagonism targeting groups of people from other places is not unique to the nations in the cases examined. Nations around the world have experienced periods when incidents of xenophobia have surfaced in communities. Such incidents will continue to surface. It is important to recognize such cycles and draw upon them as we try to predict them and better understand how we might avert such incidents in the future.

Lessons from each of the cases presented help illustrate some of why people hold views in opposition to various groups. These instances have been the result of historical experiences which have impacted how uprooted populations have been conceptualized.

Condemnation of acts of intolerance is an important part of developing strategies for addressing such intolerance. The cases presented in these pages provide an initial attempt in building an understanding of some of the underlying issues related to the tensions. Further interrogation of incidents and issues related to the cases presented and other cases illustrate some of the evolution of tolerance and tension in the countries examined and that might be considered in future cases where place of origin or migrant status is an underlying component to xenophobic notions.

Our cases present us with some background in comprehending the complexities related to the tensions that had preexisted in communities in relation to newcomers. In the case of South Africa, the challenge of xenophobia is the result of current unequal economic and social realities, and the legacies of special separation during the Apartheid and pre-Apartheid years. South Africa's inequalities of the early twenty-first century and challenges of economic integration, high unemployment rates and increased levels of poverty in communities have provided a foundation of resentment toward non-South Africans perceived as taking jobs from South Africans. Frustration of social condition bred discontent.

In Malta, historic patterns of occupation and cultural blending have been used to exacerbate a fear of the outsider. The geographic placement of Malta locates it in a space where the dynamics of movement have a historical framework that has had an influence over the years. As such, it was only until relatively recently that Malta was able to explore a conversation on what Maltese identity and nationalism looked like. This question of identity has become even more pronounced as Malta has wrestled with questions of the value of integration in a broader EU system.

Recognizing the challenge that the nation faces should it seek to fully engage in the European-wide discourse on migration issues, means also recognizing the growing pockets of both political support and political resistance that will be encountered. For some, new practices of acceptance are merely part of Malta's further integrating into a wider EU system and broader global community. For others, acceptance of other cultures, particularly those of growing migrant populations, is a barrier to enabling the nation to build its sense of its own national identity.

The United States has demonstrated a history, which, despite a celebration of the contributions of migrants, has also demonstrated periods of active hostility. In the 1800s, this hostility targeted groups of Chinese migrants, as well as those from Central, Southern, and Eastern Europe. Over the years, the United States has demonstrated that despite the ideals inscribed at the base of the Statue of Liberty, there has been a tension around how much the people who might want to enter the nation are welcomed. Recent targets for such hostilities have been youth fleeing conditions where they have felt unsafe in their home communities.

Allport's three-fold approach to addressing prejudices: recognizing human propensities toward prejudices; encouraging group interactions; and challenging incidents of demagoguery might provide a strategy for addressing the instances of rising xenophobia and prejudice in communities. While at first glance, such a three-fold approach might seem overly simplified, intentional strategies following such an approach may serve as a starting road map for addressing the challenges of hostility that largely targets outsiders.

Integration is a central reality to the dynamics of migration. As people increasingly move from locale to locale, the dynamics of how such movement is managed is crucial to the realities of twenty-first-century migration. As we think about implementing integration strategies, one of the questions to ponder is one of what institutional framework will ultimately be important for the development of such approaches. Specifically, how might theories related to group interaction be developed?

In each of the countries examined, we have witnessed components of integration that have been incorporated in different segments of conversations. In Malta, the launch of a formal integration strategy is probably the most structured and direct approach of the three nations. This is partially driven by the European Union's policies related to integration. In South Africa, questions of integration, which support and incentivize the development and implementation of such strategies underscore some of the basic propositions of equality noted in the nation's constitution. In the United States the absence of formally articulated goals of integration make achieving integration that much more elusive.

A CLOSING THOUGHT

A question posed years ago, "why do people leave," should perhaps be coupled with a reflection on a question of "why do people stay," particularly when the receiving communities have elements of hostility. Today, the particulars for flight might be different than they were several decades ago—as many of the geopolitical realities have shifted between fears driving movement. How people might be received and what might be done so people don't feel the impulse to leave are critical questions that should be explored as we try to understand flight and the people engaged in such flight.

These questions are ones that might be pondered as part of a broad imagining process that citizens of nations—whether those who have been in areas for greater periods of time, or those who are new arrivals—might consider as part of the imagining process. As nations change—the make-up of who is involved in imaginative processes around identity change as well. We are at a turning point in the choices we make in terms of how our nations and communities engage in discourse related to migration. How such discourse evolves will play a critical role in shaping future patterns of human settlement and human interaction.

NOTES

1. Gentleman, A., "More than 1,000 children left in Calais camp, say charities."
2. UN General Assembly, New York Declaration for Refugees and Migrants, 3.

Appendix I

Convention Relating to the Status of Refugees

Adopted on 28 July 1951 by the United Nations Conference of Plenipotentiaries on the Status of Refugees and Stateless Persons convened under General Assembly resolution 429 (V) of 14 December 1950

Entry into force: 22 April 1954, in accordance with article 43

Preamble

The High Contracting Parties,

Considering that the Charter of the United Nations and the Universal Declaration of Human Rights approved on 10 December 1948 by the General Assembly have affirmed the principle that human beings shall enjoy fundamental rights and freedoms without discrimination,

Considering that the United Nations has, on various occasions, manifested its profound concern for refugees and endeavoured to assure refugees the widest possible exercise of these fundamental rights and freedoms,

Considering that it is desirable to revise and consolidate previous international agreements relating to the status of refugees and to extend the scope of and protection accorded by such instruments by means of a new agreement,

Considering that the grant of asylum may place unduly heavy burdens on certain countries, and that a satisfactory solution of a problem of which the

United Nations has recognized the international scope and nature cannot therefore be achieved without international co-operation,

Expressing the wish that all States, recognizing the social and humanitarian nature of the problem of refugees, will do everything within their power to prevent this problem from becoming a cause of tension between States,

Noting that the United Nations High Commissioner for Refugees is charged with the task of supervising international conventions providing for the protection of refugees, and recognizing that the effective co-ordination of measures taken to deal with this problem will depend upon the co-operation of States with the High Commissioner,

Have agreed as follows:

Chapter I: General Provisions

Article 1
Definition of the term "refugee"

A. For the purposes of the present Convention, the term "refugee" shall apply to any person who:

1. Has been considered a refugee under the Arrangements of 12 May 1926 and 30 June 1928 or under the Conventions of 28 October 1933 and 10 February 1938, the Protocol of 14 September 1939 or the Constitution of the International Refugee Organization;

Decisions of non-eligibility taken by the International Refugee Organization during the period of its activities shall not prevent the status of refugee being accorded to persons who fulfil the conditions of paragraph 2 of this section;

2. As a result of events occurring before 1 January 1951 and owing to well-founded fear of being persecuted for reasons of race, religion, nationality, membership of a particular social group or political opinion, is outside the country of his nationality and is unable or, owing to such fear, is unwilling to avail himself of the protection of that country; or who, not having a nationality and being outside the country of his former habitual residence as a result of such events, is unable or, owing to such fear, is unwilling to return to it.

In the case of a person who has more than one nationality, the term "the country of his nationality" shall mean each of the countries of which he is a national, and a person shall not be deemed to be lacking the protection of the country of his nationality if, without any valid reason based on well-founded fear, he has not availed himself of the protection of one of the countries of which he is a national.

B.

1. For the purposes of this Convention, the words "events occurring before 1 January 1951" in article 1, section A, shall be understood to mean either:

    a. "events occurring in Europe before 1 January 1951"; or
    b. "events occurring in Europe or elsewhere before 1 January 1951", and each Contracting State shall make a declaration at the time of signature, ratification or accession, specifying which of these meanings it applies for the purpose of its obligations under this Convention.

2. Any Contracting State which has adopted alternative (a) may at any time extend its obligations by adopting alternative (b) by means of a notification addressed to the Secretary-General of the United Nations.

C. This Convention shall cease to apply to any person falling under the terms of section A if:

1. He has voluntarily re-availed himself of the protection of the country of his nationality; or

2. Having lost his nationality, he has voluntarily re-acquired it; or

3. He has acquired a new nationality, and enjoys the protection of the country of his new nationality; or

4. He has voluntarily re-established himself in the country which he left or outside which he remained owing to fear of persecution; or

5. He can no longer, because the circumstances in connection with which he has been recognized as a refugee have ceased to exist, continue to refuse to avail himself of the protection of the country of his nationality;

Provided that this paragraph shall not apply to a refugee falling under section A(1) of this article who is able to invoke compelling reasons arising out of previous persecution for refusing to avail himself of the protection of the country of nationality;

6. Being a person who has no nationality he is, because of the circumstances in connection with which he has been recognized as a refugee have ceased to exist, able to return to the country of his former habitual residence;

Provided that this paragraph shall not apply to a refugee falling under section A (1) of this article who is able to invoke compelling reasons arising out of previous persecution for refusing to return to the country of his former habitual residence.

D. This Convention shall not apply to persons who are at present receiving from organs or agencies of the United Nations other than the United Nations High Commissioner for Refugees protection or assistance.
When such protection or assistance has ceased for any reason, without the position of such persons being definitively settled in accordance with the relevant resolutions adopted by the General Assembly of the United Nations, these persons shall ipso facto be entitled to the benefits of this Convention.

E. This Convention shall not apply to a person who is recognized by the competent authorities of the country in which he has taken residence as having the rights and obligations which are attached to the possession of the nationality of that country.

F. The provisions of this Convention shall not apply to any person with respect to whom there are serious reasons for considering that:

a. he has committed a crime against peace, a war crime, or a crime against humanity, as defined in the international instruments drawn up to make provision in respect of such crimes;
b. he has committed a serious non-political crime outside the country of refuge prior to his admission to that country as a refugee;
c. he has been guilty of acts contrary to the purposes and principles of the United Nations.

Article 2
General obligations

Every refugee has duties to the country in which he finds himself, which require in particular that he conform to its laws and regulations as well as to measures taken for the maintenance of public order.

Article 3
Non-discrimination

The Contracting States shall apply the provisions of this Convention to refugees without discrimination as to race, religion or country of origin.

Article 4
Religion

The Contracting States shall accord to refugees within their territories treatment at least as favourable as that accorded to their nationals with respect to freedom to practice their religion and freedom as regards the religious education of their children.

Article 5
Rights granted apart from this Convention

Nothing in this Convention shall be deemed to impair any rights and benefits granted by a Contracting State to refugees apart from this Convention.

Article 6
The term "in the same circumstances"

For the purposes of this Convention, the term "in the same circumstances" implies that any requirements (including requirements as to length and conditions of sojourn or residence) which the particular individual would have to fulfil for the enjoyment of the right in question, if he were not a refugee, must be fulfilled by him, with the exception of requirements which by their nature a refugee is incapable of fulfilling.

Article 7
Exemption from reciprocity

1. Except where this Convention contains more favourable provisions, a Contracting State shall accord to refugees the same treatment as is accorded to aliens generally.

2. After a period of three years' residence, all refugees shall enjoy exemption from legislative reciprocity in the territory of the Contracting States.

3. Each Contracting State shall continue to accord to refugees the rights and benefits to which they were already entitled, in the absence of reciprocity, at the date of entry into force of this Convention for that State.

4. The Contracting States shall consider favourably the possibility of according to refugees, in the absence of reciprocity, rights and benefits beyond those to which they are entitled according to paragraphs 2 and 3, and to extending exemption from reciprocity to refugees who do not fulfil the conditions provided for in paragraphs 2 and 3.

5. The provisions of paragraphs 2 and 3 apply both to the rights and benefits referred to in articles 13, 18, 19, 21 and 22 of this Convention and to rights and benefits for which this Convention does not provide.

Article 8
Exemption from exceptional measures

With regard to exceptional measures which may be taken against the person, property or interests of nationals of a foreign State, the Contracting States shall not apply such measures to a refugee who is formally a national of the said State solely on account of such nationality. Contracting States which, under their legislation, are prevented from applying the general principle expressed in this article, shall, in appropriate cases, grant exemptions in favour of such refugees.

Article 9
Provisional measures

Nothing in this Convention shall prevent a Contracting State, in time of war or other grave and exceptional circumstances, from taking provisionally measures which it considers to be essential to the national security in the case of a particular person, pending a determination by the Contracting State that that person is in fact a refugee and that the continuance of such measures is necessary in his case in the interests of national security.

Article 10
Continuity of residence

1. Where a refugee has been forcibly displaced during the Second World War and removed to the territory of a Contracting State, and is resident there, the period of such enforced sojourn shall be considered to have been lawful residence within that territory.
2. Where a refugee has been forcibly displaced during the Second World War from the territory of a Contracting State and has, prior to the date of entry into force of this Convention, returned there for the purpose of taking up residence, the period of residence before and after such enforced displacement shall be regarded as one uninterrupted period for any purposes for which uninterrupted residence is required.

Article 11
Refugee seamen

In the case of refugees regularly serving as crew members on board a ship flying the flag of a Contracting State, that State shall give sympathetic consideration to their establishment on its territory and the issue of travel documents to them or their temporary admission to its territory particularly with a view to facilitating their establishment in another country.

Chapter II: Juridical Status

Article 12
Personal status

1. The personal status of a refugee shall be governed by the law of the country of his domicile or, if he has no domicile, by the law of the country of his residence.

2. Rights previously acquired by a refugee and dependent on personal status, more particularly rights attaching to marriage, shall be respected by a Contracting State, subject to compliance, if this be necessary, with the formalities required by the law of that State, provided that the right in question is one which would have been recognized by the law of that State had he not become a refugee.

Article 13
Movable and immovable property

The Contracting States shall accord to a refugee treatment as favourable as possible and, in any event, not less favourable than that accorded to aliens generally in the same circumstances, as regards the acquisition of movable and immovable property and other rights pertaining thereto, and to leases and other contracts relating to movable and immovable property.

Article 14
Artistic rights and industrial property

In respect of the protection of industrial property, such as inventions, designs or models, trade marks, trade names, and of rights in literary, artistic, and scientific works, a refugee shall be accorded in the country in which he has his habitual residence the same protection as is accorded to nationals of that country. In the territory of any other Contracting States, he shall be accorded the same protection as is accorded in that territory to nationals of the country in which he has his habitual residence.

Article 15
Right of association

As regards non-political and non-profit-making associations and trade unions the Contracting States shall accord to refugees lawfully staying in their territory the most favourable treatment accorded to nationals of a foreign country, in the same circumstances.

Article 16
Access to courts

1. A refugee shall have free access to the courts of law on the territory of all Contracting States.
2. A refugee shall enjoy in the Contracting State in which he has his habitual residence the same treatment as a national in matters pertaining to access to the Courts, including legal assistance and exemption from cautio judicatum solvi.
3. A refugee shall be accorded in the matters referred to in paragraph 2 in countries other than that in which he has his habitual residence the treatment granted to a national of the country of his habitual residence.

Chapter III: Gainful Employment

Article 17
Wage-earning employment

1. The Contracting State shall accord to refugees lawfully staying in their territory the most favourable treatment accorded to nationals of a foreign country in the same circumstances, as regards the right to engage in wage-earning employment.
2. In any case, restrictive measures imposed on aliens or the employment of aliens for the protection of the national labour market shall not be applied to a refugee who was already exempt from them at the date of entry into force of this Convention for the Contracting State concerned, or who fulfils one of the following conditions:

a. He has completed three years' residence in the country;
b. He has a spouse possessing the nationality of the country of residence. A refugee may not invoke the benefits of this provision if he has abandoned his spouse;
c. He has one or more children possessing the nationality of the country of residence.

3. The Contracting States shall give sympathetic consideration to assimilating the rights of all refugees with regard to wage-earning employment to those of nationals, and in particular of those refugees who have entered their territory pursuant to programmes of labour recruitment or under immigration schemes.

Article 18
Self-employment

The Contracting States shall accord to a refugee lawfully in their territory treatment as favourable as possible and, in any event, not less favourable than that accorded to aliens generally in the same circumstances, as regards the right to engage on his own account in agriculture, industry, handicrafts and commerce and to establish commercial and industrial companies.

Article 19
Liberal professions

1. Each Contracting State shall accord to refugees lawfully staying in their territory who hold diplomas recognized by the competent authorities of that State, and who are desirous of practicing a liberal profession, treatment as favourable as possible and, in any event, not less favourable than that accorded to aliens generally in the same circumstances.
2. The Contracting States shall use their best endeavours consistently with their laws and constitutions to secure the settlement of such refugees in the territories, other than the metropolitan territory, for whose international relations they are responsible.

Chapter IV: Welfare

Article 20
Rationing

Where a rationing system exists, which applies to the population at large and regulates the general distribution of products in short supply, refugees shall be accorded the same treatment as nationals.

Article 21
Housing

As regards housing, the Contracting States, in so far as the matter is regulated by laws or regulations or is subject to the control of public authorities, shall accord to refugees lawfully staying in their territory treatment as favourable as possible and, in any event, not less favourable than that accorded to aliens generally in the same circumstances.

Article 22
Public education

1. The Contracting States shall accord to refugees the same treatment as is accorded to nationals with respect to elementary education.

2. The Contracting States shall accord to refugees treatment as favourable as possible, and, in any event, not less favourable than that accorded to aliens generally in the same circumstances, with respect to education other than elementary education and, in particular, as regards access to studies, the recognition of foreign school certificates, diplomas and degrees, the remission of fees and charges and the award of scholarships.

Article 23
Public relief

The Contracting States shall accord to refugees lawfully staying in their territory the same treatment with respect to public relief and assistance as is accorded to their nationals.

Article 24
Labour legislation and social security

1. The Contracting States shall accord to refugees lawfully staying in their territory the same treatment as is accorded to nationals in respect of the following matters:

a. In so far as such matters are governed by laws or regulations or are subject to the control of administrative authorities: remuneration, including family allowances where these form part of remuneration, hours of work, overtime arrangements, holidays with pay, restrictions on home work, minimum age of employment, apprenticeship and training, women's work and the work of young persons, and the enjoyment of the benefits of collective bargaining;

b. Social security (legal provisions in respect of employment injury, occupational diseases, maternity, sickness, disability, old age, death, unemployment, family responsibilities and any other contingency which, according to national laws or regulations, is covered by a social security scheme), subject to the following limitations:

 (i) There may be appropriate arrangements for the maintenance of acquired rights and rights in course of acquisition;
 (ii) National laws or regulations of the country of residence may prescribe special arrangements concerning benefits or portions of ben-

efits which are payable wholly out of public funds, and concerning allowances paid to persons who do not fulfil the contribution conditions prescribed for the award of a normal pension.

2. The right to compensation for the death of a refugee resulting from employment injury or from occupational disease shall not be affected by the fact that the residence of the beneficiary is outside the territory of the Contracting State.

3. The Contracting States shall extend to refugees the benefits of agreements concluded between them, or which may be concluded between them in the future, concerning the maintenance of acquired rights and rights in the process of acquisition in regard to social security, subject only to the conditions which apply to nationals of the States signatory to the agreements in question.

4. The Contracting States will give sympathetic consideration to extending to refugees so far as possible the benefits of similar agreements which may at any time be in force between such Contracting States and non-contracting States.

Chapter V: Administrative Measures

Article 25
Administrative assistance

1. When the exercise of a right by a refugee would normally require the assistance of authorities of a foreign country to whom he cannot have recourse, the Contracting States in whose territory he is residing shall arrange that such assistance be afforded to him by their own authorities or by an international authority.

2. The authority or authorities mentioned in paragraph 1 shall deliver or cause to be delivered under their supervision to refugees such documents or certifications as would normally be delivered to aliens by or through their national authorities.

3. Documents or certifications so delivered shall stand in the stead of the official instruments delivered to aliens by or through their national authorities, and shall be given credence in the absence of proof to the contrary.

4. Subject to such exceptional treatment as may be granted to indigent persons, fees may be charged for the services mentioned herein, but such fees shall be moderate and commensurate with those charged to nationals for similar services.

5. The provisions of this article shall be without prejudice to articles 27 and 28.

Article 26
Freedom of movement

Each Contracting State shall accord to refugees lawfully in its territory the right to choose their place of residence to move freely within its territory, subject to any regulations applicable to aliens generally in the same circumstances.

Article 27
Identity papers

The Contracting States shall issue identity papers to any refugee in their territory who does not possess a valid travel document.

Article 28
Travel documents

1. The Contracting States shall issue to refugees lawfully staying in their territory travel documents for the purpose of travel outside their territory, unless compelling reasons of national security or public order otherwise require, and the provisions of the Schedule to this Convention shall apply with respect to such documents. The Contracting States may issue such a travel document to any other refugee in their territory; they shall in particular give sympathetic consideration to the issue of such a travel document to refugees in their territory who are unable to obtain a travel document from the country of their lawful residence.

2. Travel documents issued to refugees under previous international agreements by parties thereto shall be recognized and treated by the Contracting States in the same way as if they had been issued pursuant to this article.

Article 29
Fiscal charges

1. The Contracting States shall not impose upon refugees duties, charges or taxes, of any description whatsoever, other or higher than those which are or may be levied on their nationals in similar situations.

2. Nothing in the above paragraph shall prevent the application to refugees of the laws and regulations concerning charges in respect of the issue to aliens of administrative documents including identity papers.

Article 30
Transfer of assets

1. A Contracting State shall, in conformity with its laws and regulations, permit refugees to transfer assets which they have brought into its territory, to another country where they have been admitted for the purposes of resettlement.
2. A Contracting State shall give sympathetic consideration to the application of refugees for permission to transfer assets wherever they may be and which are necessary for their resettlement in another country to which they have been admitted.

Article 31
Refugees unlawfully in the country of refugee

1. The Contracting States shall not impose penalties, on account of their illegal entry or presence, on refugees who, coming directly from a territory where their life or freedom was threatened in the sense of article 1, enter or are present in their territory without authorization, provided they present themselves without delay to the authorities and show good cause for their illegal entry or presence.
2. The Contracting States shall not apply to the movements of such refugees restrictions other than those which are necessary and such restrictions shall only be applied until their status in the country is regularized or they obtain admission into another country. The Contracting States shall allow such refugees a reasonable period and all the necessary facilities to obtain admission into another country.

Article 32
Expulsion

1. The Contracting States shall not expel a refugee lawfully in their territory save on grounds of national security or public order.
2. The expulsion of such a refugee shall be only in pursuance of a decision reached in accordance with due process of law. Except where compelling reasons of national security otherwise require, the refugee shall be allowed to submit evidence to clear himself, and to appeal to and be represented for the purpose before competent authority or a person or persons specially designated by the competent authority.
3. The Contracting States shall allow such a refugee a reasonable period within which to seek legal admission into another country. The Contracting States reserve the right to apply during that period such internal measures as they may deem necessary.

Article 33
Prohibition of expulsion or return ("refoulement")

1. No Contracting State shall expel or return ("refouler") a refugee in any manner whatsoever to the frontiers of territories where his life or freedom would be threatened on account of his race, religion, nationality, membership of a particular social group or political opinion.

2. The benefit of the present provision may not, however, be claimed by a refugee whom there are reasonable grounds for regarding as a danger to the security of the country in which he is, or who, having been convicted by a final judgment of a particularly serious crime, constitutes a danger to the community of that country.

Article 34
Naturalization

The Contracting States shall as far as possible facilitate the assimilation and naturalization of refugees. They shall in particular make every effort to expedite naturalization proceedings and to reduce as far as possible the charges and costs of such proceedings.

Chapter VI: Executory and Transitory Provisions

Article 35
Co-operation of the national authorities with the United Nations

1. The Contracting States undertake to co-operate with the Office of the United Nations High Commissioner for Refugees, or any other agency of the United Nations which may succeed it, in the exercise of its functions, and shall in particular facilitate its duty of supervising the application of the provisions of this Convention.

2. In order to enable the Office of the High Commissioner or any other agency of the United Nations which may succeed it, to make reports to the competent organs of the United Nations, the Contracting States undertake to provide them in the appropriate form with information and statistical data requested concerning:

   a. The condition of refugees,
   b. The implementation of this Convention, and;
   c. Laws, regulations and decrees which are, or may hereafter be, in force relating to refugees.

Article 36
Information on national legislation

The Contracting States shall communicate to the Secretary-General of the United Nations the laws and regulations which they may adopt to ensure the application of this Convention.

Article 37
Relation to previous conventions

Without prejudice to article 28, paragraph 2, of this Convention replaces, as between Parties to it, the Arrangements of 5 July 1922, 31 May 1924, 12 May 1926, 30 June 1928 and 30 July 1935, the Conventions of 28 October 1933 and 10 February 1938, the Protocol of 14 September 1939 and the Agreement of 15 October 1946.

Chapter VII: Final Clauses

Article 38
Settlement of disputes

Any dispute between parties to this Convention relating to its interpretation or application, which cannot be settled by other means, shall be referred to the International Court of Justice at the request of any one of the parties to the dispute.

Article 39
Signature, ratification and accession

1. This Convention shall be opened for signature at Geneva on 28 July 1951 and shall thereafter be deposited with the Secretary-General of the United Nations. It shall be open for signature at the European Office of the United Nations from 28 July to 31 August 1951 and shall be re-opened for signature at the Headquarters of the United Nations from 17 September 1951 to 31 December 1952.

2. This Convention shall be open for signature on behalf of all States Members of the United Nations, and also on behalf of any other State invited to attend the Conference of Plenipotentiaries on the Status of Refugees and Stateless Persons or to which an invitation to sign will have been addressed by the General Assembly. It shall be ratified and the instruments of ratification shall be deposited with the Secretary-General of the United Nations.

3. This Convention shall be open from 28 July 1951 for accession by the States referred to in paragraph 2 of this article. Accession shall be effected by the deposit of an instrument of accession with the Secretary-General of the United Nations.

Article 40
Territorial application clause

1. Any State may, at the time of signature, ratification or accession, declare that this Convention shall extend to all or any of the territories for the international relations of which it is responsible. Such a declaration shall take effect when the Convention enters into force for the State concerned.

2. At any time thereafter any such extension shall be made by notification addressed to the Secretary-General of the United Nations and shall take effect as from the ninetieth day after the day of receipt by the Secretary-General of the United Nations of this notification, or as from the date of entry into force of the Convention for the State concerned, whichever is the later.

3. With respect to those territories to which this Convention is not extended at the time of signature, ratification or accession, each State concerned shall consider the possibility of taking the necessary steps in order to extend the application of this Convention to such territories, subject, where necessary for constitutional reasons, to the consent of the Governments of such territories.

Article 41
Federal clause

In the case of a Federal or non-unitary State, the following provisions shall apply:

a. With respect to those articles of this Convention that come within the legislative jurisdiction of the federal legislative authority, the obligations of the Federal Government shall to this extent be the same as those of Parties which are not Federal States;
b. With respect to those articles of this Convention that come within the legislative jurisdiction of constituent States, provinces or cantons which are not, under the constitutional system of the federation, bound to take legislative action, the Federal Government shall bring such articles with a favourable recommendation to the notice of the appropriate authorities of states, provinces or cantons at the earliest possible moment;
c. A Federal State Party to this Convention shall, at the request of any other Contracting State transmitted through the Secretary-General

of the United Nations, supply a statement of the law and practice of the Federation and its constituent units in regard to any particular provision of the Convention showing the extent to which effect has been given to that provision by legislative or other action.

Article 42
Reservations

1. At the time of signature, ratification or accession, any State may make reservations to articles of the Convention other than to articles 1, 3, 4, 16(1), 33, 36–46 inclusive.

2. Any State making a reservation in accordance with paragraph 1 of this article may at any time withdraw the reservation by a communication to that effect addressed to the Secretary-General of the United Nations.

Article 43
Entry into force

1. This Convention shall come into force on the ninetieth day following the day of deposit of the sixth instrument of ratification or accession.

2. For each State ratifying or acceding to the Convention after the deposit of the sixth instrument of ratification or accession, the Convention shall enter into force on the ninetieth day following the date of deposit by such State of its instrument or ratification or accession.

Article 44
Denunciation

1. Any Contracting State may denounce this Convention at any time by a notification addressed to the Secretary-General of the United Nations.

2. Such denunciation shall take effect for the Contracting State concerned one year from the date upon which it is received by the Secretary-General of the United Nations.

3. Any State which has made a declaration or notification under article 40 may, at any time thereafter, by a notification to the Secretary-General of the United Nations, declare that the Convention shall cease to extend to such territory one year after the date of receipt of the notification by the Secretary General.

Article 45
Revision

1. Any Contracting State may request revision of this Convention at any time by a notification addressed to the Secretary-General of the United Nations.

2. The General Assembly of the United Nations shall recommend the steps, if any, to be taken in respect of such request.

Article 46
Notifications by the Secretary-General of the United Nations

The Secretary-General of the United Nations shall inform all Members of the United Nations and non-member States referred to in article 39:

a. Of declarations and notifications in accordance with section B of article 1;
b. Of signatures, ratifications and accessions in accordance with article 39;
c. Of declarations and notifications in accordance with article 40;
d. Of reservations and withdrawals in accordance with article 42;
e. Of the date on which this Convention will come into force in accordance with article 43;
f. Of denunciations and notifications in accordance with article 44;
g. Of requests for revision in accordance with article 45.

In faith whereof the undersigned, duly authorized, have signed this Convention on behalf of their respective Governments.

Done at Geneva, this twenty-eighth day of July, one thousand nine hundred and fifty-one, in a single copy, of which the English and French texts are equally authentic and which shall remain deposited in the archives of the United Nations, and certified true copies of which shall be delivered to all Members of the United Nations and to the non-member States referred to in article 39.

Appendix II

Protocol Relating to the Status of Refugee

Entry into force 4 October 1967

The States Parties to the present Protocol,

Considering that the Convention relating to the Status of Refugees done at Geneva on 28 July 1951 (hereinafter referred to as the Convention) covers only those persons who have become refugees as a result of events occurring before 1 January 1951,

Considering that new refugee situations have arisen since the Convention was adopted and that the refugees concerned may therefore not fall within the scope of the Convention,

Considering that it is desirable that equal status should be enjoyed by all refugees covered by the definition in the Convention irrespective of the dateline 1 January 1951,

Have agreed as follows:

Article 1
General provision

1. The States Parties to the present Protocol undertake to apply articles 2 to 34 inclusive of the Convention to refugees as hereinafter defined.

2. For the purpose of the present Protocol, the term "refugee" shall, except as regards the application of paragraph 3 of this article, mean any person within the definition of article I of the Convention as if the words "As a result of events occurring before 1 January 1951 and . . ." and the words ". . . as a result of such events," in article 1 A (2) were omitted.

3. The present Protocol shall be applied by the States Parties hereto without any geographic limitation, save that existing declarations made by States already Parties to the Convention in accordance with article I B (I) (a) of the Convention, shall, unless extended under article I B (2) thereof, apply also under the present Protocol.

Article 2
Co-operation of the national authorities with the United Nations

1. The States Parties to the present Protocol undertake to co-operate with the Office of the United Nations High Commissioner for Refugees, or any other agency of the United Nations which may succeed it, in the exercise of its functions, and shall in particular facilitate its duty of supervising the application of the provisions of the present Protocol.

2. In order to enable the Office of the High Commissioner or any other agency of the United Nations which may succeed it, to make reports to the competent organs of the United Nations, the States Parties to the present Protocol undertake to provide them with the information and statistical data requested, in the appropriate form, concerning:

a. The condition of refugees;
b. The implementation of the present Protocol;
c. Laws, regulations and decrees which are, or may hereafter be, in force relating to refugees.

Article 3
Information on national legislation

The States Parties to the present Protocol shall communicate to the Secretary-General of the United Nations the laws and regulations which they may adopt to ensure the application of the present Protocol.

Article 4
Settlement of disputes

Any dispute between States Parties to the present Protocol which relates to its interpretation or application and which cannot be settled by other means shall be referred to the International Court of Justice at the request of any one of the parties to the dispute.

Article 5
Accession

The present Protocol shall be open for accession on behalf of all States Parties to the Convention and of any other State Member of the United Nations or member of any of the specialized agencies or to which an invitation to accede may have been addressed by the General Assembly of the United Nations. Accession shall be effected by the deposit of an instrument of accession with the Secretary-General of the United Nations.

Article 6
Federal clause

In the case of a Federal or non-unitary State, the following provisions shall apply:

a. With respect to those articles of the Convention to be applied in accordance with article I, paragraph 1, of the present Protocol that come within the legislative jurisdiction of the federal legislative authority, the obligations of the Federal Government shall to this extent be the same as those of States Parties which are not Federal States;
b. With respect to those articles of the Convention to be applied in accordance with article I, paragraph 1, of the present Protocol that come within the legislative jurisdiction of constituent States, provinces or cantons which are not, under the constitutional system of the Federation, bound to take legislative action, the Federal Government shall bring such articles with a favourable recommendation to the notice of the appropriate authorities of States, provinces or cantons at the earliest possible moment;
c. A Federal State Party to the present Protocol shall, at the request of any other State Party hereto transmitted through the Secretary-General of the United Nations, supply a statement of the law and practice of the Federation and its constituent units in regard to any particular provision of the Convention to be applied in accordance with article I, paragraph 1, of the present Protocol, showing the extent to which effect has been given to that provision by legislative or other action.

Article 7
Reservations and declarations

1. At the time of accession, any State may make reservations in respect of article IV of the present Protocol and in respect of the application in accordance with article I of the present Protocol of any provisions of the Convention other than those contained in articles 1, 3, 4, 16(1) and 33 thereof, provided that in the case of a State Party to the Convention reservations made under this article shall not extend to refugees in respect of whom the Convention applies.

2. Reservations made by States Parties to the Convention in accordance with article 42 thereof shall, unless withdrawn, be applicable in relation to their obligations under the present Protocol.

3. Any State making a reservation in accordance with paragraph I of this article may at any time withdraw such reservation by a communication to that effect addressed to the Secretary-General of the United Nations.

4. Declarations made under article 40, paragraphs I and 2, of the Convention by a State Party thereto which accedes to the present Protocol shall be deemed to apply in respect of the present Protocol, unless upon accession a notification to the contrary is addressed by the State Party concerned to the Secretary-General of the United Nations. The provisions of article 40, paragraphs 2 and 3, and of article 44, paragraph 3, of the Convention shall be deemed to apply muratis mutandis to the present Protocol.

Article 8
Entry into Protocol

1. The present Protocol shall come into force on the day of deposit of the sixth instrument of accession.

2. For each State acceding to the Protocol after the deposit of the sixth instrument of accession, the Protocol shall come into force on the date of deposit by such State of its instrument of accession.

Article 9
Denunciation

1. Any State Party hereto may denounce this Protocol at any time by a notification addressed to the Secretary-General of the United Nations.

2. Such denunciation shall take effect for the State Party concerned one year from the date on which it is received by the Secretary-General of the United Nations.

Article 10
Notifications by the Secretary-General of the United Nations

The Secretary-General of the United Nations shall inform the States referred to in article V above of the date of entry into force, accessions, reservations and withdrawals of reservations to and denunciations of the present Protocol, and of declarations and notifications relating hereto.

Article 11
Deposit in the archives of the Secretariat of the United Nations

A copy of the present Protocol, of which the Chinese, English, French, Russian and Spanish texts are equally authentic, signed by the President of the General Assembly and by the Secretary-General of the United Nations, shall be deposited in the archives of the Secretariat of the United Nations. The Secretary-General will transmit certified copies thereof to all States Members of the United Nations and to the other States referred to in article 5 above.

Appendix III

Resolution Adopted by the General Assembly on 19 September 2016

71/1. New York Declaration for Refugees and Migrants

The General Assembly

Adopts the following outcome document of the high-level plenary meeting on addressing large movements of refugees and migrants:

New York Declaration for Refugees and Migrants

We, the Heads of State and Government and High Representatives, meeting at United Nations Headquarters in New York on 19 September 2016 to address the question of large movements of refugees and migrants, have adopted the following political declaration.

I. Introduction

1. Since earliest times, humanity has been on the move. Some people move in search of new economic opportunities and horizons. Others move to escape armed conflict, poverty, food insecurity, persecution, terrorism, or human rights violations and abuses. Still others do so in response to the adverse effects of climate change, natural disasters (some of which may be linked to climate change), or other environmental factors. Many move, indeed, for a combination of these reasons.

2. We have considered today how the international community should best respond to the growing global phenomenon of large movements of refugees and migrants.

3. We are witnessing in today's world an unprecedented level of human mobility. More people than ever before live in a country other than the one in which they were born. Migrants are present in all countries in the world. Most of them move without incident. In 2015, their number surpassed 244 million, growing at a rate faster than the world's population. However, there are roughly 65 million forcibly displaced persons, including over 21 million refugees, 3 million asylum seekers and over 40 million internally displaced persons.

4. In adopting the 2030 Agenda for Sustainable Development[1] one year ago, we recognized clearly the positive contribution made by migrants for inclusive growth and sustainable development. Our world is a better place for that contribution. The benefits and opportunities of safe, orderly and regular migration are substantial and are often underestimated. Forced displacement and irregular migration in large movements, on the other hand, often present complex challenges.

5. We reaffirm the purposes and principles of the Charter of the United Nations. We reaffirm also the Universal Declaration of Human Rights[2] and recall the core international human rights treaties. We reaffirm and will fully protect the human rights of all refugees and migrants, regardless of status; all are rights holders. Our response will demonstrate full respect for international law and international human rights law and, where applicable, international refugee law and international humanitarian law.

6. Though their treatment is governed by separate legal frameworks, refugees and migrants have the same universal human rights and fundamental freedoms. They also face many common challenges and have similar vulnerabilities, including in the context of large movements. "Large movements" may be understood to reflect a number of considerations, including: the number of people arriving, the economic, social and geographical context, the capacity of a receiving State to respond and the impact of a movement that is sudden or prolonged. The term does not, for example, cover regular flows of migrants from one country to another. "Large movements" may involve mixed flows of people, whether refugees or migrants, who move for different reasons but who may use similar routes.

7. Large movements of refugees and migrants have political, economic, social, developmental, humanitarian and human rights ramifications, which cross all borders. These are global phenomena that call for global approaches and global solutions. No one State can manage such movements on its own. Neighbouring or transit countries, mostly developing countries, are disproportionately affected. Their capacities have been severely stretched in many cases, affecting their own social and economic cohesion and development. In

addition, protracted refugee crises are now commonplace, with long-term repercussions for those involved and for their host countries and communities. Greater international cooperation is needed to assist host countries and communities.

8. We declare our profound solidarity with, and support for, the millions of people in different parts of the world who, for reasons beyond their control, are forced to uproot themselves and their families from their homes.

9. Refugees and migrants in large movements often face a desperate ordeal. Many take great risks, embarking on perilous journeys, which many may not survive. Some feel compelled to employ the services of criminal groups, including smugglers, and others may fall prey to such groups or become victims of trafficking. Even if they reach their destination, they face an uncertain reception and a precarious future.

10. We are determined to save lives. Our challenge is above all moral and humanitarian. Equally, we are determined to find long-term and sustainable solutions. We will combat with all the means at our disposal the abuses and exploitation suffered by countless refugees and migrants in vulnerable situations.

11. We acknowledge a shared responsibility to manage large movements of refugees and migrants in a humane, sensitive, compassionate and people-centred manner. We will do so through international cooperation, while recognizing that there are varying capacities and resources to respond to these movements. International cooperation and, in particular, cooperation among countries of origin or nationality, transit and destination, has never been more important; "win-win" cooperation in this area has profound benefits for humanity. Large movements of refugees and migrants must have comprehensive policy support, assistance and protection, consistent with States' obligations under international law. We also recall our obligations to fully respect their human rights and fundamental freedoms, and we stress their need to live their lives in safety and dignity. We pledge our support to those affected today as well as to those who will be part of future large movements.

12. We are determined to address the root causes of large movements of refugees and migrants, including through increased efforts aimed at early prevention of crisis situations based on preventive diplomacy. We will address them also through the prevention and peaceful resolution of conflict, greater coordination of humanitarian, development and peacebuilding efforts, the promotion of the rule of law at the national and international levels and the protection of human rights. Equally, we will address movements caused by poverty, instability, marginalization and exclusion and the lack of development and economic opportunities, with particular reference to the most vulnerable populations. We will work with countries of origin to strengthen their capacities.

13. All human beings are born free and equal in dignity and rights. Everyone has the right to recognition everywhere as a person before the law. We

recall that our obligations under international law prohibit discrimination of any kind on the basis of race, colour, sex, language, religion, political or other opinion, national or social origin, property, birth or other status. Yet in many parts of the world we are witnessing, with great concern, increasingly xenophobic and racist responses to refugees and migrants.

14. We strongly condemn acts and manifestations of racism, racial discrimination, xenophobia and related intolerance against refugees and migrants, and the stereotypes often applied to them, including on the basis of religion or belief. Diversity enriches every society and contributes to social cohesion. Demonizing refugees or migrants offends profoundly against the values of dignity and equality for every human being, to which we have committed ourselves. Gathered today at the United Nations, the birthplace and custodian of these universal values, we deplore all manifestations of xenophobia, racial discrimination and intolerance. We will take a range of steps to counter such attitudes and behaviour, in particular with regard to hate crimes, hate speech and racial violence. We welcome the global campaign proposed by the Secretary-General to counter xenophobia and we will implement it in cooperation with the United Nations and all relevant stakeholders, in accordance with international law. The campaign will emphasize, inter alia, direct personal contact between host communities and refugees and migrants and will highlight the positive contributions made by the latter, as well as our common humanity.

15. We invite the private sector and civil society, including refugee and migrant organizations, to participate in multi-stakeholder alliances to support efforts to implement the commitments we are making today.

16. In the 2030 Agenda for Sustainable Development, we pledged that no one would be left behind. We declared that we wished to see the Sustainable Development Goals and their targets met for all nations and peoples and for all segments of society. We said also that we would endeavour to reach the furthest behind first. We reaffirm today our commitments that relate to the specific needs of migrants or refugees. The 2030 Agenda makes clear, inter alia, that we will facilitate orderly, safe, regular and responsible migration and mobility of people, including through the implementation of planned and well-managed migration policies. The needs of refugees, internally displaced persons and migrants are explicitly recognized.

17. The implementation of all relevant provisions of the 2030 Agenda for Sustainable Development will enable the positive contribution that migrants are making to sustainable development to be reinforced. At the same time, it will address many of the root causes of forced displacement, helping to create more favourable conditions in countries of origin. Meeting today, a year after our adoption of the 2030 Agenda, we are determined to realize the full potential of that Agenda for refugees and migrants.

18. We recall the Sendai Framework for Disaster Risk Reduction 2015–2030[3] and its recommendations concerning measures to mitigate risks associated with disasters. States that have signed and ratified the Paris Agreement on climate change[4] welcome that agreement and are committed to its implementation. We reaffirm the Addis Ababa Action Agenda of the Third International Conference on Financing for Development,[5] including its provisions that are applicable to refugees and migrants.

19. We take note of the report of the Secretary-General, entitled "In safety and dignity: addressing large movements of refugees and migrants",[6] prepared pursuant to General Assembly decision 70/539 of 22 December 2015, in preparation for this high-level meeting. While recognizing that the following conferences either did not have an intergovernmentally agreed outcome or were regional in scope, we take note of the World Humanitarian Summit, held in Istanbul, Turkey, on 23 and 24 May 2016, the high-level meeting on global responsibility-sharing through pathways for admission of Syrian refugees, convened by the Office of the United Nations High Commissioner for Refugees on 30 March 2016, the conference on "Supporting Syria and the Region", held in London on 4 February 2016, and the pledging conference on Somali refugees, held in Brussels on 21 October 2015. While recognizing that the following initiatives are regional in nature and apply only to those countries participating in them, we take note of regional initiatives such as the Bali Process on People Smuggling, Trafficking in Persons and Related Transnational Crime, the European Union-Horn of Africa Migration Route Initiative and the African Union-Horn of Africa Initiative on Human Trafficking and Smuggling of Migrants (the Khartoum Process), the Rabat Process, the Valletta Action Plan and the Brazil Declaration and Plan of Action.

20. We recognize the very large number of people who are displaced within national borders and the possibility that such persons might seek protection and assistance in other countries as refugees or migrants. We note the need for reflection on effective strategies to ensure adequate protection and assistance for internally displaced persons and to prevent and reduce such displacement.

Commitments

21. We have endorsed today a set of commitments that apply to both refugees and migrants, as well as separate sets of commitments for refugees and migrants. We do so taking into account different national realities, capacities and levels of development and respecting national policies and priorities. We reaffirm our commitment to international law and emphasize that the present declaration and its annexes are to be implemented in a manner that is consistent with the rights and obligations of States under international law. While some commitments are mainly applicable to one group, they may

also be applicable to the other. Furthermore, while they are all framed in the context of the large movements we are considering today, many may be applicable also to regular migration. Annex I to the present declaration contains a comprehensive refugee response framework and outlines steps towards the achievement of a global compact on refugees in 2018, while annex II sets out steps towards the achievement of a global compact for safe, orderly and regular migration in 2018.

II. Commitments that apply to both refugees and migrants

22. Underlining the importance of a comprehensive approach to the issues involved, we will ensure a people-centred, sensitive, humane, dignified, gender-responsive and prompt reception for all persons arriving in our countries, and particularly those in large movements, whether refugees or migrants. We will also ensure full respect and protection for their human rights and fundamental freedoms.

23. We recognize and will address, in accordance with our obligations under international law, the special needs of all people in vulnerable situations who are traveling within large movements of refugees and migrants, including women at risk, children, especially those who are unaccompanied or separated from their families, members of ethnic and religious minorities, victims of violence, older persons, persons with disabilities, persons who are discriminated against on any basis, indigenous peoples, victims of human trafficking, and victims of exploitation and abuse in the context of the smuggling of migrants.

24. Recognizing that States have rights and responsibilities to manage and control their borders, we will implement border control procedures in conformity with applicable obligations under international law, including international human rights law and international refugee law. We will promote international cooperation on border control and management as an important element of security for States, including issues relating to battling transnational organized crime, terrorism and illicit trade. We will ensure that public officials and law enforcement officers who work in border areas are trained to uphold the human rights of all persons crossing, or seeking to cross, international borders. We will strengthen international border management cooperation, including in relation to training and the exchange of best practices. We will intensify support in this area and help to build capacity as appropriate. We reaffirm that, in line with the principle of non-refoulement, individuals must not be returned at borders. We acknowledge also that, while upholding these obligations and principles, States are entitled to take measures to prevent irregular border crossings.

25. We will make efforts to collect accurate information regarding large movements of refugees and migrants. We will also take measures to identify

correctly their nationalities, as well as their reasons for movement. We will take measures to identify those who are seeking international protection as refugees.

26. We will continue to protect the human rights and fundamental freedoms of all persons, in transit and after arrival. We stress the importance of addressing the immediate needs of persons who have been exposed to physical or psychological abuse while in transit upon their arrival, without discrimination and without regard to legal or migratory status or means of transportation. For this purpose, we will consider appropriate support to strengthen, at their request, capacity-building for countries that receive large movements of refugees and migrants.

27. We are determined to address unsafe movements of refugees and migrants, with particular reference to irregular movements of refugees and migrants. We will do so without prejudice to the right to seek asylum. We will combat the exploitation, abuse and discrimination suffered by many refugees and migrants.

28. We express our profound concern at the large number of people who have lost their lives in transit. We commend the efforts already made to rescue people in distress at sea. We commit to intensifying international cooperation on the strengthening of search and rescue mechanisms. We will also work to improve the availability of accurate data on the whereabouts of people and vessels stranded at sea. In addition, we will strengthen support for rescue efforts over land along dangerous or isolated routes. We will draw attention to the risks involved in the use of such routes in the first instance.

29. We recognize and will take steps to address the particular vulnerabilities of women and children during the journey from country of origin to country of arrival. This includes their potential exposure to discrimination and exploitation, as well as to sexual, physical and psychological abuse, violence, human trafficking and contemporary forms of slavery.

30. We encourage States to address the vulnerabilities to HIV and the specific health-care needs experienced by migrant and mobile populations, as well as by refugees and crisis-affected populations, and to take steps to reduce stigma, discrimination and violence, as well as to review policies related to restrictions on entry based on HIV status, with a view to eliminating such restrictions and the return of people on the basis of their HIV status, and to support their access to HIV prevention, treatment, care and support.

31. We will ensure that our responses to large movements of refugees and migrants mainstream a gender perspective, promote gender equality and the empowerment of all women and girls and fully respect and protect the human rights of women and girls. We will combat sexual and gender-based violence to the greatest extent possible. We will provide access to sexual and reproductive health-care services. We will tackle the multiple and intersecting forms of discrimination against refugee and migrant women and girls. At the

same time, recognizing the significant contribution and leadership of women in refugee and migrant communities, we will work to ensure their full, equal and meaningful participation in the development of local solutions and opportunities. We will take into consideration the different needs, vulnerabilities and capacities of women, girls, boys and men.

32. We will protect the human rights and fundamental freedoms of all refugee and migrant children, regardless of their status, and giving primary consideration at all times to the best interests of the child. This will apply particularly to unaccompanied children and those separated from their families; we will refer their care to the relevant national child protection authorities and other relevant authorities. We will comply with our obligations under the Convention on the Rights of the Child.[7] We will work to provide for basic health, education and psychosocial development and for the registration of all births on our territories. We are determined to ensure that all children are receiving education within a few months of arrival, and we will prioritize budgetary provision to facilitate this, including support for host countries as required. We will strive to provide refugee and migrant children with a nurturing environment for the full realization of their rights and capabilities.

33. Reaffirming that all individuals who have crossed or are seeking to cross international borders are entitled to due process in the assessment of their legal status, entry and stay, we will consider reviewing policies that criminalize cross-border movements. We will also pursue alternatives to detention while these assessments are under way. Furthermore, recognizing that detention for the purposes of determining migration status is seldom, if ever, in the best interest of the child, we will use it only as a measure of last resort, in the least restrictive setting, for the shortest possible period of time, under conditions that respect their human rights and in a manner that takes into account, as a primary consideration, the best interest of the child, and we will work towards the ending of this practice.

34. Reaffirming the importance of the United Nations Convention against Transnational Organized Crime and the two relevant Protocols thereto,[8] we encourage the ratification of, accession to and implementation of relevant international instruments on preventing and combating trafficking in persons and the smuggling of migrants.

35. We recognize that refugees and migrants in large movements are at greater risk of being trafficked and of being subjected to forced labour. We will, with full respect for our obligations under international law, vigorously combat human trafficking and migrant smuggling with a view to their elimination, including through targeted measures to identify victims of human trafficking or those at risk of trafficking. We will provide support for the victims of human trafficking. We will work to prevent human trafficking among those affected by displacement.

36. With a view to disrupting and eliminating the criminal networks involved, we will review our national legislation to ensure conformity with our obligations under international law on migrant smuggling, human trafficking and maritime safety. We will implement the United Nations Global Plan of Action to Combat Trafficking in Persons.[9] We will establish or upgrade, as appropriate, national and regional anti-human trafficking policies. We note regional initiatives such as the African Union-Horn of Africa Initiative on Human Trafficking and Smuggling of Migrants, the Plan of Action Against Trafficking in Persons, Especially Women and Children, of the Association of Southeast Asian Nations, the European Union Strategy towards the Eradication of Trafficking in Human Beings 2012–2016, and the Work Plans against Trafficking in Persons in the Western Hemisphere. We welcome reinforced technical cooperation, on a regional and bilateral basis, between countries of origin, transit and destination on the prevention of human trafficking and migrant smuggling and the prosecution of traffickers and smugglers.

37. We favour an approach to addressing the drivers and root causes of large movements of refugees and migrants, including forced displacement and protracted crises, which would, inter alia, reduce vulnerability, combat poverty, improve self-reliance and resilience, ensure a strengthened humanitarian-development nexus, and improve coordination with peacebuilding efforts. This will involve coordinated prioritized responses based on joint and impartial needs assessments and facilitating cooperation across institutional mandates.

38. We will take measures to provide, on the basis of bilateral, regional and international cooperation, humanitarian financing that is adequate, flexible, predictable and consistent, to enable host countries and communities to respond both to the immediate humanitarian needs and to their longer-term development needs. There is a need to address gaps in humanitarian funding, considering additional resources as appropriate. We look forward to close cooperation in this regard among Member States, United Nations entities and other actors and between the United Nations and international financial institutions such as the World Bank, where appropriate. We envisage innovative financing responses, risk financing for affected communities and the implementation of other efficiencies such as reducing management costs, improving transparency, increasing the use of national responders, expanding the use of cash assistance, reducing duplication, increasing engagement with beneficiaries, diminishing earmarked funding and harmonizing reporting, so as to ensure a more effective use of existing resources.

39. We commit to combating xenophobia, racism and discrimination in our societies against refugees and migrants. We will take measures to improve their integration and inclusion, as appropriate, and with particular reference to access to education, health care, justice and language training. We recognize that these measures will reduce the risks of marginalization and

radicalization. National policies relating to integration and inclusion will be developed, as appropriate, in conjunction with relevant civil society organizations, including faith-based organizations, the private sector, employers' and workers' organizations and other stakeholders. We also note the obligation for refugees and migrants to observe the laws and regulations of their host countries.

40. We recognize the importance of improved data collection, particularly by national authorities, and will enhance international cooperation to this end, including through capacity-building, financial support and technical assistance. Such data should be disaggregated by sex and age and include information on regular and irregular flows, the economic impacts of migration and refugee movements, human trafficking, the needs of refugees, migrants and host communities and other issues. We will do so consistent with our national legislation on data protection, if applicable, and our international obligations related to privacy, as applicable.

III. Commitments for migrants

41. We are committed to protecting the safety, dignity and human rights and fundamental freedoms of all migrants, regardless of their migratory status, at all times. We will cooperate closely to facilitate and ensure safe, orderly and regular migration, including return and readmission, taking into account national legislation.

42. We commit to safeguarding the rights of, protecting the interests of and assisting our migrant communities abroad, including through consular protection, assistance and cooperation, in accordance with relevant international law. We reaffirm that everyone has the right to leave any country, including his or her own, and to return to his or her country. We recall at the same time that each State has a sovereign right to determine whom to admit to its territory, subject to that State's international obligations. We recall also that States must readmit their returning nationals and ensure that they are duly received without undue delay, following confirmation of their nationalities in accordance with national legislation. We will take measures to inform migrants about the various processes relating to their arrival and stay in countries of transit, destination and return.

43. We commit to addressing the drivers that create or exacerbate large movements. We will analyse and respond to the factors, including in countries of origin, which lead or contribute to large movements. We will cooperate to create conditions that allow communities and individuals to live in peace and prosperity in their homelands. Migration should be a choice, not a necessity. We will take measures, inter alia, to implement the 2030 Agenda for Sustainable Development, whose objectives include eradicating extreme poverty and inequality, revitalizing the Global Partnership for Sustainable

Development, promoting peaceful and inclusive societies based on international human rights and the rule of law, creating conditions for balanced, sustainable and inclusive economic growth and employment, combating environmental degradation and ensuring effective responses to natural disasters and the adverse impacts of climate change.

44. Recognizing that the lack of educational opportunities is often a push factor for migration, particularly for young people, we commit to strengthening capacities in countries of origin, including in educational institutions. We commit also to enhancing employment opportunities, particularly for young people, in countries of origin. We acknowledge also the impact of migration on human capital in countries of origin.

45. We will consider reviewing our migration policies with a view to examining their possible unintended negative consequences.

46. We also recognize that international migration is a multidimensional reality of major relevance for the development of countries of origin, transit and destination, which requires coherent and comprehensive responses. Migrants can make positive and profound contributions to economic and social development in their host societies and to global wealth creation. They can help to respond to demographic trends, labour shortages and other challenges in host societies, and add fresh skills and dynamism to the latter's economies. We recognize the development benefits of migration to countries of origin, including through the involvement of diasporas in economic development and reconstruction. We will commit to reducing the costs of labour migration and promote ethical recruitment policies and practices between sending and receiving countries. We will promote faster, cheaper and safer transfers of migrant remittances in both source and recipient countries, including through a reduction in transaction costs, as well as the facilitation of interaction between diasporas and their countries of origin. We would like these contributions to be more widely recognized and indeed, strengthened in the context of implementation of the 2030 Agenda for Sustainable Development.

47. We will ensure that all aspects of migration are integrated into global, regional and national sustainable development plans and into humanitarian, peacebuilding and human rights policies and programmes.

48. We call upon States that have not done so to consider ratifying, or acceding to, the International Convention on the Protection of the Rights of All Migrant Workers and Members of Their Families.[10] We call also upon States that have not done so to consider acceding to relevant International Labour Organization conventions, as appropriate. We note, in addition, that migrants enjoy rights and protection under various provisions of international law.

49. We commit to strengthening global governance of migration. We therefore warmly support and welcome the agreement to bring the International Organization for Migration, an organization regarded by its Member

States as the global lead agency on migration, into a closer legal and working relationship with the United Nations as a related organization.[11] We look forward to the implementation of this agreement, which will assist and protect migrants more comprehensively, help States to address migration issues and promote better coherence between migration and related policy domains.

50. We will assist, impartially and on the basis of needs, migrants in countries that are experiencing conflicts or natural disasters, working, as applicable, in coordination with the relevant national authorities. While recognizing that not all States are participating in them, we note in this regard the Migrants in Countries in Crisis initiative and the Agenda for the Protection of Cross-Border Displaced Persons in the Context of Disasters and Climate Change resulting from the Nansen Initiative.

51. We take note of the work done by the Global Migration Group to develop principles and practical guidance on the protection of the human rights of migrants in vulnerable situations.

52. We will consider developing non-binding guiding principles and voluntary guidelines, consistent with international law, on the treatment of migrants in vulnerable situations, especially unaccompanied and separated children who do not qualify for international protection as refugees and who may need assistance. The guiding principles and guidelines will be developed using a State-led process with the involvement of all relevant stakeholders and with input from the Special Representative of the Secretary-General on International Migration and Development, the International Organization for Migration, the Office of the United Nations High Commissioner for Human Rights, the Office of the United Nations High Commissioner for Refugees and other relevant United Nations system entities. They would complement national efforts to protect and assist migrants.

53. We welcome the willingness of some States to provide temporary protection against return to migrants who do not qualify for refugee status and who are unable to return home owing to conditions in their countries.

54. We will build on existing bilateral, regional and global cooperation and partnership mechanisms, in accordance with international law, for facilitating migration in line with the 2030 Agenda for Sustainable Development. We will strengthen cooperation to this end among countries of origin, transit and destination, including through regional consultative processes, international organizations, the International Red Cross and Red Crescent Movement, regional economic organizations and local government authorities, as well as with relevant private sector recruiters and employers, labour unions, civil society and migrant and diaspora groups. We recognize the particular needs of local authorities, who are the first receivers of migrants.

55. We recognize the progress made on international migration and development issues within the United Nations system, including the first and second High-level Dialogues on International Migration and Development.

We will support enhanced global and regional dialogue and deepened collaboration on migration, particularly through exchanges of best practice and mutual learning and the development of national or regional initiatives. We note in this regard the valuable contribution of the Global Forum on Migration and Development and acknowledge the importance of multi-stakeholder dialogues on migration and development.

56. We affirm that children should not be criminalized or subject to punitive measures because of their migration status or that of their parents.

57. We will consider facilitating opportunities for safe, orderly and regular migration, including, as appropriate, employment creation, labour mobility at all skills levels, circular migration, family reunification and education-related opportunities. We will pay particular attention to the application of minimum labour standards for migrant workers regardless of their status, as well as to recruitment and other migration-related costs, remittance flows, transfers of skills and knowledge and the creation of employment opportunities for young people.

58. We strongly encourage cooperation among countries of origin or nationality, countries of transit, countries of destination and other relevant countries in ensuring that migrants who do not have permission to stay in the country of destination can return, in accordance with international obligations of all States, to their country of origin or nationality in a safe, orderly and dignified manner, preferably on a voluntary basis, taking into account national legislation in line with international law. We note that cooperation on return and readmission forms an important element of international cooperation on migration. Such cooperation would include ensuring proper identification and the provision of relevant travel documents. Any type of return, whether voluntary or otherwise, must be consistent with our obligations under international human rights law and in compliance with the principle of non-refoulement. It should also respect the rules of international law and must in addition be conducted in keeping with the best interests of children and with due process. While recognizing that they apply only to States that have entered into them, we acknowledge that existing readmission agreements should be fully implemented. We support enhanced reception and reintegration assistance for those who are returned. Particular attention should be paid to the needs of migrants in vulnerable situations who return, such as children, older persons, persons with disabilities and victims of trafficking.

59. We reaffirm our commitment to protect the human rights of migrant children, given their vulnerability, particularly unaccompanied migrant children, and to provide access to basic health, education and psychosocial services, ensuring that the best interests of the child is a primary consideration in all relevant policies.

60. We recognize the need to address the special situation and vulnerability of migrant women and girls by, inter alia, incorporating a gender perspective into migration policies and strengthening national laws, institutions and programmes to combat gender-based violence, including trafficking in persons and discrimination against women and girls.

61. While recognizing the contribution of civil society, including non-governmental organizations, to promoting the well-being of migrants and their integration into societies, especially at times of extremely vulnerable conditions, and the support of the international community to the efforts of such organizations, we encourage deeper interaction between Governments and civil society to find responses to the challenges and the opportunities posed by international migration.

62. We note that the Special Representative of the Secretary-General on International Migration and Development, Mr. Peter Sutherland, will be providing, before the end of 2016, a report that will propose ways of strengthening international cooperation and the engagement of the United Nations on migration.

63. We commit to launching, in 2016, a process of intergovernmental negotiations leading to the adoption of a global compact for safe, orderly and regular migration at an intergovernmental conference to be held in 2018. We invite the President of the General Assembly to make arrangements for the determination of the modalities, timeline and other practicalities relating to the negotiation process. Further details regarding the process are set out in annex II to the present declaration.

IV. Commitments for refugees

64. Recognizing that armed conflict, persecution and violence, including terrorism, are among the factors which give rise to large refugee movements, we will work to address the root causes of such crisis situations and to prevent or resolve conflict by peaceful means. We will work in every way possible for the peaceful settlement of disputes, the prevention of conflict and the achievement of the long-term political solutions required. Preventive diplomacy and early response to conflict on the part of States and the United Nations are critical. The promotion of human rights is also critical. In addition, we will promote good governance, the rule of law, effective, accountable and inclusive institutions, and sustainable development at the international, regional, national and local levels. Recognizing that displacement could be reduced if international humanitarian law were respected by all parties to armed conflict, we renew our commitment to uphold humanitarian principles and international humanitarian law. We confirm also our respect for the rules that safeguard civilians in conflict.

65. We reaffirm the 1951 Convention relating to the Status of Refugees [12] and the 1967 Protocol thereto [13] as the foundation of the international refugee protection regime. We recognize the importance of their full and effective application by States parties and the values they embody. We note with satisfaction that 148 States are now parties to one or both instruments. We encourage States not parties to consider acceding to those instruments and States parties with reservations to give consideration to withdrawing them. We recognize also that a number of States not parties to the international refugee instruments have shown a generous approach to hosting refugees.

66. We reaffirm that international refugee law, international human rights law and international humanitarian law provide the legal framework to strengthen the protection of refugees. We will ensure, in this context, protection for all who need it. We take note of regional refugee instruments, such as the Organization of African Unity Convention governing the specific aspects of refugee problems in Africa [14] and the Cartagena Declaration on Refugees.

67. We reaffirm respect for the institution of asylum and the right to seek asylum. We reaffirm also respect for and adherence to the fundamental principle of non-refoulement in accordance with international refugee law.

68. We underline the centrality of international cooperation to the refugee protection regime. We recognize the burdens that large movements of refugees place on national resources, especially in the case of developing countries. To address the needs of refugees and receiving States, we commit to a more equitable sharing of the burden and responsibility for hosting and supporting the world's refugees, while taking account of existing contributions and the differing capacities and resources among States.

69. We believe that a comprehensive refugee response should be developed and initiated by the Office of the United Nations High Commissioner for Refugees, in close coordination with relevant States, including host countries, and involving other relevant United Nations entities, for each situation involving large movements of refugees. This should involve a multi-stakeholder approach that includes national and local authorities, international organizations, international financial institutions, civil society partners (including faith-based organizations, diaspora organizations and academia), the private sector, the media and refugees themselves. A comprehensive framework of this kind is annexed to the present declaration.

70. We will ensure that refugee admission policies or arrangements are in line with our obligations under international law. We wish to see administrative barriers eased, with a view to accelerating refugee admission procedures to the extent possible. We will, where appropriate, assist States to conduct early and effective registration and documentation of refugees. We will also promote access for children to child-appropriate procedures. At the same time, we recognize that the ability of refugees to lodge asylum claims in the

country of their choice may be regulated, subject to the safeguard that they will have access to, and enjoyment of, protection elsewhere.

71. We encourage the adoption of measures to facilitate access to civil registration and documentation for refugees. We recognize in this regard the importance of early and effective registration and documentation, as a protection tool and to facilitate the provision of humanitarian assistance.

72. We recognize that statelessness can be a root cause of forced displacement and that forced displacement, in turn, can lead to statelessness. We take note of the campaign of the Office of the United Nations High Commissioner for Refugees to end statelessness within a decade and we encourage States to consider actions they could take to reduce the incidence of statelessness. We encourage those States that have not yet acceded to the 1954 Convention relating to the Status of Stateless Persons[15] and the 1961 Convention on the Reduction of Statelessness[16] to consider doing so.

73. We recognize that refugee camps should be the exception and, to the extent possible, a temporary measure in response to an emergency. We note that 60 per cent of refugees worldwide are in urban settings and only a minority are in camps. We will ensure that the delivery of assistance to refugees and host communities is adapted to the relevant context. We underline that host States have the primary responsibility to ensure the civilian and humanitarian character of refugee camps and settlements. We will work to ensure that this character is not compromised by the presence or activities of armed elements and to ensure that camps are not used for purposes that are incompatible with their civilian character. We will work to strengthen security in refugee camps and surrounding local communities, at the request and with the consent of the host country.

74. We welcome the extraordinarily generous contribution made to date by countries that host large refugee populations and will work to increase the support for those countries. We call for pledges made at relevant conferences to be disbursed promptly.

75. We commit to working towards solutions from the outset of a refugee situation. We will actively promote durable solutions, particularly in protracted refugee situations, with a focus on sustainable and timely return in safety and dignity. This will encompass repatriation, reintegration, rehabilitation and reconstruction activities. We encourage States and other relevant actors to provide support through, inter alia, the allocation of funds.

76. We reaffirm that voluntary repatriation should not necessarily be conditioned on the accomplishment of political solutions in the country of origin.

77. We intend to expand the number and range of legal pathways available for refugees to be admitted to or resettled in third countries. In addition to easing the plight of refugees, this has benefits for countries that host large refugee populations and for third countries that receive refugees.

78. We urge States that have not yet established resettlement programmes to consider doing so at the earliest opportunity. Those which have already done so are encouraged to consider increasing the size of their programmes. It is our aim to provide resettlement places and other legal pathways for admission on a scale that would enable the annual resettlement needs identified by the Office of the United Nations High Commissioner for Refugees to be met.

79. We will consider the expansion of existing humanitarian admission programmes, possible temporary evacuation programmes, including evacuation for medical reasons, flexible arrangements to assist family reunification, private sponsorship for individual refugees and opportunities for labour mobility for refugees, including through private sector partnerships, and for education, such as scholarships and student visas.

80. We are committed to providing humanitarian assistance to refugees so as to ensure essential support in key life-saving sectors, such as health care, shelter, food, water and sanitation. We commit to supporting host countries and communities in this regard, including by using locally available knowledge and capacities. We will support community-based development programmes that benefit both refugees and host communities.

81. We are determined to provide quality primary and secondary education in safe learning environments for all refugee children, and to do so within a few months of the initial displacement. We commit to providing host countries with support in this regard. Access to quality education, including for host communities, gives fundamental protection to children and youth in displacement contexts, particularly in situations of conflict and crisis.

82. We will support early childhood education for refugee children. We will also promote tertiary education, skills training and vocational education. In conflict and crisis situations, higher education serves as a powerful driver for change, shelters and protects a critical group of young men and women by maintaining their hopes for the future, fosters inclusion and non-discrimination and acts as a catalyst for the recovery and rebuilding of post-conflict countries.

83. We will work to ensure that the basic health needs of refugee communities are met and that women and girls have access to essential health-care services. We commit to providing host countries with support in this regard. We will also develop national strategies for the protection of refugees within the framework of national social protection systems, as appropriate.

84. Welcoming the positive steps taken by individual States, we encourage host Governments to consider opening their labour markets to refugees. We will work to strengthen host countries' and communities' resilience, assisting them, for example, with employment creation and income generation schemes. In this regard, we recognize the potential of young people and

will work to create the conditions for growth, employment and education that will allow them to be the drivers of development.

85. In order to meet the challenges posed by large movements of refugees, close coordination will be required among a range of humanitarian and development actors. We commit to putting those most affected at the centre of planning and action. Host Governments and communities may need support from relevant United Nations entities, local authorities, international financial institutions, regional development banks, bilateral donors, the private sector and civil society. We strongly encourage joint responses involving all such actors in order to strengthen the nexus between humanitarian and development actors, facilitate cooperation across institutional mandates and, by helping to build self-reliance and resilience, lay a basis for sustainable solutions. In addition to meeting direct humanitarian and development needs, we will work to support environmental, social and infrastructural rehabilitation in areas affected by large movements of refugees.

86. We note with concern a significant gap between the needs of refugees and the available resources. We encourage support from a broader range of donors and will take measures to make humanitarian financing more flexible and predictable, with diminished earmarking and increased multi-year funding, in order to close this gap. United Nations entities such as the Office of the United Nations High Commissioner for Refugees and the United Nations Relief and Works Agency for Palestine Refugees in the Near East and other relevant organizations require sufficient funding to be able to carry out their activities effectively and in a predictable manner. We welcome the increasing engagement of the World Bank and multilateral development banks and improvements in access to concessional development financing for affected communities. It is clear, furthermore, that private sector investment in support of refugee communities and host countries will be of critical importance over the coming years. Civil society is also a key partner in every region of the world in responding to the needs of refugees.

87. We note that the United States of America, Canada, Ethiopia, Germany, Jordan, Mexico, Sweden and the Secretary-General will host a high-level meeting on refugees on 20 September 2016.

V. Follow-up to and review of our commitments

88. We recognize that arrangements are needed to ensure systematic follow-up to and review of all of the commitments we are making today. Accordingly, we request the Secretary-General to ensure that the progress made by Member States and the United Nations in implementing the commitments made at today's high-level meeting will be the subject of periodic assessments provided to the General Assembly with reference, as appropriate, to the 2030 Agenda for Sustainable Development.

89. In addition, a role in reviewing relevant aspects of the present declaration should be envisaged for the periodic High-level Dialogues on International Migration and Development and for the annual report of the United Nations High Commissioner for Refugees to the General Assembly.

90. In recognition of the need for significant financial and programme support to host countries and communities affected by large movements of refugees and migrants, we request the Secretary-General to report to the General Assembly at its seventy-first session on ways of achieving greater efficiency, operational effectiveness and system-wide coherence, as well as ways of strengthening the engagement of the United Nations with international financial institutions and the private sector, with a view to fully implementing the commitments outlined in the present declaration.

3rd plenary meeting
19 September 2016

Annex I
Comprehensive refugee response framework

1. The scale and nature of refugee displacement today requires us to act in a comprehensive and predictable manner in large-scale refugee movements. Through a comprehensive refugee response based on the principles of international cooperation and on burden- and responsibility-sharing, we are better able to protect and assist refugees and to support the host States and communities involved.

2. The comprehensive refugee response framework will be developed and initiated by the Office of the United Nations High Commissioner for Refugees, in close coordination with relevant States, including host countries, and involving other relevant United Nations entities, for each situation involving large movements of refugees. A comprehensive refugee response should involve a multi-stakeholder approach, including national and local authorities, international organizations, international financial institutions, regional organizations, regional coordination and partnership mechanisms, civil society partners, including faith-based organizations and academia, the private sector, media and the refugees themselves.

3. While each large movement of refugees will differ in nature, the elements noted below provide a framework for a comprehensive and people-centred refugee response, which is in accordance with international law and best international practice and adapted to the specific context.

4. We envisage a comprehensive refugee response framework for each situation involving large movements of refugees, including in protracted situations, as an integral and distinct part of an overall humanitarian response,

where it exists, and which would normally contain the elements set out below.

Reception and admission

5. At the outset of a large movement of refugees, receiving States, bearing in mind their national capacities and international legal obligations, in cooperation, as appropriate, with the Office of the United Nations High Commissioner for Refugees, international organizations and other partners and with the support of other States as requested, in conformity with international obligations, would:

a. Ensure, to the extent possible, that measures are in place to identify persons in need of international protection as refugees, provide for adequate, safe and dignified reception conditions, with a particular emphasis on persons with specific needs, victims of human trafficking, child protection, family unity, and prevention of and response to sexual and gender-based violence, and support the critical contribution of receiving communities and societies in this regard;
b. Take account of the rights, specific needs, contributions and voices of women and girl refugees;
c. Assess and meet the essential needs of refugees, including by providing access to adequate safe drinking water, sanitation, food, nutrition, shelter, psychosocial support and health care, including sexual and reproductive health, and providing assistance to host countries and communities in this regard, as required;
d. Register individually and document those seeking protection as refugees, including in the first country where they seek asylum, as quickly as possible upon their arrival. To achieve this, assistance may be needed, in areas such as biometric technology and other technical and financial support, to be coordinated by the Office of the United Nations High Commissioner for Refugees with relevant actors and partners, where necessary;
e. Use the registration process to identify specific assistance needs and protection arrangements, where possible, including but not exclusively for refugees with special protection concerns, such as women at risk, children, especially unaccompanied children and children separated from their families, child-headed and single-parent households, victims of trafficking, victims of trauma and survivors of sexual violence, as well as refugees with disabilities and older persons;
f. Work to ensure the immediate birth registration for all refugee children born on their territory and provide adequate assistance at the earliest opportunity with obtaining other necessary documents, as ap-

propriate, relating to civil status, such as marriage, divorce and death certificates;
g. Put in place measures, with appropriate legal safeguards, which uphold refugees' human rights, with a view to ensuring the security of refugees, as well as measures to respond to host countries' legitimate security concerns;
h. Take measures to maintain the civilian and humanitarian nature of refugee camps and settlements;
i. Take steps to ensure the credibility of asylum systems, including through collaboration among the countries of origin, transit and destination and to facilitate the return and readmission of those who do not qualify for refugee status.

Support for immediate and ongoing needs

6. States, in cooperation with multilateral donors and private sector partners, as appropriate, would, in coordination with receiving States:

a. Mobilize adequate financial and other resources to cover the humanitarian needs identified within the comprehensive refugee response framework;
b. Provide resources in a prompt, predictable, consistent and flexible manner, including through wider partnerships involving State, civil society, faith-based and private sector partners;
c. Take measures to extend the finance lending schemes that exist for developing countries to middle-income countries hosting large numbers of refugees, bearing in mind the economic and social costs to those countries;
d. Consider establishing development funding mechanisms for such countries;
e. Provide assistance to host countries to protect the environment and strengthen infrastructure affected by large movements of refugees;
f. Increase support for cash-based delivery mechanisms and other innovative means for the efficient provision of humanitarian assistance, where appropriate, while increasing accountability to ensure that humanitarian assistance reaches its beneficiaries.

7. Host States, in cooperation with the Office of the United Nations High Commissioner for Refugees and other United Nations entities, financial institutions and other relevant partners, would, as appropriate:

a. Provide prompt, safe and unhindered access to humanitarian assistance for refugees in accordance with existing humanitarian principles;

b. Deliver assistance, to the extent possible, through appropriate national and local service providers, such as public authorities for health, education, social services and child protection;
   c. Encourage and empower refugees, at the outset of an emergency phase, to establish supportive systems and networks that involve refugees and host communities and are age- and gender-sensitive, with a particular emphasis on the protection and empowerment of women and children and other persons with specific needs;
   d. Support local civil society partners that contribute to humanitarian responses, in recognition of their complementary contribution;
   e. Ensure close cooperation and encourage joint planning, as appropriate, between humanitarian and development actors and other relevant actors.

Support for host countries and communities

8. States, the Office of the United Nations High Commissioner for Refugees and relevant partners would:

   a. Implement a joint, impartial and rapid risk and/or impact assessment, in anticipation or after the onset of a large refugee movement, in order to identify and prioritize the assistance required for refugees, national and local authorities, and communities affected by a refugee presence;
   b. Incorporate, where appropriate, the comprehensive refugee response framework in national development planning, in order to strengthen the delivery of essential services and infrastructure for the benefit of host communities and refugees;
   c. Work to provide adequate resources, without prejudice to official development assistance, for national and local government authorities and other service providers in view of the increased needs and pressures on social services. Programmes should benefit refugees and the host country and communities.

Durable solutions

9. We recognize that millions of refugees around the world at present have no access to timely and durable solutions, the securing of which is one of the principal goals of international protection. The success of the search for solutions depends in large measure on resolute and sustained international cooperation and support.

Appendix III	155

10. We believe that actions should be taken in pursuit of the following durable solutions: voluntary repatriation, local solutions and resettlement and complementary pathways for admission. These actions should include the elements set out below.

11. We reaffirm the primary goal of bringing about conditions that would help refugees return in safety and dignity to their countries and emphasize the need to tackle the root causes of violence and armed conflict and to achieve necessary political solutions and the peaceful settlement of disputes, as well as to assist in reconstruction efforts. In this context, States of origin/nationality would:

   a. Acknowledge that everyone has the right to leave any country, including his or her own, and to return to his or her country;
   b. Respect this right and also respect the obligation to receive back their nationals, which should occur in a safe, dignified and humane manner and with full respect for human rights in accordance with obligations under international law;
   c. Provide necessary identification and travel documents;
   d. Facilitate the socioeconomic reintegration of returnees;
   e. Consider measures to enable the restitution of property.

12. To ensure sustainable return and reintegration, States, United Nations organizations and relevant partners would:

   a. Recognize that the voluntary nature of repatriation is necessary as long as refugees continue to require international protection, that is, as long as they cannot regain fully the protection of their own country;
   b. Plan for and support measures to encourage voluntary and informed repatriation, reintegration and reconciliation;
   c. Support countries of origin/nationality, where appropriate, including through funding for rehabilitation, reconstruction and development, and with the necessary legal safeguards to enable refugees to access legal, physical and other support mechanisms needed for the restoration of national protection and their reintegration;
   d. Support efforts to foster reconciliation and dialogue, particularly with refugee communities and with the equal participation of women and youth, and to ensure respect for the rule of law at the national and local levels;
   e. Facilitate the participation of refugees, including women, in peace and reconciliation processes, and ensure that the outcomes of such processes duly support their return in safety and dignity;

f. Ensure that national development planning incorporates the specific needs of returnees and promotes sustainable and inclusive reintegration, as a measure to prevent future displacement.

13. Host States, bearing in mind their capacities and international legal obligations, in cooperation with the Office of the United Nations High Commissioner for Refugees, the United Nations Relief and Works Agency for Palestine Refugees in the Near East, where appropriate, and other United Nations entities, financial institutions and other relevant partners, would:

a. Provide legal stay to those seeking and in need of international protection as refugees, recognizing that any decision regarding permanent settlement in any form, including possible naturalization, rests with the host country;
b. Take measures to foster self-reliance by pledging to expand opportunities for refugees to access, as appropriate, education, health care and services, livelihood opportunities and labour markets, without discriminating among refugees and in a manner which also supports host communities;
c. Take measures to enable refugees, including in particular women and youth, to make the best use of their skills and capacities, recognizing that empowered refugees are better able to contribute to their own and their communities' well-being;
d. Invest in building human capital, self-reliance and transferable skills as an essential step towards enabling long-term solutions.

14. Third countries would:

a. Consider making available or expanding, including by encouraging private sector engagement and action as a supplementary measure, resettlement opportunities and complementary pathways for admission of refugees through such means as medical evacuation and humanitarian admission programmes, family reunification and opportunities for skilled migration, labour mobility and education;
b. Commit to sharing best practices, providing refugees with sufficient information to make informed decisions and safeguarding protection standards;
c. Consider broadening the criteria for resettlement and humanitarian admission programmes in mass displacement and protracted situations, coupled with, as appropriate, temporary humanitarian evacuation programmes and other forms of admission.

15. States that have not yet established resettlement programmes are encouraged to do so at the earliest opportunity. Those that have already done so are encouraged to consider increasing the size of their programmes. Such programmes should incorporate a non-discriminatory approach and a gender perspective throughout.

16. States aim to provide resettlement places and other legal pathways on a scale that would enable the annual resettlement needs identified by the Office of the United Nations High Commissioner for Refugees to be met.

The way forward

17. We commit to implementing this comprehensive refugee response framework.

18. We invite the Office of the United Nations High Commissioner for Refugees to engage with States and consult with all relevant stakeholders over the coming two years, with a view to evaluating the detailed practical application of the comprehensive refugee response framework and assessing the scope for refinement and further development. This process should be informed by practical experience with the implementation of the framework in a range of specific situations. The objective would be to ease pressures on the host countries involved, to enhance refugee self-reliance, to expand access to third-country solutions and to support conditions in countries of origin for return in safety and dignity.

19. We will work towards the adoption in 2018 of a global compact on refugees, based on the comprehensive refugee response framework and on the outcomes of the process described above. We invite the United Nations High Commissioner for Refugees to include such a proposed global compact on refugees in his annual report to the General Assembly in 2018, for consideration by the Assembly at its seventy-third session in conjunction with its annual resolution on the Office of the United Nations High Commissioner for Refugees.

Annex II
Towards a global compact for safe, orderly and regular migration

I. Introduction

1. This year, we will launch a process of intergovernmental negotiations leading to the adoption of a global compact for safe, orderly and regular migration.

2. The global compact would set out a range of principles, commitments and understandings among Member States regarding international migration

in all its dimensions. It would make an important contribution to global governance and enhance coordination on international migration. It would present a framework for comprehensive international cooperation on migrants and human mobility. It would deal with all aspects of international migration, including the humanitarian, developmental, human rights-related and other aspects of migration. It would be guided by the 2030 Agenda for Sustainable Development[17] and the Addis Ababa Action Agenda of the Third International Conference on Financing for Development,[18] and informed by the Declaration of the High-level Dialogue on International Migration and Development adopted in October 2013.[19]

II. Context

3. We acknowledge the important contribution made by migrants and migration to development in countries of origin, transit and destination, as well as the complex interrelationship between migration and development.

4. We recognize the positive contribution of migrants to sustainable and inclusive development. We also recognize that international migration is a multidimensional reality of major relevance for the development of countries of origin, transit and destination, which requires coherent and comprehensive responses.

5. We will cooperate internationally to ensure safe, orderly and regular migration involving full respect for human rights and the humane treatment of migrants, regardless of migration status. We underline the need to ensure respect for the dignity of migrants and the protection of their rights under applicable international law, including the principle of non-discrimination under international law.

6. We emphasize the multidimensional character of international migration, the importance of international, regional and bilateral cooperation and dialogue in this regard, and the need to protect the human rights of all migrants, regardless of status, particularly at a time when migration flows have increased.

7. We bear in mind that policies and initiatives on the issue of migration should promote holistic approaches that take into account the causes and consequences of the phenomenon. We acknowledge that poverty, underdevelopment, lack of opportunities, poor governance and environmental factors are among the drivers of migration. In turn, pro-poor policies relating to trade, employment and productive investments can stimulate growth and create enormous development potential. We note that international economic imbalances, poverty and environmental degradation, combined with the absence of peace and security and lack of respect for human rights, are all factors affecting international migration.

III. Content

8. The global compact could include, but would not be limited to, the following elements:

   a. International migration as a multidimensional reality of major relevance for the development of countries of origin, transit and destination, as recognized in the 2030 Agenda for Sustainable Development;
   b. International migration as a potential opportunity for migrants and their families;
   c. The need to address the drivers of migration, including through strengthened efforts in development, poverty eradication and conflict prevention and resolution;
   d. The contribution made by migrants to sustainable development and the complex interrelationship between migration and development;
   e. The facilitation of safe, orderly, regular and responsible migration and mobility of people, including through the implementation of planned and well-managed migration policies; this may include the creation and expansion of safe, regular pathways for migration;
   f. The scope for greater international cooperation, with a view to improving migration governance;
   g. The impact of migration on human capital in countries of origin;
   h. Remittances as an important source of private capital and their contribution to development and promotion of faster, cheaper and safer transfers of remittances through legal channels, in both source and recipient countries, including through a reduction in transaction costs;
   i. Effective protection of the human rights and fundamental freedoms of migrants, including women and children, regardless of their migratory status, and the specific needs of migrants in vulnerable situations;
   j. International cooperation for border control, with full respect for the human rights of migrants;
   k. Combating trafficking in persons, smuggling of migrants and contemporary forms of slavery;
   l. Identifying those who have been trafficked and considering providing assistance, including temporary or permanent residency, and work permits, as appropriate;
   m. Reduction of the incidence and impact of irregular migration;
   n. Addressing the situations of migrants in countries in crisis;
   o. Promotion, as appropriate, of the inclusion of migrants in host societies, access to basic services for migrants and gender-responsive services;
   p. Consideration of policies to regularize the status of migrants;

q. Protection of labour rights and a safe environment for migrant workers and those in precarious employment, protection of women migrant workers in all sectors and promotion of labour mobility, including circular migration;
r. The responsibilities and obligations of migrants towards host countries;
s. Return and readmission, and improving cooperation in this regard between countries of origin and destination;
t. Harnessing the contribution of diasporas and strengthening links with countries of origin;
u. Combating racism, xenophobia, discrimination and intolerance towards all migrants;
v. Disaggregated data on international migration;
w. Recognition of foreign qualifications, education and skills and cooperation in access to and portability of earned benefits;
x. Cooperation at the national, regional and international levels on all aspects of migration.

IV. The way forward

9. The global compact would be elaborated through a process of intergovernmental negotiations, for which preparations will begin immediately. The negotiations, which will begin in early 2017, are to culminate in an intergovernmental conference on international migration in 2018 at which the global compact will be presented for adoption.

10. As the Third High-level Dialogue on International Migration and Development is to be held in New York no later than 2019,[20] a role should be envisaged for the High-level Dialogue in the process.

11. The President of the General Assembly is invited to make early arrangements for the appointment of two co-facilitators to lead open, transparent and inclusive consultations with States, with a view to the determination of modalities, a timeline, the possible holding of preparatory conferences and other practicalities relating to the intergovernmental negotiations, including the integration of Geneva-based migration expertise.

12. The Secretary-General is requested to provide appropriate support for the negotiations. We envisage that the Secretariat of the United Nations and the International Organization for Migration would jointly service the negotiations, the former providing capacity and support and the latter extending the technical and policy expertise required.

13. We envisage also that the Special Representative of the Secretary-General for International Migration and Development, Mr. Peter Sutherland, would coordinate the contributions to be made to the negotiation process by the Global Forum on Migration and Development and the Global Migration

Group. We envisage that the International Labour Organization, the United Nations Office on Drugs and Crime, the Office of the United Nations High Commissioner for Refugees, the United Nations Development Programme, the Office of the United Nations High Commissioner for Human Rights and other entities with significant mandates and expertise related to migration would contribute to the process.

14. Regional consultations in support of the negotiations would be desirable, including through existing consultative processes and mechanisms, where appropriate.

15. Civil society, the private sector, diaspora communities and migrant organizations would be invited to contribute to the process for the preparation of the global compact.

NOTES

1. Resolution 70/1.
2. Resolution 217 A (III).
3. Resolution 69/283, annex II.
4. See FCCC/CP/2015/10/Add.1, decision 1/CP.21, annex.
5. Resolution 69/313, annex.
6. A/70/59.
7. United Nations, *Treaty Series*, vol. 1577, No. 27531.
8. Ibid., vols. 2225, 2237 and 2241, No. 39574.
9. Resolution 64/293.
10. United Nations, *Treaty Series*, vol. 2220, No. 39481.
11. Resolution 70/296, annex.
12. United Nations, *Treaty Series*, vol. 189, No. 2545.
13. Ibid., vol. 606, No. 8791.
14. Ibid., vol. 1001, No. 14691.
15. Ibid., vol. 360, No. 5158.
16. Ibid., vol. 989, No. 14458.
17. Resolution 70/1.
18. Resolution 69/313, annex.
19. Resolution 68/4.
20. See resolution 69/229, para. 32.

Appendix IV

Global Compact for Safe, Orderly and Regular Migration

We, the Heads of State and Government and High Representatives, meeting in Morocco on 10 and 11 December 2018, reaffirming the New York Declaration for Refugees and Migrants and determined to make an important contribution to enhanced cooperation on international migration in all its dimensions, have adopted this Global Compact for Safe, Orderly and Regular Migration:

Preamble

1. This Global Compact rests on the purposes and principles of the Charter of the United Nations.
2. It also rests on the Universal Declaration of Human Rights; the International Covenant on Civil and Political Rights; the International Covenant on Economic, Social and Cultural Rights; the other core international human rights treaties;[1] the United Nations Convention against Transnational Organized Crime, including the Protocol to Prevent, Suppress and Punish Trafficking in Persons, Especially Women and Children, and the Protocol against the Smuggling of Migrants by Land, Sea and Air; the Slavery Convention and the Supplementary Convention on the Abolition of Slavery, the Slave Trade, and Institutions and Practices Similar to Slavery; the United Nations Framework Convention on Climate Change; the United Nations Convention to Combat Desertification in Those Countries Experiencing Serious Drought and/or Desertification, Particularly in Africa; the Paris Agreement;[2] and the International Labour Organization conventions on promoting decent work and labour migration,[3] as well as

on the 2030 Agenda for Sustainable Development; the Addis Ababa Action Agenda of the Third International Conference on Financing for Development; the Sendai Framework for Disaster Risk Reduction 2015-2030; and the New Urban Agenda.

3. Discussions about international migration at the global level are not new. We recall the advances made through the United Nations High-level Dialogues on International Migration and Development in 2006 and 2013. We also acknowledge the contributions of the Global Forum on Migration and Development, launched in 2007. These platforms paved the way for the New York Declaration for Refugees and Migrants, through which we committed to elaborate a global compact on refugees and to adopt this Global Compact for Safe, Orderly and Regular Migration, in two separate processes. The two global compacts, together, present complementary international cooperation frameworks that fulfil their respective mandates as laid out in the New York Declaration for Refugees and Migrants, which recognizes that migrants and refugees may face many common challenges and similar vulnerabilities.

4. Refugees and migrants are entitled to the same universal human rights and fundamental freedoms, which must be respected, protected and fulfilled at all times. However, migrants and refugees are distinct groups governed by separate legal frameworks. Only refugees are entitled to the specific international protection defined by international refugee law. This Global Compact refers to migrants and presents a cooperative framework addressing migration in all its dimensions.

5. As a contribution to the preparatory process for this Global Compact, we recognize the inputs shared by Member States and relevant stakeholders during the consultation and stocktaking phases, as well as the report of the Secretary-General entitled "Making migration work for all."

6. This Global Compact is a milestone in the history of the global dialogue and international cooperation on migration. It is rooted in the 2030 Agenda for Sustainable Development and the Addis Ababa Action Agenda, and informed by the Declaration of the High-level Dialogue on International Migration and Development, adopted in October 2013. It builds on the pioneering work of the former Special Representative of the Secretary-General on Migration, including his report of 3 February 2017.

7. This Global Compact presents a non-legally binding, cooperative framework that builds on the commitments agreed upon by Member States in the New York Declaration for Refugees and Migrants. It fosters international cooperation among all relevant actors on migration, acknowledging that no State can address migration alone, and upholds the sovereignty of States and their obligations under international law.

Our vision and guiding principles

8. This Global Compact expresses our collective commitment to improving cooperation on international migration. Migration has been part of the human experience throughout history, and we recognize that it is a source of prosperity, innovation and sustainable development in our globalized world, and that these positive impacts can be optimized by improving migration governance. The majority of migrants around the world today travel, live and work in a safe, orderly and regular manner. Nonetheless, migration undeniably affects our countries, communities, migrants and their families in very different and sometimes unpredictable ways.

9. It is crucial that the challenges and opportunities of international migration unite us, rather than divide us. This Global Compact sets out our common understanding, shared responsibilities and unity of purpose regarding migration, making it work for all.

Common understanding

10. This Global Compact is the product of an unprecedented review of evidence and data gathered during an open, transparent and inclusive process. We shared our realities and heard diverse voices, enriching and shaping our common understanding of this complex phenomenon. We learned that migration is a defining feature of our globalized world, connecting societies within and across all regions, making us all countries of origin, transit and destination. We recognize that there is a continuous need for international efforts to strengthen our knowledge and analysis of migration, as shared understandings will improve policies that unlock the potential of sustainable development for all. We must collect and disseminate quality data. We must ensure that current and potential migrants are fully informed about their rights, obligations and options for safe, orderly and regular migration, and are aware of the risks of irregular migration. We also must provide all our citizens with access to objective, evidence-based, clear information about the benefits and challenges of migration, with a view to dispelling misleading narratives that generate negative perceptions of migrants.

Shared responsibilities

11. This Global Compact offers a 360-degree vision of international migration and recognizes that a comprehensive approach is needed to optimize the overall benefits of migration, while addressing risks and challenges for individuals and communities in countries of origin, transit and destination. No country can address the challenges and opportunities of this global phenomenon on its own. With this comprehensive approach, we aim to facilitate

safe, orderly and regular migration, while reducing the incidence and negative impact of irregular migration through international cooperation and a combination of measures put forward in this Global Compact. We acknowledge our shared responsibilities to one another as States Members of the United Nations to address each other's needs and concerns over migration, and an overarching obligation to respect, protect and fulfil the human rights of all migrants, regardless of their migration status, while promoting the security and prosperity of all our communities.

12. This Global Compact aims to mitigate the adverse drivers and structural factors that hinder people from building and maintaining sustainable livelihoods in their countries of origin, and so compel them to seek a future elsewhere. It intends to reduce the risks and vulnerabilities migrants face at different stages of migration by respecting, protecting and fulfilling their human rights and providing them with care and assistance. It seeks to address legitimate concerns of communities, while recognizing that societies are undergoing demographic, economic, social and environmental changes at different scales that may have implications for and result from migration. It strives to create conducive conditions that enable all migrants to enrich our societies through their human, economic and social capacities, and thus facilitate their contributions to sustainable development at the local, national, regional and global levels.

Unity of purpose

13. This Global Compact recognizes that safe, orderly and regular migration works for all when it takes place in a well-informed, planned and consensual manner. Migration should never be an act of desperation. When it is, we must cooperate to respond to the needs of migrants in situations of vulnerability, and address the respective challenges. We must work together to create conditions that allow communities and individuals to live in safety and dignity in their own countries. We must save lives and keep migrants out of harm's way. We must empower migrants to become full members of our societies, highlight their positive contributions, and promote inclusion and social cohesion. We must generate greater predictability and certainty for States, communities and migrants alike. To achieve this, we commit to facilitate and ensure safe, orderly and regular migration for the benefit of all.

14. Our success rests on the mutual trust, determination and solidarity of States to fulfil the objectives and commitments contained in this Global Compact. We unite, in a spirit of win-win cooperation, to address the challenges and opportunities of migration in all its dimensions through shared responsibility and innovative solutions. It is with this sense of common purpose that we take this historic step, fully aware that the Global Compact for Safe, Orderly and Regular Migration is a milestone, but not the end to our

efforts. We commit to continue the multilateral dialogue at the United Nations through a periodic and effective follow-up and review mechanism, ensuring that the words in this document translate into concrete actions for the benefit of millions of people in every region of the world.

15. We agree that this Global Compact is based on a set of cross-cutting and interdependent guiding principles:

People-centred. The Global Compact carries a strong human dimension, inherent to the migration experience itself. It promotes the well-being of migrants and the members of communities in countries of origin, transit and destination. As a result, the Global Compact places individuals at its core;

International cooperation. The Global Compact is a non-legally binding cooperative framework that recognizes that no State can address migration on its own because of the inherently transnational nature of the phenomenon. It requires international, regional and bilateral cooperation and dialogue. Its authority rests on its consensual nature, credibility, collective ownership, joint implementation, follow-up and review;

National sovereignty. The Global Compact reaffirms the sovereign right of States to determine their national migration policy and their prerogative to govern migration within their jurisdiction, in conformity with international law. Within their sovereign jurisdiction, States may distinguish between regular and irregular migration status, including as they determine their legislative and policy measures for the implementation of the Global Compact, taking into account different national realities, policies, priorities and requirements for entry, residence and work, in accordance with international law;

Rule of law and due process. The Global Compact recognizes that respect for the rule of law, due process and access to justice are fundamental to all aspects of migration governance. This means that the State, public and private institutions and entities, as well as persons themselves, are accountable to laws that are publicly promulgated, equally enforced and independently adjudicated, and are consistent with international law;

Sustainable development. The Global Compact is rooted in the 2030 Agenda for Sustainable Development, and builds upon its recognition that migration is a multidimensional reality of major relevance for the sustainable development of countries of origin, transit and destination, which requires coherent and comprehensive responses. Migration contributes to positive development outcomes and to realizing the goals of the 2030 Agenda for Sustainable Development, especially when it is properly managed. The Global Compact aims to leverage the potential of migration for the achievement of all Sustainable Development Goals, as well as the impact this achievement will have on migration in the future;

Human rights. The Global Compact is based on international human rights law and upholds the principles of non-regression and non-discrimination. By implementing the Global Compact, we ensure effective respect for and protection and fulfilment of the human rights of all migrants, regardless of their migration status, across all stages of the migration cycle. We also reaffirm the commitment to eliminate all forms of discrimination, including racism, xenophobia and intolerance, against migrants and their families;

Gender-responsive. The Global Compact ensures that the human rights of women, men, girls and boys are respected at all stages of migration, that their specific needs are properly understood and addressed and that they are empowered as agents of change. It mainstreams a gender perspective and promotes gender equality and the empowerment of all women and girls, recognizing their independence, agency and leadership in order to move away from addressing migrant women primarily through a lens of victimhood;

Child-sensitive. The Global Compact promotes existing international legal obligations in relation to the rights of the child, and upholds the principle of the best interests of the child at all times, as a primary consideration in all situations concerning children in the context of international migration, including unaccompanied and separated children;

Whole-of-government approach. The Global Compact considers that migration is a multidimensional reality that cannot be addressed by one government policy sector alone. To develop and implement effective migration policies and practices, a whole-of-government approach is needed to ensure horizontal and vertical policy coherence across all sectors and levels of government;

Whole-of-society approach. The Global Compact promotes broad multi-stakeholder partnerships to address migration in all its dimensions by including migrants, diasporas, local communities, civil society, academia, the private sector, parliamentarians, trade unions, national human rights institutions, the media and other relevant stakeholders in migration governance.

Our cooperative framework

16. With the New York Declaration for Refugees and Migrants, we adopted a political declaration and a set of commitments. Reaffirming that Declaration in its entirety, we build upon it by laying out the following cooperative framework, comprising 23 objectives, implementation, as well as follow-up and review. Each objective contains a commitment, followed by a range of actions considered to be relevant policy instruments and best practices. To fulfil the 23 objectives, we will draw from these actions to achieve safe, orderly and regular migration along the migration cycle.

OBJECTIVES FOR SAFE, ORDERLY AND REGULAR MIGRATION

1. Collect and utilize accurate and disaggregated data as a basis for evidence-based policies
2. Minimize the adverse drivers and structural factors that compel people to leave their country of origin
3. Provide accurate and timely information at all stages of migration
4. Ensure that all migrants have proof of legal identity and adequate documentation
5. Enhance availability and flexibility of pathways for regular migration
6. Facilitate fair and ethical recruitment and safeguard conditions that ensure decent work
7. Address and reduce vulnerabilities in migration
8. Save lives and establish coordinated international efforts on missing migrants
9. Strengthen the transnational response to smuggling of migrants
10. Prevent, combat and eradicate trafficking in persons in the context of international migration
11. Manage borders in an integrated, secure and coordinated manner
12. Strengthen certainty and predictability in migration procedures for appropriate screening, assessment and referral
13. Use migration detention only as a measure of last resort and work towards alternatives
14. Enhance consular protection, assistance and cooperation throughout the migration cycle
15. Provide access to basic services for migrants
16. Empower migrants and societies to realize full inclusion and social cohesion
17. Eliminate all forms of discrimination and promote evidence-based public discourse to shape perceptions of migration
18. Invest in skills development and facilitate mutual recognition of skills, qualifications and competences
19. Create conditions for migrants and diasporas to fully contribute to sustainable development in all countries
20. Promote faster, safer and cheaper transfer of remittances and foster financial inclusion of migrants
21. Cooperate in facilitating safe and dignified return and readmission, as well as sustainable reintegration

22. Establish mechanisms for the portability of social security entitlements and earned benefits

23. Strengthen international cooperation and global partnerships for safe, orderly and regular migration

Objectives and commitments

Objective 1: Collect and utilize accurate and disaggregated data as a basis for evidence-based policies

17. We commit to strengthen the global evidence base on international migration by improving and investing in the collection, analysis and dissemination of accurate, reliable and comparable data, disaggregated by sex, age, migration status and other characteristics relevant in national contexts, while upholding the right to privacy under international human rights law and protecting personal data. We further commit to ensure that this data fosters research, guides coherent and evidence-based policymaking and well-informed public discourse, and allows for effective monitoring and evaluation of the implementation of commitments over time.

To realize this commitment, we will draw from the following actions:

a. Elaborate and implement a comprehensive strategy for improving migration data at the local, national, regional and global levels, with the participation of all relevant stakeholders, under the guidance of the Statistical Commission of the United Nations, by harmonizing methodologies for data collection, and strengthening analysis and dissemination of migration-related data and indicators;
b. Improve international comparability and compatibility of migration statistics and national data systems, including by further developing and applying the statistical definition of an international migrant, elaborating a set of standards to measure migrant stocks and flows, and documenting migration patterns and trends, characteristics of migrants, as well as drivers and impacts of migration;
c. Develop a global programme to build and enhance national capacities in data collection, analysis and dissemination to share data, address data gaps and assess key migration trends, that encourages collaboration between relevant stakeholders at all levels, provides dedicated training, financial support and technical assistance, leverages new data

sources, including big data, and is reviewed by the Statistical Commission on a regular basis;
d. Collect, analyse and use data on the effects and benefits of migration, as well as the contributions of migrants and diasporas to sustainable development, with a view to informing the implementation of the 2030 Agenda for Sustainable Development and related strategies and programmes at the local, national, regional and global levels;
e. Support further development of and collaboration between existing global and regional databases and depositories, including the International Organization for Migration (IOM) Global Migration Data Portal and the World Bank Global Knowledge Partnership on Migration and Development, with a view to systematically consolidating relevant data in a transparent and user-friendly manner, while encouraging inter-agency collaboration to avoid duplication;
f. Establish and strengthen regional centres for research and training on migration or migration observatories, such as the African Observatory for Migration and Development, to collect and analyse data in line with United Nations standards, including on best practices, the contributions of migrants, the overall economic, social and political benefits and challenges of migration in countries of origin, transit and destination, as well as drivers of migration, with a view to establishing shared strategies and maximizing the value of disaggregated migration data, in coordination with existing regional and subregional mechanisms;
g. Improve national data collection by integrating migration-related topics into national censuses, as early as practicable, such as on country of birth, country of birth of parents, country of citizenship, country of residence five years prior to the census, most recent arrival date and reason for migrating, to ensure timely analysis and dissemination of results, disaggregated and tabulated in accordance with international standards, for statistical purposes;
h. Conduct household, labour force and other surveys to collect information on the social and economic integration of migrants or add standard migration modules to existing household surveys to improve national, regional and international comparability, and make collected data available through public use of statistical microdata files;
i. Enhance collaboration between State units responsible for migration data and national statistical offices to produce migration-related statistics, including by using administrative records for statistical purposes, such as border records, visas, resident permits, population registers and other relevant sources, while upholding the right to privacy and protecting personal data;
j. Develop and use country-specific migration profiles, which include disaggregated data on all migration-relevant aspects in a national con-

text, including those on labour market needs, demand for and availability of skills, the economic, environmental and social impacts of migration, remittance transfer costs, health, education, occupation, living and working conditions, wages, and the needs of migrants and receiving communities, in order to develop evidence-based migration policies;

k. Cooperate with relevant stakeholders in countries of origin, transit and destination to develop research, studies and surveys on the interrelationship between migration and the three dimensions of sustainable development, the contributions and skills of migrants and diasporas, as well as their ties to the countries of origin and destination.

Objective 2: Minimize the adverse drivers and structural factors that compel people to leave their country of origin

18. We commit to create conducive political, economic, social and environmental conditions for people to lead peaceful, productive and sustainable lives in their own country and to fulfil their personal aspirations, while ensuring that desperation and deteriorating environments do not compel them to seek a livelihood elsewhere through irregular migration. We further commit to ensure timely and full implementation of the 2030 Agenda for Sustainable Development, as well as to build upon and invest in the implementation of other existing frameworks, in order to enhance the overall impact of the Global Compact to facilitate safe, orderly and regular migration.

To realize this commitment, we will draw from the following actions:

a. Promote the implementation of the 2030 Agenda for Sustainable Development, including the Sustainable Development Goals and the Addis Ababa Action Agenda, and the commitment to reach the furthest behind first, as well as the Paris Agreement and the Sendai Framework for Disaster Risk Reduction 2015–2030;
b. Invest in programmes that accelerate States' fulfilment of the Sustainable Development Goals with the aim of eliminating the adverse drivers and structural factors that compel people to leave their country of origin, including through poverty eradication, food security, health and sanitation, education, inclusive economic growth, infrastructure, urban and rural development, employment creation, decent work, gender equality and empowerment of women and girls, resilience and disaster risk reduction, climate change mitigation and adaptation, addressing the socioeconomic effects of all forms of violence, non-discrimination, the rule of law and good governance, access to justice and

protection of human rights, as well as creating and maintaining peaceful and inclusive societies with effective, accountable and transparent institutions;

c. Establish or strengthen mechanisms to monitor and anticipate the development of risks and threats that might trigger or affect migration movements, strengthen early warning systems, develop emergency procedures and toolkits, launch emergency operations and support post-emergency recovery, in close cooperation with and in support of other States, relevant national and local authorities, national human rights institutions and civil society;

d. Invest in sustainable development at the local and national levels in all regions, allowing all people to improve their lives and meet their aspirations, by fostering sustained, inclusive and sustainable economic growth, including through private and foreign direct investment and trade preferences, to create conducive conditions that allow communities and individuals to take advantage of opportunities in their own countries and drive sustainable development;

e. Invest in human capital development by promoting entrepreneurship, education, vocational training and skills development programmes and partnerships, productive employment creation, in line with labour market needs, as well as in cooperation with the private sector and trade unions, with a view to reducing youth unemployment, avoiding brain drain and optimizing brain gain in countries of origin, and harnessing the demographic dividend;

f. Strengthen collaboration between humanitarian and development actors, including by promoting joint analysis, multi-donor approaches and multi-year funding cycles, in order to develop long-term responses and outcomes that ensure respect for the rights of affected individuals, resilience and coping capacities of populations, as well as economic and social self-reliance, and by ensuring that these efforts take migration into account;

g. Account for migrants in national emergency preparedness and response, including by taking into consideration relevant recommendations from State-led consultative processes, such as the Guidelines to Protect Migrants in Countries Experiencing Conflict or Natural Disaster (Migrants in Countries in Crisis Initiative Guidelines);

Natural disasters, the adverse effects of climate change, and environmental degradation

h. Strengthen joint analysis and sharing of information to better map, understand, predict and address migration movements, such as those that may result from sudden-onset and slow-onset natural disasters, the adverse effects of climate change, environmental degradation, as well as other precarious situations, while ensuring effective respect for and protection and fulfilment of the human rights of all migrants;

i. Develop adaptation and resilience strategies to sudden-onset and slow-onset natural disasters, the adverse effects of climate change, and environmental degradation, such as desertification, land degradation, drought and sea level rise, taking into account the potential implications for migration, while recognizing that adaptation in the country of origin is a priority;

j. Integrate displacement considerations into disaster preparedness strategies and promote cooperation with neighbouring and other relevant countries to prepare for early warning, contingency planning, stockpiling, coordination mechanisms, evacuation planning, reception and assistance arrangements, and public information;

k. Harmonize and develop approaches and mechanisms at the subregional and regional levels to address the vulnerabilities of persons affected by sudden-onset and slow-onset natural disasters, by ensuring that they have access to humanitarian assistance that meets their essential needs with full respect for their rights wherever they are, and by promoting sustainable outcomes that increase resilience and self-reliance, taking into account the capacities of all countries involved;

l. Develop coherent approaches to address the challenges of migration movements in the context of sudden-onset and slow-onset natural disasters, including by taking into consideration relevant recommendations from State-led consultative processes, such as the Agenda for the Protection of Cross-Border Displaced Persons in the Context of Disasters and Climate Change, and the Platform on Disaster Displacement.

Objective 3: Provide accurate and timely information at all stages of migration

19. We commit to strengthen our efforts to provide, make available and disseminate accurate, timely, accessible and transparent information on migration-related aspects for and between States, communities and migrants at all stages of migration. We further commit to use this information to develop migration policies that provide a high degree of predictability and certainty for all actors involved.

To realize this commitment, we will draw from the following actions:

a. Launch and publicize a centralized and publicly accessible national website to make information available on regular migration options, such as on country-specific immigration laws and policies, visa requirements, application formalities, fees and conversion criteria, em-

ployment permit requirements, professional qualification requirements, credential assessment and equivalences, training and study opportunities, and living costs and conditions, in order to inform the decisions of migrants;
b. Promote and improve systematic bilateral, regional and international cooperation and dialogue to exchange information on migration-related trends, including through joint databases, online platforms, international training centres and liaison networks, while upholding the right to privacy and protecting personal data;
c. Establish open and accessible information points along relevant migration routes that can refer migrants to child-sensitive and gender-responsive support and counselling, offer opportunities to communicate with consular representatives of the country of origin, and make available relevant information, including on human rights and fundamental freedoms, appropriate protection and assistance, options and pathways for regular migration, and possibilities for return, in a language that the person concerned understands;
d. Provide newly arrived migrants with targeted, gender-responsive, child-sensitive, accessible and comprehensive information and legal guidance on their rights and obligations, including on compliance with national and local laws, obtaining of work and resident permits, status adjustments, registration with authorities, access to justice to file complaints about rights violations, as well as access to basic services;
e. Promote multilingual, gender-responsive and evidence-based information campaigns and organize awareness-raising events and pre-departure orientation training in countries of origin, in cooperation with local authorities, consular and diplomatic missions, the private sector, academia, migrant and diaspora organizations and civil society, in order to promote safe, orderly and regular migration, as well as to highlight the risks associated with irregular and unsafe migration.

Objective 4: Ensure that all migrants have proof of legal identity and adequate documentation

20. We commit to fulfil the right of all individuals to a legal identity by providing all our nationals with proof of nationality and relevant documentation, allowing national and local authorities to ascertain a migrant's legal identity upon entry, during stay and for return, as well as to ensure effective migration procedures, efficient service provision and improved public safety. We further commit to ensure, through appropriate measures, that migrants are issued adequate documentation and civil registry documents, such as birth, marriage and death certificates, at all stages of migration, as a means to empower migrants to effectively exercise their human rights.

To realize this commitment, we will draw from the following actions:

a. Improve civil registry systems, with a particular focus on reaching unregistered persons and our nationals residing in other countries, including by providing relevant identity and civil registry documents, strengthening capacities, and investing in information and communications technology solutions, while upholding the right to privacy and protecting personal data;
b. Harmonize travel documents in line with the specifications of the International Civil Aviation Organization to facilitate interoperable and universal recognition of travel documents, as well as to combat identity fraud and document forgery, including by investing in digitalization, and strengthening mechanisms for biometric data-sharing, while upholding the right to privacy and protecting personal data;
c. Ensure adequate, timely, reliable and accessible consular documentation to our nationals residing in other countries, including identity and travel documents, making use of information and communications technology, as well as community outreach, particularly in remote areas;
d. Facilitate access to personal documentation, such as passports and visas, and ensure that relevant regulations and criteria for obtaining such documentation are non-discriminatory, by undertaking a gender-responsive and age-sensitive review in order to prevent increased risk of vulnerabilities throughout the migration cycle;
e. Strengthen measures to reduce statelessness, including by registering migrants' births, ensuring that women and men can equally confer their nationality on their children, and providing nationality to children born in another State's territory, especially in situations where a child would otherwise be stateless, fully respecting the human right to a nationality and in accordance with national legislation;
f. Review and revise requirements to prove nationality at service delivery centres to ensure that migrants without proof of nationality or legal identity are not precluded from accessing basic services nor denied their human rights;
g. Build upon existing practices at the local level that facilitate participation in community life, such as interaction with authorities and access to relevant services, through the issuance of registration cards to all persons living in a municipality, including migrants, that contain basic personal information, while not constituting entitlements to citizenship or residency.

Objective 5: Enhance availability and flexibility of pathways for regular migration

21. We commit to adapt options and pathways for regular migration in a manner that facilitates labour mobility and decent work reflecting demographic and labour market realities, optimizes education opportunities, upholds the right to family life, and responds to the needs of migrants in a situation of vulnerability, with a view to expanding and diversifying availability of pathways for safe, orderly and regular migration.

To realize this commitment, we will draw from the following actions:

a. Develop human rights-based and gender-responsive bilateral, regional and multilateral labour mobility agreements with sector-specific standard terms of employment in cooperation with relevant stakeholders, drawing on relevant International Labour Organization (ILO) standards, guidelines and principles, in compliance with international human rights and labour law;
b. Facilitate regional and cross-regional labour mobility through international and bilateral cooperation arrangements, such as free movement regimes, visa liberalization or multiple-country visas, and labour mobility cooperation frameworks, in accordance with national priorities, local market needs and skills supply;
c. Review and revise existing options and pathways for regular migration, with a view to optimizing skills-matching in labour markets and addressing demographic realities and development challenges and opportunities, in accordance with local and national labour market demands and skills supply, in consultation with the private sector and other relevant stakeholders;
d. Develop flexible, rights-based and gender-responsive labour mobility schemes for migrants, in accordance with local and national labour market needs and skills supply at all skills levels, including temporary, seasonal, circular and fast-track programmes in areas of labour shortages, by providing flexible, convertible and non-discriminatory visa and permit options, such as for permanent and temporary work, multiple-entry study, business, visit, investment and entrepreneurship;
e. Promote effective skills-matching in the national economy by involving local authorities and other relevant stakeholders, particularly the private sector and trade unions, in the analysis of the local labour market, identification of skills gaps, definition of required skills profiles, and evaluation of the efficacy of labour migration policies, in

order to ensure market-responsive contractual labour mobility through regular pathways;

f. Foster efficient and effective skills-matching programmes by reducing visa and permit processing time frames for standard employment authorizations, and by offering accelerated and facilitated visa and permit processing for employers with a track record of compliance;

g. Develop or build on existing national and regional practices for admission and stay of appropriate duration based on compassionate, humanitarian or other considerations for migrants compelled to leave their countries of origin owing to sudden-onset natural disasters and other precarious situations, such as by providing humanitarian visas, private sponsorships, access to education for children, and temporary work permits, while adaptation in or return to their country of origin is not possible;

h. Cooperate to identify, develop and strengthen solutions for migrants compelled to leave their countries of origin owing to slow-onset natural disasters, the adverse effects of climate change, and environmental degradation, such as desertification, land degradation, drought and sea level rise, including by devising planned relocation and visa options, in cases where adaptation in or return to their country of origin is not possible;

i. Facilitate access to procedures for family reunification for migrants at all skills levels through appropriate measures that promote the realization of the right to family life and the best interests of the child, including by reviewing and revising applicable requirements, such as on income, language proficiency, length of stay, work authorization, and access to social security and services;

j. Expand available options for academic mobility, including through bilateral and multilateral agreements that facilitate academic exchanges, such as scholarships for students and academic professionals, visiting professorships, joint training programmes and international research opportunities, in cooperation with academic institutions and other relevant stakeholders.

Objective 6: Facilitate fair and ethical recruitment and safeguard conditions that ensure decent work

22. We commit to review existing recruitment mechanisms to guarantee that they are fair and ethical, and to protect all migrant workers against all forms of exploitation and abuse in order to guarantee decent work and maximize the socioeconomic contributions of migrants in both their countries of origin and destination.

To realize this commitment, we will draw from the following actions:

a. Promote signature and ratification of, accession to and implementation of relevant international instruments related to international labour migration, labour rights, decent work and forced labour;
b. Build upon the work of existing bilateral, subregional and regional platforms that have overcome obstacles and identified best practices in labour mobility, by facilitating cross-regional dialogue to share this knowledge, and to promote full respect for the human and labour rights of migrant workers at all skills levels, including migrant domestic workers;
c. Improve regulations on public and private recruitment agencies in order to align them with international guidelines and best practices, and prohibit recruiters and employers from charging or shifting recruitment fees or related costs to migrant workers in order to prevent debt bondage, exploitation and forced labour, including by establishing mandatory, enforceable mechanisms for effective regulation and monitoring of the recruitment industry;
d. Establish partnerships with all relevant stakeholders, including employers, migrant workers' organizations and trade unions, to ensure that migrant workers are provided with written contracts and are made aware of the provisions therein, the regulations relating to international labour recruitment and employment in the country of destination, and their rights and obligations, as well as of how to access effective complaint and redress mechanisms, in a language they understand;
e. Enact and implement national laws that sanction human and labour rights violations, especially in cases of forced and child labour, and cooperate with the private sector, including employers, recruiters, subcontractors and suppliers, to build partnerships that promote conditions for decent work, prevent abuse and exploitation, and ensure that the roles and responsibilities within the recruitment and employment processes are clearly outlined, thereby enhancing supply chain transparency;
f. Strengthen the enforcement of fair and ethical recruitment and decent work norms and policies by enhancing the abilities of labour inspectors and other authorities to better monitor recruiters, employers and service providers in all sectors, ensuring that international human rights and labour law is observed to prevent all forms of exploitation, slavery, servitude and forced, compulsory or child labour;
g. Develop and strengthen labour migration and fair and ethical recruitment processes that allow migrants to change employers and modify

the conditions or length of their stay with minimal administrative burden, while promoting greater opportunities for decent work and respect for international human rights and labour law;
h. Take measures that prohibit the confiscation or non-consensual retention of work contracts and travel or identity documents from migrants, in order to prevent abuse, all forms of exploitation, forced, compulsory and child labour, extortion and other situations of dependency, and to allow migrants to fully exercise their human rights;
i. Provide migrant workers engaged in remunerated and contractual labour with the same labour rights and protections extended to all workers in the respective sector, such as the rights to just and favourable conditions of work, to equal pay for work of equal value, to freedom of peaceful assembly and association, and to the highest attainable standard of physical and mental health, including through wage protection mechanisms, social dialogue and membership in trade unions;
j. Ensure that migrants working in the informal economy have safe access to effective reporting, complaint and redress mechanisms in cases of exploitation, abuse or violations of their rights in the workplace, in a manner that does not exacerbate vulnerabilities of migrants who denounce such incidents and allows them to participate in respective legal proceedings whether in the country of origin or the country of destination;
k. Review relevant national labour laws, employment policies and programmes to ensure that they include considerations of the specific needs and contributions of women migrant workers, especially in domestic work and lower-skilled occupations, and adopt specific measures to prevent, report, address and provide effective remedy for all forms of exploitation and abuse, including sexual and gender-based violence, as a basis to promote gender-responsive labour mobility policies;
l. Develop and improve national policies and programmes relating to international labour mobility, including by taking into consideration relevant recommendations of the ILO General Principles and Operational Guidelines for Fair Recruitment, the United Nations Guiding Principles on Business and Human Rights and the IOM International Recruitment Integrity System (IRIS).

Objective 7: Address and reduce vulnerabilities in migration

23. We commit to respond to the needs of migrants who face situations of vulnerability, which may arise from the circumstances in which they travel or the conditions they face in countries of origin, transit and destination, by

assisting them and protecting their human rights, in accordance with our obligations under international law. We further commit to uphold the best interests of the child at all times, as a primary consideration in situations where children are concerned, and to apply a gender-responsive approach in addressing vulnerabilities, including in responses to mixed movements.

To realize this commitment, we will draw from the following actions:

a. Review relevant policies and practices to ensure that they do not create, exacerbate or unintentionally increase vulnerabilities of migrants, including by applying a human rights-based, gender- and disability-responsive, as well as age- and child-sensitive approach;
b. Establish comprehensive policies and develop partnerships that provide migrants in a situation of vulnerability, regardless of their migration status, with necessary support at all stages of migration, through identification and assistance, as well as protection of their human rights, in particular in cases related to women at risk, children, especially those unaccompanied or separated from their families, members of ethnic and religious minorities, victims of violence, including sexual and gender-based violence, older persons, persons with disabilities, persons who are discriminated against on any basis, indigenous peoples, workers facing exploitation and abuse, domestic workers, victims of trafficking in persons, and migrants subject to exploitation and abuse in the context of smuggling of migrants;
c. Develop gender-responsive migration policies to address the particular needs and vulnerabilities of migrant women, girls and boys, which may include assistance, health care, psychological and other counselling services, as well as access to justice and effective remedies, especially in cases of sexual and gender-based violence, abuse and exploitation;
d. Review relevant existing labour laws and work conditions to identify and effectively address workplace-related vulnerabilities and abuses of migrant workers at all skills levels, including domestic workers, and those working in the informal economy, in cooperation with relevant stakeholders, particularly the private sector;
e. Account for migrant children in national child protection systems by establishing robust procedures for the protection of migrant children in relevant legislative, administrative and judicial proceedings and decisions, as well as in all migration policies and programmes that impact children, including consular protection policies and services, as well as cross-border cooperation frameworks, in order to ensure that the best interests of the child are appropriately integrated, consistently

interpreted and applied in coordination and cooperation with child protection authorities;
f. Protect unaccompanied and separated children at all stages of migration through the establishment of specialized procedures for their identification, referral, care and family reunification, and provide access to health-care services, including mental health, education, legal assistance and the right to be heard in administrative and judicial proceedings, including by swiftly appointing a competent and impartial legal guardian, as essential means to address their particular vulnerabilities and discrimination, protect them from all forms of violence and provide access to sustainable solutions that are in their best interests;
g. Ensure that migrants have access to public or affordable independent legal assistance and representation in legal proceedings that affect them, including during any related judicial or administrative hearing, in order to safeguard that all migrants, everywhere, are recognized as persons before the law and that the delivery of justice is impartial and non-discriminatory;
h. Develop accessible and expedient procedures that facilitate transitions from one status to another and inform migrants of their rights and obligations, so as to prevent migrants from falling into an irregular status in the country of destination, to reduce precariousness of status and related vulnerabilities, as well as to enable individual status assessments for migrants, including for those who have fallen out of regular status, without fear of arbitrary expulsion;
i. Build on existing practices to facilitate access for migrants in an irregular status to an individual assessment that may lead to regular status, on a case-by-case basis and with clear and transparent criteria, especially in cases where children, youth and families are involved, as an option for reducing vulnerabilities, as well as for States to ascertain better knowledge of the resident population;
j. Apply specific support measures to ensure that migrants caught up in situations of crisis in countries of transit and destination have access to consular protection and humanitarian assistance, including by facilitating cross-border and broader international cooperation, as well as by taking migrant populations into account in crisis preparedness, emergency response and post-crisis action;
k. Involve local authorities and relevant stakeholders in the identification, referral and assistance of migrants in a situation of vulnerability, including through agreements with national protection bodies, legal aid and service providers, as well as the engagement of mobile response teams, where they exist;

l. Develop national policies and programmes to improve national responses that address the needs of migrants in situations of vulnerability, including by taking into consideration relevant recommendations of the Global Migration Group's Principles and Guidelines, Supported by Practical Guidance, on the Human Rights Protection of Migrants in Vulnerable Situations.

Objective 8: Save lives and establish coordinated international efforts on missing migrants

24. We commit to cooperate internationally to save lives and prevent migrant deaths and injuries through individual or joint search and rescue operations, standardized collection and exchange of relevant information, assuming collective responsibility to preserve the lives of all migrants, in accordance with international law. We further commit to identify those who have died or gone missing, and to facilitate communication with affected families.

To realize this commitment, we will draw from the following actions:

a. Develop procedures and agreements on search and rescue of migrants, with the primary objective of protecting migrants' right to life, that uphold the prohibition of collective expulsion, guarantee due process and individual assessments, enhance reception and assistance capacities, and ensure that the provision of assistance of an exclusively humanitarian nature for migrants is not considered unlawful;
b. Review the impacts of migration-related policies and laws to ensure that these do not raise or create the risk of migrants going missing, including by identifying dangerous transit routes used by migrants, by working with other States as well as relevant stakeholders and international organizations to identify contextual risks and establishing mechanisms for preventing and responding to such situations, with particular attention to migrant children, especially those unaccompanied or separated;
c. Enable migrants to communicate with their families without delay to inform them that they are alive by facilitating access to means of communication along routes and at their destination, including in places of detention, as well as access to consular missions, local authorities and organizations that can provide assistance with family contacts, especially in cases of unaccompanied or separated migrant children, as well as adolescents;

d. Establish transnational coordination channels, including through consular cooperation, and designate contact points for families looking for missing migrants, through which families can be kept informed on the status of the search and obtain other relevant information, while respecting the right to privacy and protecting personal data;
e. Collect, centralize and systematize data regarding corpses and ensure traceability after burial, in accordance with internationally accepted forensic standards, and establish coordination channels at the transnational level to facilitate identification and the provision of information to families;
f. Make all efforts, including through international cooperation, to recover, identify and repatriate to their countries of origin the remains of deceased migrants, respecting the wishes of grieving families, and, in the case of unidentified individuals, facilitate the identification and subsequent recovery of the mortal remains, ensuring that the remains of deceased migrants are treated in a dignified, respectful and proper manner.

Objective 9: Strengthen the transnational response to smuggling of migrants

25. We commit to intensify joint efforts to prevent and counter smuggling of migrants by strengthening capacities and international cooperation to prevent, investigate, prosecute and penalize the smuggling of migrants in order to end the impunity of smuggling networks. We further commit to ensure that migrants shall not become liable to criminal prosecution for the fact of having been the object of smuggling, notwithstanding potential prosecution for other violations of national law. We also commit to identify smuggled migrants to protect their human rights, taking into consideration the special needs of women and children, and assisting in particular those migrants subject to smuggling under aggravating circumstances, in accordance with international law.

To realize this commitment, we will draw from the following actions:

a. Promote ratification of, accession to and implementation of the Protocol against the Smuggling of Migrants by Land, Sea and Air, supplementing the United Nations Convention against Transnational Organized Crime;
b. Use transnational, regional and bilateral mechanisms to share relevant information and intelligence on smuggling routes, modus operandi and financial transactions of smuggling networks, vulner-

abilities faced by smuggled migrants, and other data to dismantle the smuggling networks and enhance joint responses;

c. Develop gender-responsive and child-sensitive cooperation protocols along migration routes that outline step-by-step measures to adequately identify and assist smuggled migrants, in accordance with international law, as well as to facilitate cross-border law enforcement and intelligence cooperation in order to prevent and counter smuggling of migrants so as to end impunity for smugglers and prevent irregular migration, while ensuring that counter-smuggling measures are in full respect for human rights;

d. Adopt legislative and other measures as may be necessary to establish the smuggling of migrants as a criminal offence, when committed intentionally and in order to obtain, directly or indirectly, a financial or other material benefit for the smuggler, and include enhanced penalties for smuggling of migrants under aggravating circumstances, in accordance with international law;

e. Design, review or amend relevant policies and procedures to distinguish between the crimes of smuggling of migrants and trafficking in persons by using the correct definitions and applying distinct responses to these separate crimes, while recognizing that smuggled migrants might also become victims of trafficking in persons, therefore requiring appropriate protection and assistance;

f. Take measures to prevent the smuggling of migrants along the migration cycle, in partnership with other States and relevant stakeholders, including by cooperating in the fields of development, public information, justice, as well as training and technical capacity-building at the national and local levels, paying special attention to geographical areas from which irregular migration systematically originates.

Objective 10: Prevent, combat and eradicate trafficking in persons in the context of international migration

26. We commit to take legislative or other measures to prevent, combat and eradicate trafficking in persons in the context of international migration by strengthening capacities and international cooperation to investigate, prosecute and penalize trafficking in persons, discouraging demand that fosters exploitation leading to trafficking, and ending impunity of trafficking networks. We further commit to enhance the identification and protection of, and assistance to, migrants who have become victims of trafficking, paying particular attention to women and children.

To realize this commitment, we will draw from the following actions:

a. Promote ratification of, accession to and implementation of the Protocol to Prevent, Suppress and Punish Trafficking in Persons, Especially Women and Children, supplementing the United Nations Convention against Transnational Organized Crime;
b. Promote the implementation of the United Nations Global Plan of Action to Combat Trafficking in Persons and take into consideration relevant recommendations of the United Nations Office on Drugs and Crime (UNODC) Toolkit to Combat Trafficking in Persons and other relevant UNODC documents when developing and implementing national and regional policies and measures relating to trafficking in persons;
c. Monitor irregular migration routes which may be exploited by human trafficking networks to recruit and victimize smuggled or irregular migrants, in order to strengthen cooperation at the bilateral, regional and cross-regional levels on prevention, investigation and prosecution of perpetrators, as well as on identification and protection of, and assistance to, victims of trafficking in persons;
d. Share relevant information and intelligence through transnational and regional mechanisms, including on the modus operandi, economic models and conditions driving trafficking networks, strengthen cooperation between all relevant actors, including financial intelligence units, regulators and financial institutions, to identify and disrupt financial flows associated with trafficking in persons, and enhance judicial cooperation and enforcement so as to ensure accountability and end impunity;
e. Apply measures that address the particular vulnerabilities of women, men, girls and boys, regardless of their migration status, who have become or are at risk of becoming victims of trafficking in persons and other forms of exploitation, by facilitating access to justice and safe reporting without fear of detention, deportation or penalty, focusing on prevention, identification, appropriate protection and assistance, and addressing specific forms of abuse and exploitation;
f. Ensure that definitions of trafficking in persons used in legislation, migration policy and planning, as well as in judicial prosecutions, are in accordance with international law, in order to distinguish between the crimes of trafficking in persons and smuggling of migrants;
g. Strengthen legislation and relevant procedures to enhance prosecution of traffickers, avoid criminalization of migrants who are victims of trafficking in persons for trafficking-related offences, and ensure that the victim

receives appropriate protection and assistance, not conditional upon cooperation with the authorities against suspected traffickers;

h. Provide migrants who have become victims of trafficking in persons with protection and assistance, such as measures for physical, psychological and social recovery, as well as measures that permit them to remain in the country of destination, temporarily or permanently, in appropriate cases, facilitating victims' access to justice, including redress and compensation, in accordance with international law;

i. Create national and local information systems and training programmes which alert and educate citizens, employers, as well as public officials and law enforcement officers, and strengthen capacities to identify signs of trafficking in persons, such as forced, compulsory or child labour, in countries of origin, transit and destination;

j. Invest in awareness-raising campaigns, in partnership with relevant stakeholders, for migrants and prospective migrants on the risks and dangers of trafficking in persons, and provide them with information on preventing and reporting trafficking activities.

Objective 11: Manage borders in an integrated, secure and coordinated manner

27. We commit to manage our national borders in a coordinated manner, promoting bilateral and regional cooperation, ensuring security for States, communities and migrants, and facilitating safe and regular cross-border movements of people while preventing irregular migration. We further commit to implement border management policies that respect national sovereignty, the rule of law, obligations under international law, and the human rights of all migrants, regardless of their migration status, and are non-discriminatory, gender-responsive and child-sensitive.

To realize this commitment, we will draw from the following actions:

a. Enhance international, regional and cross-regional border management cooperation, taking into consideration the particular situation of countries of transit, on proper identification, timely and efficient referral, assistance and appropriate protection of migrants in situations of vulnerability at or near international borders, in compliance with international human rights law, by adopting whole-of-government approaches, implementing joint cross-border training and fostering capacity-building measures;

b. Establish appropriate structures and mechanisms for effective integrated border management by ensuring comprehensive and efficient border crossing procedures, including through pre-screening of arriving persons, pre-reporting by carriers of passengers, and use of information and communications technology, while upholding the principle of non-discrimination, respecting the right to privacy and protecting personal data;

c. Review and revise relevant national procedures for border screening, individual assessment and interview processes to ensure due process at international borders and that all migrants are treated in accordance with international human rights law, including through cooperation with national human rights institutions and other relevant stakeholders;

d. Develop technical cooperation agreements that enable States to request and offer assets, equipment and other technical assistance to strengthen border management, particularly in the area of search and rescue as well as other emergency situations;

e. Ensure that child protection authorities are promptly informed and assigned to participate in procedures for the determination of the best interests of the child once an unaccompanied or separated child crosses an international border, in accordance with international law, including by training border officials in the rights of the child and child-sensitive procedures, such as those that prevent family separation and reunite families when family separation occurs;

f. Review and revise relevant laws and regulations to determine whether sanctions are appropriate to address irregular entry or stay and, if so, to ensure that they are proportionate, equitable, non-discriminatory and fully consistent with due process and other obligations under international law;

g. Improve cross-border collaboration among neighbouring and other States relating to the treatment given to persons crossing or seeking to cross international borders, including by taking into consideration relevant recommendations from the Office of the United Nations High Commissioner for Human Rights Recommended Principles and Guidelines on Human Rights at International Borders when identifying best practices.

Objective 12: Strengthen certainty and predictability in migration procedures for appropriate screening, assessment and referral

28. We commit to increase legal certainty and predictability of migration procedures by developing and strengthening effective and human rights-

based mechanisms for the adequate and timely screening and individual assessment of all migrants for the purpose of identifying and facilitating access to the appropriate referral procedures, in accordance with international law.

To realize this commitment, we will draw from the following actions:

a. Increase transparency and accessibility of migration procedures by communicating the requirements for entry, admission, stay, work, study or other activities, and introducing technology to simplify application procedures, in order to avoid unnecessary delays and expenses for States and migrants;
b. Develop and conduct intra- and cross-regional specialized human rights and trauma-informed training for first responders and government officials, including law enforcement authorities, border officials, consular representatives and judicial bodies, to facilitate and standardize identification and referral of, as well as appropriate assistance and counselling in a culturally sensitive way to, victims of trafficking in persons, migrants in situations of vulnerability, including children, in particular those unaccompanied or separated, and persons affected by any form of exploitation and abuse related to smuggling of migrants under aggravating circumstances;
c. Establish gender-responsive and child-sensitive referral mechanisms, including improved screening measures and individual assessments at borders and places of first arrival, by applying standardized operating procedures developed in coordination with local authorities, national human rights institutions, international organizations and civil society;
d. Ensure that migrant children are promptly identified at places of first arrival in countries of transit and destination, and, if unaccompanied or separated, are swiftly referred to child protection authorities and other relevant services as well as appointed a competent and impartial legal guardian, that family unity is protected, and that anyone legitimately claiming to be a child is treated as such unless otherwise determined through a multidisciplinary, independent and child-sensitive age assessment;
e. Ensure that, in the context of mixed movements, relevant information on rights and obligations under national laws and procedures, including on entry and stay requirements, available forms of protection, as well as options for return and reintegration, is appropriately, promptly and effectively communicated, and is accessible.

Objective 13: Use immigration detention only as a measure of last resort and work towards alternatives

29. We commit to ensure that any detention in the context of international migration follows due process, is non-arbitrary, is based on law, necessity, proportionality and individual assessments, is carried out by authorized officials and is for the shortest possible period of time, irrespective of whether detention occurs at the moment of entry, in transit or in proceedings of return, and regardless of the type of place where the detention occurs. We further commit to prioritize non-custodial alternatives to detention that are in line with international law, and to take a human rights-based approach to any detention of migrants, using detention as a measure of last resort only.

To realize this commitment, we will draw from the following actions:

a. Use existing relevant human rights mechanisms to improve independent monitoring of migrant detention, ensuring that it is a measure of last resort, that human rights violations do not occur, and that States promote, implement and expand alternatives to detention, favouring non-custodial measures and community-based care arrangements, especially in the case of families and children;
b. Consolidate a comprehensive repository to disseminate best practices of human rights-based alternatives to detention in the context of international migration, including by facilitating regular exchanges and the development of initiatives based on successful practices among States, and between States and relevant stakeholders;
c. Review and revise relevant legislation, policies and practices related to immigration detention to ensure that migrants are not detained arbitrarily, that decisions to detain are based on law, are proportionate, have a legitimate purpose, and are taken on an individual basis, in full compliance with due process and procedural safeguards, and that immigration detention is not promoted as a deterrent or used as a form of cruel, inhumane or degrading treatment of migrants, in accordance with international human rights law;
d. Provide access to justice for all migrants in countries of transit and destination who are or may be subject to detention, including by facilitating access to free or affordable legal advice and assistance of a qualified and independent lawyer, as well as access to information and the right to regular review of a detention order;
e. Ensure that all migrants in detention are informed about the reasons for their detention, in a language they understand, and facilitate the

exercise of their rights, including to communicate with the respective consular or diplomatic missions without delay, legal representatives and family members, in accordance with international law and due process guarantees;
f. Reduce the negative and potentially lasting effects of detention on migrants by guaranteeing due process and proportionality, that it is for the shortest period of time, that it safeguards physical and mental integrity, and that, at a minimum, access to food, basic health care, legal orientation and assistance, information and communication as well as adequate accommodation is granted, in accordance with international human rights law;
g. Ensure that all governmental authorities and private actors duly charged with administering immigration detention do so in a way consistent with human rights and are trained on non-discrimination and the prevention of arbitrary arrest and detention in the context of international migration, and are held accountable for violations or abuses of human rights;
h. Protect and respect the rights and best interests of the child at all times, regardless of migration status, by ensuring availability and accessibility of a viable range of alternatives to detention in non-custodial contexts, favouring community-based care arrangements, that ensure access to education and health care, and respect the right to family life and family unity, and by working to end the practice of child detention in the context of international migration.

Objective 14: Enhance consular protection, assistance and cooperation throughout the migration cycle

30. We commit to strengthen consular protection of and assistance to our nationals abroad, as well as consular cooperation between States, in order to better safeguard the rights and interests of all migrants at all times, and to build upon the functions of consular missions to enhance interactions between migrants and State authorities of countries of origin, transit and destination, in accordance with international law.

To realize this commitment, we will draw from the following actions:

a. Cooperate to build consular capacities, train consular officers, promote arrangements for providing consular services collectively where individual States lack capacity, including through technical assistance,

and develop bilateral or regional agreements on various aspects of consular cooperation;
b. Involve relevant consular and immigration personnel in existing global and regional forums on migration in order to exchange information and best practices about issues of mutual concern that pertain to citizens abroad and contribute to comprehensive and evidence-based migration policy development;
c. Conclude bilateral or regional agreements on consular assistance and representation in places where States have an interest in strengthening effective consular services related to migration, but do not have a diplomatic or consular presence;
d. Strengthen consular capacities in order to identify, protect and assist our nationals abroad who are in a situation of vulnerability, including victims of human and labour rights violations or abuse, victims of crime, victims of trafficking in persons, migrants subject to smuggling under aggravating circumstances, and migrant workers exploited in the process of recruitment, by providing training to consular officers on human rights-based, gender-responsive and child-sensitive actions in this regard;
e. Provide our nationals abroad with the opportunity to register with the country of origin, in close cooperation with consular, national and local authorities, as well as relevant migrant organizations, as a means to facilitate information, services and assistance to migrants in emergency situations and ensure migrants' accessibility to relevant and timely information, such as by establishing helplines and consolidating national digital databases, while upholding the right to privacy and protecting personal data;
f. Provide consular support to our nationals through advice, including on local laws and customs, interaction with authorities, financial inclusion and business establishment, as well as through the issuance of relevant documentation, such as travel documents and consular identity documents that may facilitate access to services, assistance in emergency situations, the opening of a bank account, and access to remittance facilities.

Objective 15: Provide access to basic services for migrants

31. We commit to ensure that all migrants, regardless of their migration status, can exercise their human rights through safe access to basic services. We further commit to strengthen migrant-inclusive service delivery systems, notwithstanding that nationals and regular migrants may be entitled to more comprehensive service provision, while ensuring that any differential treat-

ment must be based on law, be proportionate and pursue a legitimate aim, in accordance with international human rights law.

To realize this commitment, we will draw from the following actions:

a. Enact laws and take measures to ensure that service delivery does not amount to discrimination against migrants on the grounds of race, colour, sex, language, religion, political or other opinion, national or social origin, property, birth, disability or other grounds irrespective of cases where differential provision of services based on migration status might apply;
b. Ensure that cooperation between service providers and immigration authorities does not exacerbate vulnerabilities of irregular migrants by compromising their safe access to basic services or by unlawfully infringing upon the human rights to privacy, liberty and security of person at places of basic service delivery;
c. Establish and strengthen holistic and easily accessible service points at the local level that are migrant-inclusive, offer relevant information on basic services in a gender- and disability-responsive as well as child-sensitive manner, and facilitate safe access thereto;
d. Establish or mandate independent institutions at the national or local level, such as national human rights institutions, to receive, investigate and monitor complaints about situations in which migrants' access to basic services is systematically denied or hindered, facilitate access to redress, and work towards a change in practice;
e. Incorporate the health needs of migrants into national and local health-care policies and plans, such as by strengthening capacities for service provision, facilitating affordable and non-discriminatory access, reducing communication barriers, and training health-care providers on culturally sensitive service delivery, in order to promote the physical and mental health of migrants and communities overall, including by taking into consideration relevant recommendations from the World Health Organization Framework of Priorities and Guiding Principles to Promote the Health of Refugees and Migrants;
f. Provide inclusive and equitable quality education to migrant children and youth, as well as facilitate access to lifelong learning opportunities, including by strengthening the capacities of education systems and by facilitating non-discriminatory access to early childhood development, formal schooling, non-formal education programmes for children for whom the formal system is inaccessible, on-the-job and vocational training, technical education and language training, as well as

Objective 16: Empower migrants and societies to realize full inclusion and social cohesion

32. We commit to foster inclusive and cohesive societies by empowering migrants to become active members of society and promoting the reciprocal engagement of receiving communities and migrants in the exercise of their rights and obligations towards each other, including observance of national laws and respect for customs of the country of destination. We further commit to strengthen the welfare of all members of societies by minimizing disparities, avoiding polarization and increasing public confidence in policies and institutions related to migration, in line with the acknowledgement that fully integrated migrants are better positioned to contribute to prosperity.

To realize this commitment, we will draw from the following actions:

a. Promote mutual respect for the cultures, traditions and customs of communities of destination and of migrants by exchanging and implementing best practices on integration policies, programmes and activities, including on ways to promote acceptance of diversity and facilitate social cohesion and inclusion;

b. Establish comprehensive and needs-based pre-departure and post-arrival programmes that may include rights and obligations, basic language training, as well as orientation about social norms and customs in the country of destination;

c. Develop national short-, medium- and long-term policy goals regarding the inclusion of migrants in societies, including on labour market integration, family reunification, education, non-discrimination and health, including by fostering partnerships with relevant stakeholders;

d. Work towards inclusive labour markets and full participation of migrant workers in the formal economy by facilitating access to decent work and employment for which they are most qualified, in accordance with local and national labour market demands and skills supply;

e. Empower migrant women by eliminating gender-based discriminatory restrictions on formal employment, ensuring the right to freedom of association and facilitating access to relevant basic services, as measures to promote their leadership and guarantee their full, free and equal participation in society and the economy;

f. Establish community centres or programmes at the local level to facilitate migrant participation in the receiving society by involving migrants, community members, diaspora organizations, migrant associations and local authorities in intercultural dialogue, sharing of stories, mentorship programmes and development of business ties that improve integration outcomes and foster mutual respect;
g. Capitalize on the skills, cultural and language proficiency of migrants and receiving communities by developing and promoting peer-to-peer training exchanges, gender-responsive, vocational and civic integration courses and workshops;
h. Support multicultural activities through sports, music, arts, culinary festivals, volunteering and other social events that will facilitate mutual understanding and appreciation of migrant cultures and those of destination communities;
i. Promote school environments that are welcoming and safe, and support the aspirations of migrant children by enhancing relationships within the school community, incorporating evidence-based information about migration into education curricula, and dedicating targeted resources to schools with a high concentration of migrant children for integration activities in order to promote respect for diversity and inclusion, and to prevent all forms of discrimination, including racism, xenophobia and intolerance.

Objective 17: Eliminate all forms of discrimination and promote evidence-based public discourse to shape perceptions of migration

33. We commit to eliminate all forms of discrimination, condemn and counter expressions, acts and manifestations of racism, racial discrimination, violence, xenophobia and related intolerance against all migrants in conformity with international human rights law. We further commit to promote an open and evidence-based public discourse on migration and migrants in partnership with all parts of society, that generates a more realistic, humane and constructive perception in this regard. We also commit to protect freedom of expression in accordance with international law, recognizing that an open and free debate contributes to a comprehensive understanding of all aspects of migration.

To realize this commitment, we will draw from the following actions:

a. Enact, implement or maintain legislation that penalizes hate crimes and aggravated hate crimes targeting migrants, and train law enforce-

ment and other public officials to identify, prevent and respond to such crimes and other acts of violence that target migrants, as well as to provide medical, legal and psychosocial assistance for victims;
b. Empower migrants and communities to denounce any acts of incitement to violence directed towards migrants by informing them of available mechanisms for redress, and ensure that those who actively participate in the commission of a hate crime targeting migrants are held accountable, in accordance with national legislation, while upholding international human rights law, in particular the right to freedom of expression;
c. Promote independent, objective and quality reporting of media outlets, including Internet-based information, including by sensitizing and educating media professionals on migration-related issues and terminology, investing in ethical reporting standards and advertising, and stopping allocation of public funding or material support to media outlets that systematically promote intolerance, xenophobia, racism and other forms of discrimination towards migrants, in full respect for the freedom of the media;
d. Establish mechanisms to prevent, detect and respond to racial, ethnic and religious profiling of migrants by public authorities, as well as systematic instances of intolerance, xenophobia, racism and all other multiple and intersecting forms of discrimination, in partnership with national human rights institutions, including by tracking and publishing trend analyses, and ensuring access to effective complaint and redress mechanisms;
e. Provide migrants, especially migrant women, with access to national and regional complaint and redress mechanisms with a view to promoting accountability and addressing governmental actions related to discriminatory acts and manifestations carried out against migrants and their families;
f. Promote awareness-raising campaigns targeted at communities of origin, transit and destination in order to inform public perceptions regarding the positive contributions of safe, orderly and regular migration, based on evidence and facts, and to end racism, xenophobia and stigmatization against all migrants;
g. Engage migrants, political, religious and community leaders, as well as educators and service providers, to detect and prevent incidences of intolerance, racism, xenophobia and other forms of discrimination against migrants and diasporas, and support activities in local communities to promote mutual respect, including in the context of electoral campaigns.

Objective 18: Invest in skills development and facilitate mutual recognition of skills, qualifications and competences

34. We commit to invest in innovative solutions that facilitate mutual recognition of skills, qualifications and competences of migrant workers at all skills levels, and promote demand-driven skills development to optimize the employability of migrants in formal labour markets in countries of destination and in countries of origin upon return, as well as to ensure decent work in labour migration.

To realize this commitment, we will draw from the following actions:

a. Develop standards and guidelines for the mutual recognition of foreign qualifications and non-formally acquired skills in different sectors in collaboration with the respective industries with a view to ensuring worldwide compatibility based on existing models and best practices;
b. Promote transparency of certifications and compatibility of national qualifications frameworks by agreeing on standard criteria, indicators and assessment parameters, and by creating and strengthening national skills profiling tools, registries or institutions in order to facilitate effective and efficient mutual recognition procedures at all skills levels;
c. Conclude bilateral, regional or multilateral mutual recognition agreements or include recognition provisions in other agreements, such as labour mobility or trade agreements, in order to provide equivalence or comparability in national systems, such as automatic or managed mutual recognition mechanisms;
d. Use technology and digitalization to evaluate and mutually recognize skills more comprehensively on the basis of formal credentials as well as non-formally acquired competences and professional experience at all skills levels;
e. Build global skills partnerships among countries that strengthen training capacities of national authorities and relevant stakeholders, including the private sector and trade unions, and foster skills development of workers in countries of origin and migrants in countries of destination with a view to preparing trainees for employability in the labour markets of all participating countries;
f. Promote inter-institutional networks and collaborative programmes for partnerships between the private sector and educational institutions in countries of origin and destination to enable mutually beneficial skills development opportunities for migrants, communities and par-

ticipating partners, including by building on the best practices of the Business Mechanism developed in the context of the Global Forum on Migration and Development;

g. Engage in bilateral partnerships and programmes in cooperation with relevant stakeholders that promote skills development, mobility and circulation, such as student exchange programmes, scholarships, professional exchange programmes and trainee- or apprenticeships that include options for beneficiaries, after successful completion of these programmes, to seek employment and engage in entrepreneurship;

h. Cooperate with the private sector and employers to make available easily accessible and gender-responsive remote or online skills development and matching programmes to migrants at all skills levels, including early and occupation-specific language training, on-the-job training and access to advanced training programmes, to enhance their employability in sectors with demand for labour on the basis of the industry's knowledge of labour market dynamics, especially to promote the economic empowerment of women;

i. Enhance the ability of migrant workers to transition from one job or employer to another by making available documentation that recognizes skills acquired on the job or through training in order to optimize the benefits of upskilling;

j. Develop and promote innovative ways to mutually recognize and assess formally and informally acquired skills, including through timely and complementary training for job seekers, mentoring, and internship programmes in order to fully recognize existing credentials and provide certificates of proficiency for the validation of newly acquired skills;

k. Establish screening mechanisms for credentials and offer information to migrants on how to have their skills and qualifications assessed and recognized prior to departure, including in recruitment processes or at an early stage after arrival to improve employability;

l. Cooperate to promote documentation and information tools, in partnership with relevant stakeholders, that provide an overview of a worker's credentials, skills and qualifications, recognized in countries of origin, transit and destination, in order to enable employers to evaluate the suitability of migrant workers in job application processes.

Objective 19: Create conditions for migrants and diasporas to fully contribute to sustainable development in all countries

35. We commit to empower migrants and diasporas to catalyse their development contributions, and to harness the benefits of migration as a

source of sustainable development, reaffirming that migration is a multidimensional reality of major relevance to the sustainable development of countries of origin, transit and destination.

To realize this commitment, we will draw from the following actions:

a. Ensure the full and effective implementation of the 2030 Agenda for Sustainable Development and the Addis Ababa Action Agenda by fostering and facilitating the positive effects of migration for the realization of all Sustainable Development Goals;
b. Integrate migration into development planning and sectoral policies at the local, national, regional and global levels, taking into consideration relevant existing policy guidelines and recommendations, such as the Global Migration Group's Mainstreaming Migration into Development Planning: A Handbook for Policymakers and Practitioners, in order to strengthen policy coherence and effectiveness of development cooperation;
c. Invest in research on the impact of non-financial contributions of migrants and diasporas to sustainable development in countries of origin and destination, such as knowledge and skills transfer, social and civic engagement, and cultural exchange, with a view to developing evidence-based policies and strengthening global policy discussions;
d. Facilitate the contributions of migrants and diasporas to their countries of origin, including by establishing or strengthening government structures or mechanisms at all levels, such as dedicated diaspora offices or focal points, diaspora policy advisory boards for Governments to account for the potential of migrants and diasporas in migration and development policymaking, and dedicated diaspora focal points in diplomatic or consular missions;
e. Develop targeted support programmes and financial products that facilitate migrant and diaspora investments and entrepreneurship, including by providing administrative and legal support in business creation and granting seed capital-matching, establish diaspora bonds, diaspora development funds and investment funds, and organize dedicated trade fairs;
f. Provide easily accessible information and guidance, including through digital platforms, as well as tailored mechanisms for the coordinated and effective financial, voluntary or philanthropic engagement of migrants and diasporas, especially in humanitarian emergencies in their countries of origin, including by involving consular missions;
g. Enable political participation and engagement of migrants in their countries of origin, including in peace and reconciliation processes, in

elections and political reforms, such as by establishing voting registries for citizens abroad, and through parliamentary representation, in accordance with national legislation;

h. Promote migration policies that optimize the benefits of diasporas for countries of origin and destination and their communities, by facilitating flexible modalities to travel, work and invest with minimal administrative burdens, including by reviewing and revising visa, residency and citizenship regulations, as appropriate;

i. Cooperate with other States, the private sector and employers' organizations to enable migrants and diasporas, especially those in highly technical fields and in high demand, to carry out some of their professional activities and engage in knowledge transfer in their home countries, without necessarily losing employment, residence status or earned social benefits;

j. Build partnerships between local authorities, local communities, the private sector, diasporas, hometown associations and migrant organizations to promote knowledge and skills transfer between their countries of origin and their countries of destination, including by mapping the diasporas and their skills, as a means to maintain the link between diasporas and their country of origin.

Objective 20: Promote faster, safer and cheaper transfer of remittances and foster financial inclusion of migrants

36. We commit to promote faster, safer and cheaper remittances by further developing existing conducive policy and regulatory environments that enable competition, regulation and innovation on the remittance market and by providing gender-responsive programmes and instruments that enhance the financial inclusion of migrants and their families. We further commit to optimize the transformative impact of remittances on the well-being of migrant workers and their families, as well as on the sustainable development of countries, while respecting that remittances constitute an important source of private capital and cannot be equated to other international financial flows, such as foreign direct investment, official development assistance or other public sources of financing for development.

To realize this commitment, we will draw from the following actions:

a. Develop a road map to reduce the transaction costs of migrant remittances to less than 3 per cent and eliminate remittance corridors with costs higher than 5 percent by 2030 in line with target 10.c of the 2030 Agenda for Sustainable Development;

b. Promote and support the United Nations International Day of Family Remittances and the International Fund for Agricultural Development Global Forum on Remittances, Investment and Development as an important platform to build and strengthen partnerships for innovative solutions on cheaper, faster and safer transfer of remittances with all relevant stakeholders;

c. Harmonize remittance market regulations and increase the interoperability of remittance infrastructure along corridors by ensuring that measures to combat illicit financial flows and money-laundering do not impede migrant remittances through undue, excessive or discriminatory policies;

d. Establish conducive policy and regulatory frameworks that promote a competitive and innovative remittance market, remove unwarranted obstacles to non-bank remittance service providers in accessing payment system infrastructure, apply tax exemptions or incentives to remittance transfers, promote market access to diverse service providers, incentivize the private sector to expand remittance services, and enhance the security and predictability of low-value transactions by bearing in mind de-risking concerns, and developing a methodology to distinguish remittances from illicit flows, in consultation with remittance service providers and financial regulators;

e. Develop innovative technological solutions for remittance transfer, such as mobile payments, digital tools or e-banking, to reduce costs, improve speed, enhance security, increase transfer through regular channels and open up gender-responsive distribution channels to underserved populations, including persons in rural areas, persons with low levels of literacy and persons with disabilities;

f. Provide accessible information on remittance transfer costs by provider and channel, such as comparison websites, in order to increase the transparency and competition on the remittance transfer market, and promote financial literacy and inclusion of migrants and their families through education and training;

g. Develop programmes and instruments to promote investments from remittance senders in local development and entrepreneurship in countries of origin, such as through matching-grant mechanisms, municipal bonds and partnerships with hometown associations, in order to enhance the transformative potential of remittances beyond the individual households of migrant workers at all skills levels;

h. Enable migrant women to access financial literacy training and formal remittance transfer systems, as well as to open a bank account and own and manage financial assets, investments and businesses as means to address gender inequalities and foster their active participation in the economy;

i. Provide access to and develop banking solutions and financial instruments for migrants, including low-income and female-headed households, such as bank accounts that permit direct deposits by employers, savings accounts, loans and credits in cooperation with the banking sector.

Objective 21: Cooperate in facilitating safe and dignified return and readmission, as well as sustainable reintegration

37. We commit to facilitate and cooperate for safe and dignified return and to guarantee due process, individual assessment and effective remedy, by upholding the prohibition of collective expulsion and of returning migrants when there is a real and foreseeable risk of death, torture and other cruel, inhuman and degrading treatment or punishment, or other irreparable harm, in accordance with our obligations under international human rights law. We further commit to ensure that our nationals are duly received and readmitted, in full respect for the human right to return to one's own country and the obligation of States to readmit their own nationals. We also commit to create conducive conditions for personal safety, economic empowerment, inclusion and social cohesion in communities, in order to ensure that reintegration of migrants upon return to their countries of origin is sustainable.

To realize this commitment, we will draw from the following actions:

a. Develop and implement bilateral, regional and multilateral cooperation frameworks and agreements, including readmission agreements, ensuring that return and readmission of migrants to their own country is safe, dignified and in full compliance with international human rights law, including the rights of the child, by determining clear and mutually agreed procedures that uphold procedural safeguards, guarantee individual assessments and legal certainty, and by ensuring that they also include provisions that facilitate sustainable reintegration;

b. Promote gender-responsive and child-sensitive return and reintegration programmes that may include legal, social and financial support, guaranteeing that all returns in the context of such voluntary programmes effectively take place on the basis of the migrant's free, prior and informed consent, and that returning migrants are assisted in their reintegration process through effective partnerships, including to avoid their becoming displaced in the country of origin upon return;

c. Cooperate on identification of nationals and issuance of travel documents for safe and dignified return and readmission in cases of persons who do not have the legal right to stay on another State's territory, by establishing reliable and efficient means of identification of our own nationals such as through the addition of biometric identifiers in population registries, and by digitalizing civil registry systems, with full respect for the right to privacy and protection of personal data;
d. Foster institutional contacts between consular authorities and relevant officials from countries of origin and destination, and provide adequate consular assistance to returning migrants prior to return by facilitating access to documentation, travel documents and other services, in order to ensure predictability, safety and dignity in return and readmission;
e. Ensure that the return of migrants who do not have the legal right to stay on another State's territory is safe and dignified, follows an individual assessment, is carried out by competent authorities through prompt and effective cooperation between countries of origin and destination, and allows all applicable legal remedies to be exhausted, in compliance with due process guarantees and other obligations under international human rights law;
f. Establish or strengthen national monitoring mechanisms on return, in partnership with relevant stakeholders, that provide independent recommendations on ways and means to strengthen accountability, in order to guarantee the safety, dignity and human rights of all returning migrants;
g. Ensure that return and readmission processes involving children are carried out only after a determination of the best interests of the child and take into account the right to family life and family unity, and that a parent, legal guardian or specialized official accompanies the child throughout the return process, ensuring that appropriate reception, care and reintegration arrangements for children are in place in the country of origin upon return;
h. Facilitate the sustainable reintegration of returning migrants into community life by providing them with equal access to social protection and services, justice, psychosocial assistance, vocational training, employment opportunities and decent work, recognition of skills acquired abroad, and financial services, in order to fully build upon their entrepreneurship, skills and human capital as active members of society and contributors to sustainable development in the country of origin upon return;
i. Identify and address the needs of the communities to which migrants return by including respective provisions in national and local development strategies, infrastructure planning, budget allocations and oth-

er relevant policy decisions and cooperating with local authorities and relevant stakeholders.

Objective 22: Establish mechanisms for the portability of social security entitlements and earned benefits

38. We commit to assist migrant workers at all skills levels to have access to social protection in countries of destination and profit from the portability of applicable social security entitlements and earned benefits in their countries of origin or when they decide to take up work in another country.

To realize this commitment, we will draw from the following actions:

a. Establish or maintain non-discriminatory national social protection systems, including social protection floors for nationals and migrants, in line with the ILO Social Protection Floors Recommendation, 2012 (No. 202);
b. Conclude reciprocal bilateral, regional or multilateral social security agreements on the portability of earned benefits for migrant workers at all skills levels, that refer to applicable social protection floors in the respective States and applicable social security entitlements and provisions, such as pensions, health care or other earned benefits, or integrate such provisions into other relevant agreements, such as those on long-term and temporary labour migration;
c. Integrate provisions on the portability of entitlements and earned benefits into national social security frameworks, designate focal points in countries of origin, transit and destination that facilitate portability requests from migrants, address the difficulties women and older persons can face in accessing social protection, and establish dedicated instruments, such as migrant welfare funds in countries of origin, that support migrant workers and their families.

Objective 23: Strengthen international cooperation and global partnerships for safe, orderly and regular migration

39. We commit to support each other in the realization of the objectives and commitments laid out in this Global Compact through enhanced international cooperation, a revitalized global partnership and, in the spirit of solidarity, reaffirming the centrality of a comprehensive and integrated approach to facilitate safe, orderly and regular migration and recognizing that we are

all countries of origin, transit and destination. We further commit to take joint action, in addressing the challenges faced by each country, to implement this Global Compact, underscoring the specific challenges faced in particular by African countries, least developed countries, landlocked developing countries, small island developing States and middle-income countries. We also commit to promote the mutually reinforcing nature between the Global Compact and existing international legal and policy frameworks, by aligning the implementation of this Global Compact with such frameworks, particularly the 2030 Agenda for Sustainable Development as well as the Addis Ababa Action Agenda, and their recognition that migration and sustainable development are multidimensional and interdependent.

To realize this commitment, we will draw from the following actions:

a. Support other States as we collectively implement the Global Compact, including through the provision of financial and technical assistance, in line with national priorities, policies, action plans and strategies, through a whole-of-government and whole-of-society approach;
b. Increase international and regional cooperation to accelerate the implementation of the 2030 Agenda for Sustainable Development in geographical areas from which irregular migration systematically originates owing to consistent impacts of poverty, unemployment, climate change and disasters, inequality, corruption and poor governance, among other structural factors, through appropriate cooperation frameworks, innovative partnerships and the involvement of all relevant stakeholders, while upholding national ownership and shared responsibility;
c. Involve and support local authorities in the identification of needs and opportunities for international cooperation for the effective implementation of the Global Compact and integrate their perspectives and priorities into development strategies, programmes and planning on migration, as a means to ensure good governance as well as policy coherence across levels of government and policy sectors, and maximize the effectiveness and impact of international development cooperation;
d. Make use of the capacity-building mechanism and build upon other existing instruments to strengthen the capacities of relevant authorities by mobilizing technical, financial and human resources from States, international financial institutions, the private sector, international organizations and other sources in order to assist all States in fulfilling the commitments outlined in this Global Compact;

e. Conclude bilateral, regional or multilateral mutually beneficial, tailored and transparent partnerships, in line with international law, that develop targeted solutions to migration policy issues of common interest and address opportunities and challenges of migration in accordance with the Global Compact.

Implementation

40. For the effective implementation of the Global Compact, we require concerted efforts at the global, regional, national and local levels, including a coherent United Nations system.

41. We commit to fulfil the objectives and commitments outlined in the Global Compact, in line with our vision and guiding principles, by taking effective steps at all levels to facilitate safe, orderly and regular migration at all stages. We will implement the Global Compact, within our own countries and at the regional and global levels, taking into account different national realities, capacities and levels of development, and respecting national policies and priorities. We reaffirm our commitment to international law and emphasize that the Global Compact is to be implemented in a manner that is consistent with our rights and obligations under international law.

42. We will implement the Global Compact through enhanced bilateral, regional and multilateral cooperation and a revitalized global partnership in a spirit of solidarity. We will continue building on existing mechanisms, platforms and frameworks to address migration in all its dimensions. Recognizing the centrality of international cooperation for the effective fulfilment of the objectives and commitments, we will strive to reinforce our engagement in North-South, South-South and triangular cooperation and assistance. Our cooperation efforts in this regard will be aligned with the 2030 Agenda for Sustainable Development and the Addis Ababa Action Agenda.

43. We decide to establish a capacity-building mechanism in the United Nations, building upon existing initiatives, that supports efforts of Member States to implement the Global Compact. It allows Member States, the United Nations and other relevant stakeholders, including the private sector and philanthropic foundations, to contribute technical, financial and human resources on a voluntary basis in order to strengthen capacities and foster multi-partner cooperation. The capacity-building mechanism will consist of:

a. A connection hub that facilitates demand-driven, tailor-made and integrated solutions, by:

(i) Advising on, assessing and processing country requests for the development of solutions;

(ii) Identifying main implementing partners within and outside of the United Nations system, in line with their comparative advantages and operational capacities;
(iii) Connecting the request to similar initiatives and solutions for peer-to-peer exchange and potential replication, where existing and relevant;
(iv) Ensuring effective set-up for multi-agency and multi-stakeholder implementation;
(v) Identifying funding opportunities, including by initiating the start-up fund;

b. A start-up fund for initial financing to realize project-oriented solutions, by:

(i) Providing seed funding, where needed, to jump-start a specific project;
(ii) Complementing other funding sources;
(iii) Receiving voluntary financial contributions by Member States, the United Nations, international financial institutions and other stakeholders, including the private sector and philanthropic foundations;

c. A global knowledge platform as an online open data source, by:

(i) Serving as a repository of existing evidence, practices and initiatives;
(ii) Facilitating the accessibility of knowledge and sharing of solutions;
(iii) Building on the Global Forum on Migration and Development Platform for Partnerships and other relevant sources.

44. We will implement the Global Compact in cooperation and partnership with migrants, civil society, migrant and diaspora organizations, faith-based organizations, local authorities and communities, the private sector, trade unions, parliamentarians, national human rights institutions, the International Red Cross and Red Crescent Movement, academia, the media and other relevant stakeholders.

45. We welcome the decision of the Secretary-General to establish a United Nations network on migration to ensure effective and coherent system-wide support for implementation, including the capacity-building mechanism, as well as follow-up and review of the Global Compact, in response to the needs of Member States. In this regard, we note that:

a. IOM will serve as the coordinator and secretariat of the network;
b. The network will fully draw from the technical expertise and experience of relevant entities within the United Nations system;

c. The work of the network will be fully aligned with existing coordination mechanisms and the repositioning of the United Nations development system.

46. We request the Secretary-General, drawing on the network, to report to the General Assembly on a biennial basis on the implementation of the Global Compact, the activities of the United Nations system in this regard, as well as the functioning of the institutional arrangements.

47. Further recognizing the important role of State-led processes and platforms at the global and regional levels in advancing the international dialogue on migration, we invite the Global Forum on Migration and Development, regional consultative processes and other global, regional and subregional forums to provide platforms to exchange experiences on the implementation of the Global Compact, share good practices on policies and cooperation, promote innovative approaches, and foster multi-stakeholder partnerships around specific policy issues.

Follow-up and review

48. We will review the progress made at the local, national, regional and global levels in implementing the Global Compact in the framework of the United Nations through a State-led approach and with the participation of all relevant stakeholders. For follow-up and review, we agree on intergovernmental measures that will assist us in fulfilling our objectives and commitments.

49. Considering that international migration requires a forum at the global level through which Member States can review the implementation progress and guide the direction of the work of the United Nations, we decide that:

a. The High-level Dialogue on International Migration and Development, currently scheduled to take place every fourth session of the General Assembly, shall be repurposed and renamed "International Migration Review Forum";
b. The International Migration Review Forum shall serve as the primary intergovernmental global platform for Member States to discuss and share progress on the implementation of all aspects of the Global Compact, including as it relates to the 2030 Agenda for Sustainable Development, and with the participation of all relevant stakeholders;
c. The International Migration Review Forum shall take place every four years beginning in 2022;
d. The International Migration Review Forum shall discuss the implementation of the Global Compact at the local, national, regional and global levels, as well as allow for interaction with other relevant stake-

holders with a view to building upon accomplishments and identifying opportunities for further cooperation;

e. Each edition of the International Migration Review Forum will result in an intergovernmentally agreed Progress Declaration, which may be taken into consideration by the high-level political forum on sustainable development.

50. Considering that most international migration takes place within regions, we invite relevant subregional, regional and cross-regional processes, platforms and organizations, including the United Nations regional economic commissions or regional consultative processes, to review the implementation of the Global Compact within the respective regions, beginning in 2020, alternating with discussions at the global level at a four-year interval, in order to effectively inform each edition of the International Migration Review Forum, with the participation of all relevant stakeholders.

51. We invite the Global Forum on Migration and Development to provide a space for annual informal exchange on the implementation of the Global Compact, and to report the findings, best practices and innovative approaches to the International Migration Review Forum.

52. Recognizing the important contributions of State-led initiatives on international migration, we invite forums such as the IOM International Dialogue on Migration, regional consultative processes and others to contribute to the International Migration Review Forum by providing relevant data, evidence, best practices, innovative approaches and recommendations as they relate to the implementation of the Global Compact for Safe, Orderly and Regular Migration.

53. We encourage all Member States to develop, as soon as practicable, ambitious national responses for the implementation of the Global Compact, and to conduct regular and inclusive reviews of progress at the national level, such as through the voluntary elaboration and use of a national implementation plan. Such reviews should draw on contributions from all relevant stakeholders, as well as parliaments and local authorities, and serve to effectively inform the participation of Member States in the International Migration Review Forum and other relevant fora.

54. We request the President of the General Assembly to launch and conclude, in 2019, open, transparent and inclusive intergovernmental consultations to determine the precise modalities and organizational aspects of the International Migration Review Forums and articulate how the contributions of the regional reviews and other relevant processes will inform the Forums, as a means to further strengthen the overall effectiveness and consistency of the follow-up and review outlined in the Global Compact.

NOTES

1. International Convention on the Elimination of All Forms of Racial Discrimination, Convention on the Elimination of All Forms of Discrimination against Women, Convention against Torture and Other Cruel, Inhuman or Degrading Treatment or Punishment, Convention on the Rights of the Child, International Convention on the Protection of the Rights of All Migrant Workers and Members of Their Families, International Convention for the Protection of All Persons from Enforced Disappearance, and Convention on the Rights of Persons with Disabilities.

2. Adopted under the United Nations Framework Convention on Climate Change in FCCC/CP/2015/10/Add.1 , decision 1/CP.21.

3. Migration for Employment Convention (Revised), 1949 (No. 97), Migrant Workers (Supplementary Provisions) Convention, 1975 (No. 143), Equality of Treatment (Social Security) Convention, 1962 (No. 118), and Domestic Workers Convention, 2011 (No. 189).

Bibliography

A/70/59—Report of the Secretary General—In Safety and Dignity: Addressing Large Movements of Refugees and Migrants (April 21. 2016), https://refugeesmigrants.un.org/sites/default/files/in_safety_and_dignity_-_addressing_large_movements_of_refugees_and_migrants.pdf.

Abela, Joseph S. *Malta: A Brief History*. Hal Tarxien, Malta: Gutenberg Press, 2015.

Ager, Alastair, and Alison Strang. "Understanding Integration: A Conceptual Framework," *Journal of Refugee Studies*. 21 no. 2 (June 2008): 166–191.

Adjai, Carol, and Gabriella Lazaridis. "Migration, Xenophobia and New Racism in Post-Apartheid South Africa," *International Journal of Social Science Studies*. 1 no. 1 (November 2013) 192.

Aliens Control Act 96 of 1991 § 55.

Allport, Gordon W. *The Nature of Race Prejudice*, New York: Perseus Books, 1979.

Anderson, Benedict. *Imagined Communities: Reflections on the Origin and Spread of Nationalism*. Brooklyn, NY: Verso Books, 2016.

Barzun, Jacques. *Race: A Study in Superstition*. New York: Harper and Row, 1965.

Beirich, Heidi, and Susy Buchanan. "2017: The Year in Hate and Extremism," *The Intelligence Report*, February 11, 2018 (downloaded January 27, 2018 https://www.splcenter.org/fighting-hate/intelligence-report/2018/2017-year-hate-and-extremism).

Bell, Daniel. "The Dispossessed." In Daniel Bell, ed., *The Radical Right*. New York: Anchor Books, 1964.

Boddy-Evans, Alistair. "Harold Macmillan's 'Wind of Change' Speech." ThoughtCo. https://www.thoughtco.com/harold-macmillans-wind-of-change-speech-43760 (accessed January 21, 2019).

Bonner, Philip, and Noor Nieftagodien. *Alexandra: A History*. Johannesburg, South Africa: Wits University Press, 2008.

Borgeson, Kevin, and Robin Valeri. "Faces of Hate," *Journal of Applied Sociology, 21*(2), 99–111, 2004.

Bordeau, Jamie. *Xenophobia: The Violence of Fear and Hate*. New York: The Rosen Publishing Group, Inc., 2010.

Bozzoli, Belinda. *Theatres of Struggle and the End of Apartheid*. Athens, OH: Ohio University Press, 2004.

Brimelow, Peter. *Alien Nation: Common Sense About America's Immigration Disaster*. New York, Random House, 1995.

Camilleri-Cassar, Frances. "Living on the Edge: Migrant Women in Malta," *International Journal of Comparative and Applied Criminal Justice*, 35 no. 3 (August 2011): 193–206.

Carciotto, Sergio, and Mike Mavura. "The Evolution of Migration Policy in Post-Apartheid South Africa: Emerging Themes and New Challenges." Scalabrini Institute for Human Mobility in Africa. February 2016. http://sihma.org.za/reports/the-evolution-of-migration-policy-in-post-apartheid-south-africa/.

Cartagena Declaration on Refugees.

Castles, Stephen et al. *Integration: Mapping the Field* (Oxford, England: Centre for Migration and Policy Research and Refugee Studies Centre, December 2002).

Children on the Run: Unaccompanied Children Leaving Central America and Mexico and the Need for International Protection, Washington, DC: United Nations High Commissioner for Refugees Washington, DC, Regional Office. March 20, 2016.

Ciaccia, Kimberly, and Rita Marie John. "Unaccompanied Immigrant Minors: Where to Begin." *Journal of Pediatric Health Care*, 30 no. 3 (May–June 2016): 231–240.

Cini, Michelle. "The Europeanization of Malta: Adaptation, Identity, and Party Politics," *South European Society and Politics* 5 no. 2 (December 2000): 261–276.

Convention Relating to the Status of Refugees, 1951.

Cooper, James Fenimore. *The American Democrat, or Hints on the Social and Civic Relations of the United States of America*, Cooperstown, NY: H.E. and Phinney, 1838.

Crush, Jonathan. *The Perfect Storm: The Realities of Xenophobia in Contemporary South Africa*, Cape Town: Southern African Migration Project, 2008.

Debono, Daniela. "In Search of the Building Blocks of a Human Rights Culture: Lessons from the Treatment of Irregular Immigrants in Malta" (Ph.D. diss., University of Sussex, 2012).

De Jager, Justin. "Addressing Xenophobia in the Equality Courts of South Africa," *Refuge*, 28 no. 2 (2011) 107–116.

Dodson, Belinda. "Locating Xenophobia: Debate, Discourse, and Everyday Experience in Cape Town, South Africa," *Africa Today* 56 no. 3 (2010): 3–22.

"Donald Trump Transcript: 'Our Country Needs a Great Leader,'" *Wall Street Journal*, June 16, 2015, https://blogs.wsj.com/washwire/2015/06/16/donald-trump-transcript-our-country-needs-a-truly-great-leader/.

Donato, Katherine M., and Blake Sisk. "Children's Migration to the United States from Mexico and Central America: Evidence from the Mexican and Latin American Migration Projects," *Journal on Migration and Human Security*. 3 no. 1 (2015): 58–79.

Eiselein, Gregory (ed.). *Emma Lazarus: Selected Poems and Other Writings*, Peterborough, ON: Broadview Press, 2002.

Falzon, Mark Anthony, and Mark Micallef. "Sacred Island or World Empire? Locating Far-Right Movements In and Beyond Malta," *Journal of Contemporary European Studies*. 16 no. 3 (December 2008): 393–406.

FCC/CP/2015/10/Add1, Report of the Conference of the Parties on its twenty-first session, held in Paris from 30 November to 13 December 2015 (January 26, 2016), https://unfccc.int/resource/docs/2015/cop21/eng/10a01.pdf.

Fiott, Daniel. "How Europeanized Has Maltese Foreign Policy Become," *Mediterranean Quarterly*, 21 no. 3 (Summer 2010): 104–118.

Forbes, Susan, and Patricia Weiss Fagnin. *Unaccompanied Refugee Children: The Evolution of US Policies 1939 to 1984*, Washington, DC: Refugee Studies Center/Refugee Policy Group, January 8, 1984.

Ford, Glyn. "In the Wake of Xenophobia: The New Racism in Europe," UN Chronicle, XLIV no. 3 (September 2007). Accessed January 27, 2019: https://unchronicle.un.org/article/wake-xenophobia-new-racism-europe.

Frederickson, George. *Racism: A Short History*. Princeton, NJ: Princeton University Press, 2002.

Freeman, Colin, and Nick Squires. "EU Immigration: 'Malta is the Smallest State, and We Are Carrying a Burden That is Much Larger than Any Other Country,'" *The Telegraph*, July 21, 2013. https://www.telegraph.co.uk/news/worldnews/europe/malta/10192458/EU-immigration-Malta-is-the-smallest-state-and-we-are-carrying-a-burden-that-is-much-bigger-than-any-other-country.html.

Frey, William H. *Diversity Explosion: How New Racial Demographics Are Remaking America*. Brookings Institution Press, 2018.

Friedman, Dan. "Congress Hears from the Children that Fled Violence at Home for the U.S. Border," *New York Daily News*, July 30, 2014 Accessed January 27, 2019: https://www.nydailynews.com/news/politics/congress-hears-children-fled-u-s-border-article-1.1885043.

General Assembly Resolution 428 (V) of 14 December 1950, "Statute for the Office of the United Nations High Commissioner for Refugees."

Grant, Madison. *The Passing of the Great Race or the Racial Basis of European History*, New York: Charles Scribner's Sons, 1922.

Grech, Herman. "Illegal Immigrants Drift into Xlandi Bay," *Times of Malta*, March 5, 2002.

Hall, Prescott Farnsworth. *Immigration and Its Effects Upon the United States*, New York: Henry Holt and Company, 1906.

Hanekom, Braam and Leigh Ann Webster. "The Role of South Africa's Government in the Xenophobic Violence of May 2008," *University of Pennsylvania Journal of Law and Social Change* 13 (2009): 91–117.

Higham, John. "Politics of Immigration Restriction," *Immigration and Nationality Review* 1. (1976) 1–38.

Holborn, Loiuse W. "The League of Nations and the Refugee Problem," *The Annals of the American Academy of Political and Social Science* 203 (May 1939): 124–135.

Horn, Heather. "Is Eastern Europe Any More Xenophobic than Western Europe," *The Atlantic*, October 16, 2015, Downloaded January 27, 2019 https://www.theatlantic.com/international/archive/2015/10/xenophobia-eastern-europe-refugees/410800/.

Human Rights Watch. *"Prohibited Persons": Abuse of Undocumented Migrants, Asylum Seekers, and Refugees in South Africa* (New York: Human Rights Watch, March 1998).

Human Sciences Research Council. *Citizenship, Violence and Xenophobia in South Africa: Perceptions from South African Communities.* (Pretoria, SA: Human Sciences Research Council, June 2008).

Huntington, Samuel. *Who Are We? The Challenges to America's National Identity*, New York: Simon & Schuster, 2005.

International Labour Office, International Organization for Migration, Office of the United Nations High Commissioner for Human Rights, *International Migration, Racism, Discrimination and Xenophobia*, Geneva, Switzerland: Office of the UN High Commissioner for Refugees, 2001.

"Irregular Immigrants, Refugees and Integration: Policy Document" Ministry for Justice and Home Affairs and Ministry for the Family and Social Solidarity. Valetta, Malta, 2005.

"Italian Navy Recovers Ship That Sank with Over 800 People on Board." *The Guardian*, June 26, 2016.

Kandel, William, A. *Unaccompanied Alien Children: An Overview*. Washington, DC: Congressional Research Service, January 18, 2017.

Kennedy, John. *A Nation of Immigrants*, New York: Harper and Row Publishers, 1964.

Kerr, Philippa, and Kevin Durrheim. "The Dilemma of Anti-Xenophobia Discourse in the Aftermath of Violence in the De Doorns," *Journal of Southern African Studies,* (2013) 39 no. 3: 577–596.

Khosa v. Minister of Social Development and Others, 2004 6 SA(CC).

King, Russell. "Geography, Islands and Migration in an Era of Global Mobility," *Island Studies Journal*, 4 no. 1 (May 2009): 53–84.

King, Russell. and Ronald. Skeldon 'Mind the Gap!' Integrating Approaches to Internal and International Migration. *Journal of Ethnic and Migration Studies*. 36 no. 10 (June 2010): 1619–1646.

Kingsley, Patrick *The New Odyssey: The Story of Europe's Refugee Crisis*. London: Guardian Books, 2016.

Klepp, Silja. "Free Content A Contested Asylum System: The European Union between Refugee Protection and Border Control in the Mediterranean Sea," *European Journal of Migration and Law*, 12 no. 1 (2010): 1–21.

Klepp, Silja. "A Double Bind: Malta and the Rescue of Unwanted Migrants at Sea, a Legal Anthropological Perspective on the Humanitarian Law of the Sea," *International Journal of Refugee Law* 23 no. 3 (July 2011): 538–557.

Koessler, Maximillian (1946) "Subject," "Citizen," "National," and "Permanent Allegiance," *The Yale Law Journal* 56(1): 58–76.

"Landed on Ellis Island: New Immigration Building Opened Yesterday A Rosy-Cheeked Irish Girl the First Registered—Room Enough for All Arrivals Only Railroad People Find Fault," *New York Times*. January 2, 1892.

Lawyers for Human Rights v. Minister for Home Affairs, 2004 7, SA 125 (CC).

Lazarus, Emma. "The New Colossus" in *The Poems of Emma Lazarus: Jewish Poems*, Alexandria, VA: Library of Alexandria, 2009.

Lowenthal, Leo, and Norbert Guterman. *Prophets of Deceit: A Study of the Techniques of the American Agitator*. Palo Alto, CA: Pacific Books Publishers, 1970.

Lutterbeck, D. "Small Frontier Island: Malta and the Challenge of Irregular Immigration," *Mediterranean Quarterly* 2009 20 no. 1 (2009): 119–144.

Mainwaring, Cetta "Constructing a Crisis: The Role of Immigration Detention in Malta," *Population, Space and Place* 18 no. 6 (November 2012): 687–700.

Mainwaring, Cetta. "Resisting Distalization? Malta and Cyprus' Influence on EU Migration and Asylum Policies," *Refugee Survey Quarterly*. 31 no. 4 (December 2012): 38–66.

"Malta and European Migration," *The Sunday Times*, September 29, 2002, 35.

Mandela, Nelson. "Statement of the President of the African National Congress." Statement given at his Inauguration as President of the Democratic Republic of South Africa, Union Buildings, Pretoria, May 1994. https://www.gov.za/statement-president-african-national-congress-nelson-mandela-his-inauguration-president-democratic-0.

"Man's Inhumanity," Editorial, *New York Times*, June 9, 1939, 20.

Martin, Susan F. *A Nation of Immigrants*, New York: Cambridge University Press, 2011.

Mbeki, Thabo. "Address of the President of South Africa." Address given at the National Tribute in remembrance of the victims of attacks on foreign nationals, July 2008.

McDonald-Gibson, Charlotte. *Cast Away: True Stories of Survival from Europe's Refugee Crisis*. New York: The New Press, 2016.

McGlashan, Neil. "White Immigration into South Africa," *Geography*, 51, no. 4 (November 1966): 383–384.

Migration Policy Institute *Before the Boat: Understanding the Migrant Journey* (Washington, DC: Migration Policy Institute, May 2015).

Minister of Home Affairs v. Watchenuka, 2003 10 SA 21 (SCA).

Ministry for European Affairs and Equality. *Integration=Belonging: Migrant Integration Strategy and Action Plan*, Valetta, Malta: Ministry of European Affairs and Equality, 2017.

Misago, J.-P., Monson, T., Polzer, T., et al. *May 2008 Violence Against Foreign Nationals in South Africa: Understanding Causes and Evaluating Responses*. (Johannesburg: Consortium for Refugees and Migrants in South Africa / University of the Witwatersrand, 2010).

Morehead, Caroline *Human Cargo: A Journey Among Refugees*, New York: Picador, 2006.

Morse, Arthur D. *While Six Million Died: A Chronicle of American Apathy*. New York: Abrams Press, 1998.

Ndou, Clive. "Foreigners Must Go Home—King Zwelithini," *The Citizen*, March 23, 2015.

"Not Here to Stay: Report of the International Commission of Jurists on its Visit to Malta on 26–30 September, 2011" Geneva, Switzerland: International Commission of Jurists, 2012.

Nyar, Annsilla. "Synthesis Report: What Happened?': Narrative of the May 2008 Xenophobic Violence." In *South African Civil Society and Xenophobia* (New York: The Atlantic Philanthropies. July 2010).

OAU Convention Governing the Specific Aspects of Refugee Problems in Africa.

Pace, Roderick. "Malta and EU Membership: Overcoming 'Vulnerabilities,' Strengthening 'Resilience,'" *European Integration*, 28 no. 1 (March 2006): 33–49.

Peberdy, Sally. *Selecting Immigrants: National Identity and South Africa's Immigration Policies 1910–2008*, Johannesburg: Wits University Press, 2009.

Peberdy, Sally, and Mazibuko K. Jara. "Humanitarian and Social Mobilization in Cape Town: Civil Society and the May 2008 Xenophobic Violence," *Politikon* 2011, 38 no. 1 (April 2011): 37–57.

Phillmore, J., and Goodson, L. "Making a Place in the Global City: The Relevance of Indicators of Integration," *Journal of Refugee Studies* 21 no.3 (September 2008): 305–325.

Bibliography

Pisani, Maria. "Addressing the 'Citizenship Assumption' in Critical Pedagogy: Exploring the Case of Rejected Female Sub-Saharan African Asylum Seekers in Malta," *Power and Education* 4 no 2 (June 2012): 185–195.

"Pope Francis Visits Italy's Migrant Island of Lampedusa," *BBC News*, July 8, 2013, https://www.bbc.com/news/world-europe-23224010.

Public Papers of the Presidents of the United States: Lyndon B. Johnson, 1965. Volume II, entry 546 (Washington, DC: Government Printing Office, 1966), 1037–1040.

Saenger, Gerhart. *The Social Psychology of Prejudice: Achieving Intercultural Understanding and Cooperation in a Democracy*. New York NY: Harper and Row Publishers, 1953.

Schembri, Gabriel, and Julian Bonnici "Update: You're All Dirty' Remarks Demonstrator During Protest Against Bugubba Prayer Room," *Independent*, October, 2016.

Schierup, Carl-Ulrik, and Peo Hansen. *Migration, Citizenship, and the European Welfare State: A European Dilemma*. Oxford: Oxford University Press, 2006.

Separated Children Placed in Office of Refugee Resettlement Care, U.S. Department of Health and Human Services, Office of the Inspector General, HHS OIG Brief—OEI-BL-18-00511, January 2019.

Sessions, Jeff. "Attorney General Sessions Delivers Remarks on Immigration Enforcement." Remarks given in Las Cruces, NM, April 2018. https://www.justice.gov/opa/speech/attorney-general-sessions-delivers-remarks-immigration-enforcement.

Simpson, John Hope. "The Refugee Problem," *International Affairs* 17 no. 5 (September 1938): 607–628.

Skott, Christina. "Linnaeus and the Troglodyte: Early European Encounters with the Malay World and the Natural History of Man," *Indonesia and the Malay World* 42 no. 123 (2015): 141–161.

Smith, Alex Duval. Zimbabweans Flee Shanty Town Attacks in South Africa, *Independent*, October 24, 2001.

South African Const. ch 2.

Spiteri, Damian. (2012) "The Evolving Identities of Unaccompanied Young Male Asylum Seekers in Malta," *Journal of Immigrant & Refugee Studies* 10 no. 4 (December 2012): 362–379.

Strang, Alison, and Alastair Ager. "Refugee Integration: Emerging Trends and Remaining Agendas," *Journal of Refugee Studies* 23 no. 4 (November 2010): 589–607.

Suso v. Malta, 23 July 2013, European Court of Human Rights.

Thomson, M. (2006) Migrants on the Edge of Europe: Perspectives from Malta, Cyprus and Slovenia. Sussex Migration Working Paper No. 35.

Trump, Donald. "Address to the Nation on the Crisis at the Border." Address given in the Oval Office, January 2019. https://www.whitehouse.gov/briefings-statements/president-donald-j-trumps-address-nation-crisis-border/.

Trump, Donald. "Our Country Needs a Great Leader," (Presidential Campaign launch speech, New York, NY, June 16, 2015).

UN General Assembly. "Report of the Special Representative of the Secretary General on Migration." A/71/728 (February 3, 2017), http://www.un.org/en/development/desa/population/migration/events/coordination/15/documents/Report%20of%20SRSG%20on%20Migration%20-%20A.71.728_ADVANCE.pdf.

UN General Assembly. "Strengthening of the United Nations: an agenda for further change." A/57/387 (September 9, 2002), http://unpan1.un.org/intradoc/groups/public/documents/un/unpan005675.pdf.

UN General Assembly, Resolution 64/293, United Nations Global Plan of Action to Combat Trafficking in Persons, A/RES/64/293 (August 12, 2010), https://www.unodc.org/documents/human-trafficking/United_Nations_Global_Plan_of_Action_to_Combat_Trafficking_in_Persons.pdf.

UN General Assembly, Resolution 68/4, Declaration of the High-level Dialogue on International Migration and Development, A/RES/68/4 (January 21, 2014), https://undocs.org/A/RES/68/4.

UN General Assembly, Resolution 69/229, International Migration and Development, A/RES/69/229 (February 4, 2015), http://www.un.org/en/ga/search/view_doc.asp?symbol=A/RES/69/229.

UN General Assembly, Resolution 69/283, Sendai Framework for Disaster Risk Reduction 2015–2030, A/RES/69/283 (June 23, 2015), https://www.un.org/en/development/desa/population/migration/generalassembly/docs/globalcompact/A_RES_69_283.pdf.

UN General Assembly, Resolution 69/313, Addis Ababa Action Agenda of the Third International Conference on Financing for Development (Addis Ababa Action Agenda), A/RES/69/313 (July 27, 2015), http://www.un.org/en/development/desa/population/migration/generalassembly/docs/globalcompact/A_RES_69_313.pdf.

UN General Assembly, Resolution 70/1, Transforming our World: the 2030 Agenda for Sustainable Development, A/70/L.1 (October 21, 2015), http://www.un.org/en/ga/search/view_doc.asp?symbol=A/RES/70/1.

UN General Assembly, Resolution 70/296, Agreement Concerning the Relationship between the United Nations and the International Organization for Migration, A/RES/70/296 (August 5, 2016), http://www.un.org/en/ga/search/view_doc.asp?symbol=A/RES/70/296.

UN General Assembly, Resolution 71/1, New York Declaration for Refugees and Migrants, A/RES/71/1 (October 3, 2016), http://undocs.org/a/res/71/1.

UN General Assembly, Resolution 217 A (III), Universal Declaration of Human Rights, A/RES/3/217A (December 10, 1948), https://documents-dds-ny.un.org/doc/RESOLUTION/GEN/NR0/043/88/IMG/NR004388.pdf?OpenElement.

United Nations Commission on Human Rights. Sub-Commission on Prevention of Discrimination and Protection of Minorities, *The Main Types and Causes of Discrimination*. Lake Success, NY: United Nations Publications, 1949.

United Nations, Treaty Series. New York: United Nations, 1999.

Walker, Francis A. "The Restriction of Immigration," *Atlantic Monthly* (June 1896): 822–829.

Walker-Leigh, Vanya. "Tunis Declaration 'will help Malta cope with illegal immigrants,'" *Sunday Times*, October 17, 2002.

Wang, Amy B. "A Ship Full of Refugees Fleeing the Nazis Once Begged the U.S. for Entry. They Were Turned Back," *Washington Post*, January 29, 2017.

World Migration Report—2010: The Future of Migration: Building Capacities for Change Geneva, International Organization for Migration, 2010.

Xuereb, Peter (ed.). *Migration and Asylum in Malta and the European Union: Rights and Realities 2002–2011*. Valetta, Malta: Midsea Books, 2018.

Zammit, David E. "Vernacularizing Asylum Law in Malta," in Valentina Colcelli and Ranier Arnold (eds.) *Europeanization Through Private Law Instruments*, Regensburg, Germany: University of Regensburg Press, 2016.

Index

Aghlabid, 68–69
Alexandra, 44, 45, 46, 57, 57–58, 58, 60, 61, 62
Aliens Act of 1937, 49
Aliens Control Act of 1991, 51, 55, 57
Allport, Gordon, 23–24, 24, 24–25, 107
A Nation of Immigrants, 90
Anderson, Benedict, 5
Annan, Kofi, 38, 39

Barzan, Jacques, 19, 20
Bill of Rights, Section 9, 52
Bill of Rights, Section 10, 53, 54
Bill of Rights, Section 12(1), 53
Bonaparte, Napoleon, 69
Borg, Tony, 72–73
Brexit, 7
Brimelow, Peter, 93, 94, 98
Bugibba, 65, 76
Bush, George H.W., 93
Byzantine Empire, 68

Calais, 103
Carter, Jimmy, 92
Chinese Exclusion Act, 84
Citizenship Act (Malta), 70, 71
Convention Relating to the Status of Refugees (1951 Refugee Convention), 12, 34, 56
Cooper, James Fenimore, 25

Dalli, Helena, 76
Darwin, Charles, 18
Democratic Party, 84
Dillingham Commission, 86
Dillingham, William Paul, 86
Displaced Person Act, 89
Duncan, Patrick, 47–48, 48

Education Section Code Section 21.03, 92
European Union, 7, 11, 34, 66, 72, 73, 75, 77, 107
Evian France, 33
Executive Order 13767: Border Security and Immigration Enforcement Improvements, 95
Executive Order 13841, 96

Frey, William, 98

Galton, Francis, 18
Geary Act, 84
Global Compact for Safe, Orderly and Regular Migration, 10, 11, 41, 103
Global Compact on Refugees, 10, 11, 41, 103
Grant, Madison, 18, 19, 85
Great Depression, 87
Green Paper on International Migration, 55–56, 56, 59

Hall, Prescott, 85

Hart-Celler Immigration and Nationality Act, 83, 91
Hernandez, Mayeli, 94, 95, 99
Hitler, Adolf, 32, 33
Human Rights Watch, 61
Huntington, Samuel, 94, 98

International Organization for Migration, 4, 12, 75, 104
Immigrant Quota Act, 48
Immigration Act (Malta), 71
Immigration Act of 1924 (1924 Immigration Act), 11
Immigration Act of 1965 (1965 Immigration Act), 11, 97, 105
Immigration Act of 1990 (1990 Immigration Act), 93
Immigration and Regulation Act (1913), 46, 48
Immigration Restriction League, 85
International Commission of Jurists, 74
International Organization for Migration, 75
Immigration Quota Act (1924), 86
Immigration Reform Control Act (1986), 93
International Refugee Organization, 33

Jewish Joint Distribution Committee, 89
Johnson, Lyndon, 91
Johnson Reed Act, 82–83, 86, 87

Kennedy, John, 90, 91
Kennedy, Ted, 93
Khosa v. Minister of Social Development, 55
Kinnicutt, Francis H., 88
Knights Hospitaller, 69
Kristallnacht, 87

Lampedusa, 1
Lawyers for Human Rights v. Minister of Home Affairs, 54
Lazarus, Emma, 83, 84
Linnaeus, Carl, 17
Lodge, Henry Cabot, 85
Lowell, A. Lawrence, 85

MacMillan, Harold, 22

Malta Muslim Council, 65
Mbeki, Thabo, 58
Millennial Development Goals, 10, 38
Ministry of European Affairs and Equality, 105
Minister of Home Affairs v. Watchenuka, 53
Ministry for Social Dialogue, Consumer Affairs, and Civil Liberties, 76
Modise, Joe, 61
Moore, Annie, 81, 82, 83, 99
Moviment Patrijotti, 65, 68
Murrieta, California, 81–82, 83

Nansen, Fridtjof, 31
Nationalist Party, 49–50, 50
New Colossus, 83, 84
New York Declaration for Refugees and Migrants, 10, 39, 41, 103, 133
New York Times, 81, 89
Nhamuave, Ernesto Alfabeto, 43, 44–45, 50
Norman, 69

Obama Administration, 95
Office of Refugee Resettlement, 92
Organization of African Union Convention Governing the Specific Aspects of Refugee Problems in Africa, 51

Park, Robert, 20
Pasha, Mustafa, 69
Paul of Tarsus (St. Paul), 67, 68, 77
Plyler, James, 92
Plyler v. Doe, 92, 92–93
Population Registration Act (1950), 50
Proposition 187, 93
Protocol Relating to the Status of Refugees (1967), 35, 51

Ramaphosa, 43, 43–44, 45, 58, 60, 61, 62
Refugee Act 130, 56
Refugee Act (1980), 92, 105
Refugee Act (Malta), 71, 72
Refugee White Paper, 56
Republican Party, 84
Restriction of Immigration, 85
Roger of Normandy, 69
Rogers, Edith, 87

Roosevelt, Franklin, 33

Sabraw, Dana, 96
Secretary General, Office of the, 38
Siege of Malta, 69
Simpson, John Hope, 32
Southern Poverty Law Center, 26
St. Louis, 88, 89
Sustainable Development Goals, 10, 38
Sutherland, Peter, 39

Treaty of Westphalia, 30
Truman, Harry, 90
Trump, Donald, 4, 95, 96, 97
Turner, Frederick Jackson, 85

United Nations Commission on Human Rights' Sub-Commission on Prevention of Discrimination and Protection of Minorities, 21
United Nations Relief and Rehabilitation Agency (UNRRA), 33
Universal Declaration of Human Rights, 21

United Nations High Commission for Refugees (UNHCR), 5, 33, 40, 51, 104
UN Summit for Refugees and Migrants, 103
United States Immigration Commission, 86

Verwoerd, Hendrick, 50
Valetta Summit, 75–76, 78
Von Hompesh, Ferdinand, 69

Wagner, Robert F., 87, 88
Wagner-Rogers Bill, 88, 89
Walker, Francis, 85
Ward, Robert, 85
Warren, Charles, 85
White Paper on International Migration, 46, 56, 57, 59
Who Are We, 94
World Conference on Racism and Xenophobia, 25

Xlendi Bay, 72, 73

Zwelithini, Goodwill, 62

About the Author

Kyle Farmbry, JD, PhD, is a professor in the School of Public Affairs and Administration at Rutgers University-Newark. In 2017–2018, he served as an American Council on Education Fellow at the University of Pretoria in South Africa. In 2016 he served as a Fulbright Fellow examining European Union immigration policies—with an emphasis on the challenges and management of refugee movement and integration in the nation of Malta. In February of 2009, Dr. Farmbry was selected as one of thirty-five people from around the world to serve as a Fulbright New Century Scholar. In this role, he was engaged in research examining factors of youth entrepreneurial and civic engagement in South Africa. In addition to *Migration and Xenophobia: A Three Country Exploration*, he is the author or editor of three other books: *Administration and the Other: Explorations of Diversity and Marginalization in the Political Administrative State* (2009); *Crisis, Disaster, and Risk: Institutional Response and Emergence* (2012); and *The War on Poverty: A Retrospective* (2014). Dr. Farmbry received his BA, MPA, and PhD degrees from The George Washington University. He completed his JD degree at the Rutgers University School of Law.